Security and Defence Related Treaties of India

DISCLAIMER

Security and Defence Related Treaties of India

Brig V P Malhotra (Retd)

Vij Books India Pvt Ltd
21 Ansari Road, Darya Ganj
New Delhi - 110002

Security and Defence Related Treaties of India

Editor: Brig (Retd) V P Malhotra

Published By:

Vij Books India Pvt Ltd
4675-A, 21 Ansari Road, Darya Ganj
New Delhi - 110002
Ph: 43596460, 65449971, 9811094883
Fax: 91-11-30126465
Email: vijbooks@rediffmail.com

ISBN: 978-93-80177-17-5

Dedicated to My Father
Shri Vidya Parkash Malhotra

PREFACE

India has disputed borders with China and Pakistan. Agreements on maritime boundary with Pakistan and Bangladesh have yet to be reached. We have disturbed conditions in Jammu & Kashmir and in some of our North Eastern States. Tibetan Government in exile functions from Indian soil. There are other security-related issues arising out of the geo-strategic location of India and its smaller neighbours. There are issues of river waters, uneven economic development and demographic issues with their resonance on security. It is as such essential that a general security overview is provided to those who wish to study this vital subject.

Only factual defence-related treaties, agreements and other documents have been included and no effort has been made to express opinions or carry out analysis, which has been left to the wisdom of readers. The book is set out in a sequence so as to provide a platform for research. The book also provides a ready reference material at the macro level. Where the full length of some of the treaties, agreements and documents is not included due to reasons of space, the core issues have been brought out in the form of extracts/brief descriptions. For the same reason the voluminous Geneva Conventions as they relate to war have not been included, as, in their case the extracts will not do. If the readers wish to go into details of such treaties and agreements, the same are readily available in the ten volumes brought out by the MEA as also in various other books and publications given in the bibliography.

Those involved in geo-political and geo-strategic studies, whether in universities or in professional fields, particularly the defence services officers and officers from the para-military organisations, will find the book useful.

I must make a mention of the valuable contribution made by my wife, Indu and my daughters, Ruchi and Nidhi. My job was greatly facilitated.

New Delhi
March 2010

V P Malhotra

9818205817, 26897422

CONTENTS

Page(s)

III India–Neighbouring Countries–Others

IV Important River Water Treaties/Agreements

DEFINITIONS/EXPLANATIONS

1. Accession.

The term *Accession* is used to describe the practice, where a state, which is not party to a treaty, later on joins such a treaty.

2. Agreement.

The term *Agreement* in strict sense of the word applies to inter-state compacts which are signed for or on behalf of the governments and which as a rule are not subject to ratification. There are, however, exceptions where agreements have been concluded which are subject to ratifications.

3. Cease Fire Line (CFL).

A military line resulting from a military conflict.

4. Convention.

The term *Convention* usually means a compact which determines the inter-state relations in a special field.

5. Confederation.

A Confederation is created by a number of independent states bound together by an independent treaty or Compact in to a union with organs of government extending over the member states. A Confederation is not a state in the international law The individual states maintain their independent personality.

6. Declaration.

It applies to a statement by two or more states regarding specic political, economic and legal questions. *Declarations,* as a rule, set out general principles of international relations and international law.

7. Demarcate.

The frontier is said to have been *demarcated* when it has been physically set out on ground and not just marked on map.

8. Delimit.

When the boundary can be drawn on a map and is accepted by the states which are divided by it, even though it is not marked on ground, it is said to have been *delimited.*

9. Exchange of Notes.

The term *Exchange of Notes* means the procedure of reaching agreements by means of written statements with identical texts.

10. Federation.

A federal st ate is a real st ate in the international law . Federal organ has direct power, not only on the member st ates but also over the citizens of the member states.

11. Frontier.

It denotes the limits of the country's political and military influence.

12. International Border.

International Border defines the territorial limit of national sovereignty of a country

13. Line of Actual Control.

A bilateral political line which is not an international border

14. Pact.

The term *Pact* is usually applied to bilateral or multilateral inter-state compacts* regarding some aspects of political relations e.g. a non- aggression pact.

15. Plebiscite.

Plebiscite involves putting a whole nation or the people of a region to vote directly on a special point such as whether a contested region should be attached to one country or the other or in some cases become independent autonomous.

---

*The dictionary meaning of Compact is mutual bargain or agreement: a league, treaty or union.

16. Protectorate.

Protectorate denotes a relation assumed by a s tate over a territory,which it administers without annexation and admitting the inhabitants to citizenship. It is a form of dependence by which one state on the basis of a treaty concluded with another, hands over the management of its foreign affairs and may receive an adviser to deal with its internal affairs.

17. Protocol.

The most varied agreements between governments in which they set on record their statements regarding adherence to a treaty, reservations, prolongation, transference of rights, etc., are usually formulated in the form of *Protocols.*

18. Ratification.

(a) *Ratification* is an international act whereby a state establishes its consent to a treaty on international plane.

(b) Executive in India is competent to enter into treaties which would be binding on the State. Legislation is however necessary when a treaty involves providing for money to a foreign power which must be withdrawn from the Consolidated Fund of India; where the treaty affects the justiable rights of a citizen of India; and, where it requires the taking of property, life or liberty or the imposition of a tax.

(c) In case Indian territory is to be ceded to a foreign power, an amendment to the Constitution would be required by reason of Article 1 of the Constitution. But no amendment of the Constitution nor even legislation is necessary for an agreement to refer a dispute regarding boundaries with a foreign state, as settlement of boundary disputes does not amount to cession of territory.

19. Referendum.

The principle or practice of submitting a question directly to the vote of the entire electorate is known as *Referendum.*

20. Sovereign.

A *Sovereign* is a supreme leader or a monarch, or a supreme and independent power.

21. Suzerain.

It is a kind of international guardianship of a State which is known as Vassal. A Vassal is represented internationally by a *Suzerain.* Suzerainty, however, is not sovereignty.

22. Treaty.

An international *treaty* is a formally expressed agreement between two or more States regarding the establishment, amendment or termination of their reciprocal rights and obligations. The most important principle of the international law is that the international treaties must be observed. The treaties must be concluded on the basis of sovereign equality. Unequal treaties or treaties which are imposed, do not full these elementary requirements. International treaties could be in the form of documents like treaty, pact, convention, agreement, protocol, declaration, memorandum of understanding, exchange of notes etc.— have no essential legal signicance.

23. Vassal.

While it is difficult to define a *Vassal* in precise terms, the status of a Vassal is a form of political dependence characteristic of the epoch of feudalism in which the dependent state (Vassal) is obliged to give the stronger state (Suzerain) military assistance, pay tribute and swear fealty. A vassal has no international relationship as that is absorbed by the Suzerain. Yet a vassal is a half Sovereign on account of its internal independence.

MAIN PROVISIONS OF THE INDIAN INDEPENDENCE ACT, 1947

The Indian Independence Bill was introduced in the House of Commons on 4 July 1947 and received the Royal Assent on 18 July 1947. The main features of the Indian Independence Act, 1947 are as follows:

1. Two independent Dominions will be set up in India with effect from 15 August 1947, to be known respectively as India and Pakistan.
2. The territory of India shall include all British Indian Provinces less those that comprise Pakistan.
3. The territory of Pakistan shall include the areas covered by the Provinces of East Bengal, West Punjab, Sind, Baluchistan and North West Frontier Province (The Province of East Bengal shall include the district of Sylhet).
4. The Indian States are free to accede to either of the two new Dominions.
5. There shall be a Governor General appointed by His Majesty for each of the two Dominions and shall represent His Majesty for the purposes of the Government of the Dominions.
6. The Legislature of the new Dominions shall have full powers to make laws for the Dominions, including laws having extra-territorial operations. No such law shall be void on the grounds that the same is repugnant to the laws of England nor any Order-in-Council shall extend to the new Dominions.
7. With effect from 15 August 1947, the Government of the United Kingdom will have no responsibility towards the governance of the erstwhile British Empire in India.
8. The suzerainty of His Majesty over the Indian States lapses on passing of this Act and with it all Treaties and Agreements between His Majesty and the Rulers of Indian States.
9. The Constituent Assembly of each Dominion shall exercise all powers exercised by the Legislature of the Dominion.
10. The Governor General shall make such provisions as to make this Act effectively operative.

I

INDIA–J&K–PAKISTAN–OTHERS

EXTRACT OF TREATY OF LAHORE, MARCH 9, 1846

The British Government demanded from the Lahore State, as indemnification for the expenses of the war which included the cession of territory described in Article 3 of the Treaty and payment of one and a half crores of rupees. Lahore Government having failed to pay this amount, the Maharaja ceded to the Company in perpetual sovereignty, as equivalent to the sum demanded, all his forts, territories, rights and interests in the hill countries which are situated between the river Beas and Indus, including the provinces of Kashmir and Hazara.

TREATY BETWEEN EAST INDIA COMPANY AND MAHARAJA GULAB SINGH OF JAMMU, AMRITSAR, 16 MARCH 1846

Article 1

The British Government transfers and makes over for ever , in independent possession, to Maharajah Golab Sing and the heirs mail of his body, all the hilly or mountainous country, with its dependencies, situated to the east- ward of the River Indus and westward of River Ravi, including Chamba and excluding Lahaul, being part of territories ceded to the British Government by the Lahore State, according to the provision of Article IV of the Treaty of Lahore, dated 9 March 1846.

Article 2

The eastern boundary of the tract transferred by the foregoing article of Maharajah Golab Sing shall be laid down by Commissioners appointed by the British Government and Maharajah Golab Sing respectively for the purpose and shall be defined in a separate engagement after survey.

Article 3

In consideration of the transfer made to him and his heirs by the provision for the foregoing article, Maharajah Golab Sing will pay to the British Government the sum of seventy-five lakhs of rupees (Nanukshahee), fifty lakhs to be paid on ratification of this treaty and twenty five lakhs on or before 1st October of the current year AD 1846.

Article 4

The limits of territory of Maharajah Golab Sing shall not be, at any time changed without concurrence of the British Government.

Article 5

Maharajah Golab Sing will refer to arbitration of the British Government any disputes or question that may arise between himself and Government of Lahore or any other neighbouring State, and will abide by the decision of the British Government.

Article 6

Maharajah Golab Sing engages for himself and heirs to join, with the whole of the military force, the British troops, when employed within the hills or in the territories adjoining his possessions.

Article 7

Maharajah Golab Sing engages never to take or retain in his service, any British subject, nor the subject of any European or American State, without the consent of British Government.

Article 8

Maharajah Golab Sing engages to respect, in regard to the territory transferred to him, the provisions of Articles V, VI and VII of the separate engagement between the British Government and the Lahore Durbar, dated March 11th, 1846.

Article 9

The British government will give its aid to Maharajah Golab Sing in protecting his territories from external enemies.

Article 10

Maharajah Golab Sing acknowledges the supremacy of the British Government and will, in token of such supremacy, present annually to the British Government one horse, twelve perfect shawl goats of approved breed (six male and six female) and three pairs of Cashmere Shawls.

The Treaty, consisting of ten articles, has been this day settled by Fredrick Currie, Esquire, and Brevet Major Henry Montgomery Lawrence, acting under the directions of the Right Honourable Sir Henry Hardinge, G.C.B., Governor General on the part of the British Government, and Maharaja Golab Sing in person; and the said Treaty has been this day ratified by the seal of Right Honourable Sir Henry Hardinge, G.C.B., Governor-General.

Done at Amritsar, the sixteenth day of March, in the year of our Lord one thousand eight hundred forty-six corresponding with the seventeenth day of Rabi-ul-awal 1262 Hijri.

F Currie
HM Lawrence

Hardinge

By order of the Right Honourable the Governor-General of India.

F CURRIE
Secretary to the Government of India, with the Governor-General.

STANDSTILL AGREEMENT BETWEEN JAMMU & KASHMIR AND INDIA AND PAKISTAN

Identical telegrams were sent by the Prime Minister of Kashmir to the Dominions of India and Pakistan on August 12, 1947. The text is as follows:

> "Jammu and Kashmir Government would welcome Standstill Agreement with India (Pakistan) on all matters on which these exist at present moment with outgoing British Government. It is suggested that existing arrangements should continue pending settlement of details and formal execution of fresh agreement."

Reply from Government of Pakistan sent on August 15, 1947:

> "Your telegram of 12th. The Government of Pakistan agree to have a Standstill Agreement with the Government of Jammu and Kashmir for the continuance of the existing arrangements pending settlement of details and formal execution."

Reply from the Government of India:

> "Government of India would be glad if you or some other minister duly authorized in this behalf could fly to Delhi for negotiating Standstill Agreement between Kashmir Government and India Dominion. Early action desirable to maintain intact the existing arrangements."

The representative of Kashmir did not visit Delhi and no Standstill Agreement was concluded between the State and the Dominion of India.

INSTRUMENT OF ACCESSION OF THE STATE OF JAMMU & KASHMIR

Where as the Indian Independence Act 1947, provides that as from the fifteenth day of August 1947, there shall be set up an independent Dominion known as India, and that the Government of India Act, 1935, shall with such omissions, additions, adaptations and modifications as the Governor General may by order specify be applicable to the Dominion of India;

And whereas the Government of India Act, 1935 as so adopted by the Governor General provides that an Indian State may accede to the Dominion of India by an Instrument of Accession executed by the Ruler thereof:

Now therefore, I Shriman Indar Mahandar Rajrajeshwar Maharajadhiraj Shri Hari Singhji, Jammu and Kashmir Naresh Tatha Tibbet Adi Deshadhi- pathi, Ruler of Jammu and Kashmir State, in the exercise of my sovereignty in and over my State do hereby execute my this Instrument of Accession; and

1. I hereby declare that I accede to the Dominion of India with the intent that the Governor General of India, the Dominion Legislature, the Federal Court and any other Dominion authority established for the purpose of the Dominion shall, by virtue of this my Instrument of Accession but subject always to the terms thereof, and for the purposes only of the Dominion, exercise in relation to the State of Jammu and Kashmir (here- in after referred to as "this State") such functions as may be vested in them by or under the Government of India Act 1935 as in force in the Dominion of India, on the 15th day of August 1947 (which Act as so in force is hereafter referred to as "the Act").

2. I hereby assume the obligation of ensuring that due effect is given to the provisions of the Act within this State so far as they are applicable therein by virtue of my Instrument of Accession.

3. I accept the matters specified in the schedule hereto as the matters with respect to which the Dominion Legislature may make laws for this State.

4. I hereby declare that I accede to the Dominion of India on the assurance that if an agreement is made between the Governor General and the Ruler of this

State whereby any functions in relation to the administration in this State of any law of the Dominion Legislature shall be exercised by the Ruler of this State, then any such agreement shall be deemed to form part of this Instrument and shall be construed and have effect accordingly.

5. The terms of this my Instrument of Accession shall not be varied by any amendment of the Act or of the Indian Independence Act, 1947 unless such amendment is accepted by me by an Instrument supplementary to this Instrument.

6. Nothing in this Instrument shall empower the Dominion Legislature to make any law for this state authorizing the compulsory acquisition of land for any purpose, but I hereby undertake that should the Dominion for the purpose of a Dominion law which applies in this State deem it necessary to acquire land, I will at their request acquire the land at their expense or if the land belongs to me transfer it to them on such terms as may be agreed, or, in default of the agreement, determined by an arbitrator to be appointed by the Chief Justice of India.

7. Nothing in this Instrument shall be deemed to commit me in any way to acceptance of any future Constitution of India or to fetter my discretion to enter into arrangements with the Government of India under any such future constitution.

8. Nothing in this Instrument affects the continuance of my sovereignty in and over this State, or, save as provided by or under this instrument, the exercise of any powers, authority and rights now enjoyed by me as a ruler of this State or the validity of any law at present in force in this State.

9. I hereby declare that I execute this Instrument on behalf of this State and that any reference in this Instrument to me or to the ruler of the State is to be construed as including a reference to my heirs and successors.

Given under my hand this 26th day of October, nineteen hundred and forty seven.

(Sd) Hari Singh
Maharajadhiraj of Jammu and Kashmir State

SCHEDULE

The matters with respect to which the Dominion Legislature may make laws for the State:

A. Defence

1. The naval, military and air forces of the Dominion and any other armed forces, including forces raised or maintained by the Dominion; any armed forces, including forces raised or maintained by an acceding State, which are attached to, or operating with, any of the armed forces of the Dominion.

2. Naval, military and air force works, administration of cantonment areas.

3. Arms, firearms, ammunition.

4. Explosives.

B. External affairs

1. External affairs; the implementation of treaties and agreements with other countries; extradition, including the surrender of criminal and accused persons to parts of His Majesty's Dominions outside India.

2. Admission into, and emigration and expulsion from India including relations thereto, the regulation of the movements in India of persons who are not British subjects domiciled in India or subjects of any acceding State, pilgrimages to places beyond India.

3. Naturalization.

C. Communications

1. Posts and telegraphs, including telephones, wireless, broadcasting, and other like forms of communication.

2. Federal railways; the regulation of all railways other than minor railways in respect of safety, maximum and minimum rates and fare, station and services terminal charges, interchange of traffic and responsibility of railway administrations as carriers of goods and passengers; the regulation of minor railways in respect of safety and the responsibility of the administration

of such railway as carriers of goods and passengers.

3. Maritime shipping and navigation, including shipping and navigation on tidal waters; Admiralty jurisdiction.

4. Port quarantine.

5. Major ports, that is to say, the declaration and delimitation of such ports, and the constitution and powers of Port Authorities therein.

6. Aircraft and air navigation; the provision of aerodromes; regulation and organizations of air traffic and of aerodromes.

7. Lighthouses, including lightships, beacons and other provisions for the safety of shipping and aircraft.

8. Carriage of passengers and goods by sea or by air.

9. Extension of the powers and jurisdiction of members of police force belonging to any unit to railway area outside that unit.

D. Ancillary

1. Elections to the Dominion Legislature, subject to the provisions of the Act and of any Order made thereunder.

2. Offences against laws with respect to any of the aforesaid matters.

3. Inquiries and statistics for the purposes of any of the aforesaid matters.

4. Jurisdiction and powers of all court s with respect to any of the aforesaid matters but, except with the consent of the Ruler of the Acceding State, not so as to confer any jurisdiction or powers upon any courts other than ordinarily exercising jurisdiction in or in relation to that State.

ACCEPTANCE OF INSTRUMENT OF ACCESSION

My dear Maharajah Sahib,

Your Highness' letter, dated the 26th October, has been delivered to me by Mr. V. P. Menon.

In the special circumstances mentioned by Your Highness, my Government has decided to accept the accession of Kashmir state to the Dominion of India.

Consistently with their policy that in the case of any state where the issue of accession has been the subject of dispute, the question of accession should be decided in accordance with the wishes of the people of the state, it is my government's wish that, as soon as law and order have been restored in Kashmir and her soil cleared of the invader, the question of the state's accession should be settled by a reference to the people. Meanwhile, in response to Your Highness' appeal for military aid, action has been taken today to send troops to defend your territory and to protect the lives, property and honour of your people.

My government and I note with satisfaction that Your Highness has decided to invite Sheikh Abdullah to form an Interim Government to work with your Prime Minister.

Yours sincerely,

Sd/

Mountbatten of Burma

LETTER OF THE PRIME MINISTER OF INDIA TO THE PRIME MINISTER OF PAKISTAN ON 22 DECEMBER 1947

(1) On various occasions, I have drawn your attention to the aid which the raiders into Kashmir State are deriving from Pakistan. They have free transit through Pakistan territory. They are operating against Kashmir from bases in Pakistan. Their modern military equipment could only have been obtained from Pakistan sources; mortars, artillery and Mark V mines are not normally the kind of armament which tribesmen possess. Motor transport, which the raiders have been using, and the petrol required for it, could also be obtained in Pakistan only. Food and other supplies are also secured from Pakistan; indeed, we have reliable reports that the raiders get their rations from military messes in Pakistan. According to our information, large number of these raiders are receiving military training in Pakistan, which could only be under officers of the Pakistan Army.

(2) The forms of aid, enumerated inthe preceding paragraph, which the raiders are receiving, constitute an act of aggression against India because they are being used against a State which has acceded to the Indian Dominion. The Government of India, while protesting against the action of the Pakistan Government in furnishing or allowing such assistance to be furnished, and urging that the Pakistan Government should stop such help and at least urge the raiders to withdraw, has so far taken no action itself which might involve entry by Indian forces into Pakistan territory. They have been hoping, all these weeks, though with diminishing hope, that the Pakistan Government themselves would put a stop to aid to the raiders which is of the nature of help to India's enemies. Since protests have failed to bear fruit, the Government oflndia now formally ask the Government of Pakistan to deny to the raiders:

(i) all access to and use of Pakistan territory for operations against Kashmir;

(ii) all military and other supplies; and

(iii) all other kinds of aid that might tend to prolong the present struggle.

(3) The Government of India have always desired and still earnestly desire to live on terms of friendship with Pakistan. They sincerely hope that the request which they have now formally made will be acceded to promptly and without reserve. Failing such response, they will be compelled to take such action, consistently with the provisions of the United Nations Charter, as they may consider necessary to protect their interests, and to discharge their obligations to the Government and people of Kashmir.

LETTER OF THE PRIME MINISTER OF PAKISTAN TO THE PRIME MINISTER OF INDIA ON 30 DECEMBER 1947

(1) Please refer to your demi-official letter, dated the 22nd December, in which you have brought formal charges against the Pakistan Government for aiding and abetting the so-called 'invaders' of Kashmir in their fight against the forces of the Maharaja and of the Indian Dominion.

(2) Despite the ominous hint contained in paragraph three, I trust I am right in assuming that your letter is not an 'Ultimatum' but a forerunner of a formal reference of the matter to the UNO. If so, nothing could be more welcome, for, you will recollect, this is exactly what the Pakistan Government has been suggesting throughout as the most effective method of ironing out our mutual differences. I am therefore sincerely glad to find that you propose at last to adopt this particular line of approach to our problems.

(3) I must, however, confess my disappointment that your proposal apparently restricts the reference to the single issue of Kashmir. The episode of Kashmir considered by itself would look like a sentence torn out of its context. It is but an act in the unparalleled tragedy which is being enacted before our eyes ever since the announcement of the scheme of partition. A reference to the UNO therefore in my opinion must cover much larger ground and embrace all the fundamentals of the differences between the two Dominions. As I see it, it is neither Kashmir alone nor Junagadh and Manavadar, nor even the terrible tragedy of wholesale massacres of Muslim men, women and children in extensive areas of the Indian Dominion, but a totality of these horrors and iniquities, indicating but one consistent, sinister pattern which should rightly form the subject matter of international investigation. If the root causes of the evil which is vitiating our relations are not determined and removed it is much to be feared that fresh incidents will continue to threaten the peace not only between the two Dominions, but in a much wider field.

(4) The case of Kashmir is simple and our attitude has been explained frankly and repeatedly both in our communications to you and our official statements to

the press. The Pakistan Government has not accepted and cannot accept the so-called 'accession' of the Jammu and Kashmir State to India. We have said it before and repeat that the 'accession' was fraudulent in as muchas it was achieved by deliberately creating certain conditions, with the object of finding an excuse to stage the 'accession'. It was based on violence because it furthered the plan of the Kashmir Government to liquidate the Muslim population of the State. The accession was against the well- known will of an overwhelming majority of the population and could not be justified on any grounds whether moral or constitutional, geographical or economic, cultural or religious.

(5) The sole responsibility for the disturbances which occurred in the State much squarely lie on the Maharaja and his Government who, despite the advice tendered by the Pakistan Government, persisted in their policy of repression of Muslims. Repression was followed by resistance, particularly in the area of Poonch which is inhabited by a large number of ex-soldiers. The resistance in its turn was met with more repression till the Dogra savagery supported by the brutality of Sikh and Rashtriya Sewak bands created a reign of terror in the State. This state of affairs naturally aroused strong feelings of sympathy throughout Pakistan, particularly among the Muslims living in the continuous areas who had numerous ties of relationship with the persecuted people of the State. Some of these people went across to assist their kinsmen in their struggle for freedom and indeed for existence it self. The stage was thus set for the pre planned intervention by the forces of the Indian Dominion to quell this spontaneous popular rising against the culmination of the age long tyranny of the Dogra rule. The repeated warnings of the Pakistan Government went unheeded. This hasty and ill advised action completely changed the picture and the Frontier tribesmen, a ferociously freedom-loving people, naturally took up the challenge in support of their Kashmir co-religionists fighting for their survival and liberation. If the Government of India had extended to the Pakistan Government the courtesy of consulting it before embarking on its enterprise and suddenly landing troops in Kashmir, or even notifying Pakistan of its proposed action, thus providing an opportunity for discussion and consultation, it might have been possible to avert the tragedy of Kashmir. The action of the Government of India served to swell the torrent of popular resentment until it became impossible for the Pakistan Government to stem it without embarking on large scale military operations.

(6) As regards the charges of aid and assistance to the 'invaders' by the Pakistan Government we emphatically repudiate them. On the contrary, and solely with the object o f maintaining friendly relations between the two Dominions, the Pakistan Government have continued to do all in their power to discourage the tribal movements by all means short of war. This has caused bitter resentment throughout the countr y, but despite a very serious risk of large scale internal disturbances the Pakistan Government has not deviated from the policy.

In view of this background it would not be surprising if some nationals of Pakistan were taking part in the struggle for the liberation of Kashmir along with the forces of the Azad Kashmir Government. You must have already heard of an International Brigade composed of representatives of many nations in the world who are likewise fighting on the side of the Azad Kashmir Government. In regard to the modern military equipment that you allege to be in the possession of the Azad Kashmir forces, our information i s that these forces are poorly equipped and such few modern weapons as they might possess have either been captured from the Dogra and Indian troops or have been in the possession of the ex-soldiers of Poonch since the days of the British. As you know there are large number of Poonchis in the Pakistan Army and if some of them while on leave in their homes rendered assistance to their kith and kin in defence of their hearths and homes, it is scarcely to be wondered at.

(7) On the contrary, it is the Indian Government which must answer the charge of conspiracy with the Maharaja of Kashmir in repudiation of the very principles on which it had only one month before opposed Junagadh's accession to Pakistan. The plea that the accession i s only temporary pending restoration of peaceful conditions i s too flimsy to stand examination, p articularly in the light of recent negotiations in the course of which a perfectly fair and workable plan of withdrawal of opposing forces followed by a referendum under impartial aegis, suggested by us, was turned down by your Government. But all this fits in with the general 'pattern' of the India Government's political attitude towards Pakistan ever since it became evident that partition was the only possible solution of our constitutional problems.

(8) The story begins as early as the middle of 1946, following the demonstration of Muslim solidarity throughout the country after the last provincial elections. It became clear that Pakistan was the unalterable goal of the Muslims.

The inevitability of the partition of the country which now became evident to all gave rise to a wave of deep resentment among the Hindu and Sikh population of the sub-continent. As a direct result of this, severe communal rioting occurred in several towns and provinces of India such as Calcutta, Noakhali, Bihar, Bombay, Garhmukteshwar, Rawalpindi, Lahore and Amritsar. Such communal strife had not been unknown previously, but what was astonishing was the unprecedented scale of killings that took place in Bihar and Garhmukteshwar , proving beyond doubt the existence of a well-settled plan of extermination of the Muslims. It was during these disturbances that the Rashtriya Sewak Sangh came to be known as the author of some of the most brutal massacres. The orgy of blood, however, died down in due course, but, as later events proved, only temporarily.

(9) The political activity which took place in the early part of 1947 produced a lull, but soon after the partition plan was announced on 3 June 1947, clear indications began to be received that the country was going to be plunged into a blood bath by the fanatical Sikhs and the militant Hindu groups headed by the Rashtriya Sewak Sangh who had made no secret of their opposition to the Partition scheme, in spite of its being accepted by the representatives of all the three major communities.

(10) The process of Partition itself was marked by all manner of obstructions aimed at depriving Pakistan of its rightful share of financial and other assets. Even in cases in which agreement was reached the implementation was delayed or sabotaged.

(11) At this stage the main chain of events which eventually brought untold suffering to millions of people of East Punjab, Rajputana and the United Provinces was set in motion with a carefully prepared attack on a special train carrying Pakistan Government employees and their families from Delhi to Karachi on 9 August 47. As the plan unfolded itself, it became clear that the Sikhs, encouraged and actively assisted by the Hindus, had determined to liquidate by violent and bloody means the entire Muslim population of East Punjab. The object of the plan was to kill or drive out Mussalmans in order to settle the Sikh population which was being pulled out of West Punjab under a planned scheme. The modus operandi was to disarm the Muslim population and then to leave it at the mercy of armed bands who were actively assisted by the army and the police. There is abundant evidence that this plan had the full support and active assistance not only of the

officers of the Provincial Government but also of the Sikh States such as Patiala, Kapurthala, and Faridkot. Alwar and Bharatpur had already set the example in eliminating their entire Muslim population, but they were soon outdone. Kapurthala, which like Kashmir was a Muslim-majority State, has today not a single Muslim left. Similarly, large tracts of Muslim-majority areas which under the Boundary Award had been most unjustly included in East Punjab were depopulated. The whole country was ravaged by fire and sword, vast numbers were butchered and countless women were abducted. Indeed decency forbids mention of some crimes committed against women. Millions were forcibly and ruthlessly driven out of their homes. The process went on sector by sector and culminated in the tragedy that was enacted in Delhi, the capital of India. According to the Government of India itself, there was a complete breakdown of administration for a number of days. The destruction and desecration of mosques, tombs and holy places and forcible conversions on a mass scale were special features of these happenings.

(12) This plan of liquidation of the Muslim population is still proceeding despite the pious professions of the Government of India. The latest example of this is provided by the happenings in the holy city of Ajmer. The Government of Pakistan find it difficult to believe that under the circumstances the Government of India are innocent of all complicity in this vast scheme of 'genocide' started by the Sikhs and Hindus and encouraged and supported by persons in authority as a means of destroying the newly created State of Pakistan. The Mussalmans of India are being subjected to calculated insults and humiliations. All sorts of tests of loyalty are being demanded from them. The one on which particular emphasis is laid is that they should denounce Pakistan and try to undo the Partition and express their readiness to fight Pakistan on the side of India in the event of war between the two Dominions. It is a matter for deep regret that even today responsible members of the Government of India, including yourself, openly declare their intention or hope of bringing Pakistan back into the Indian Union, well knowing that this can be done only through conquest by arms. Such an attitude can only mean that Hindu and Sikh leaders, while giving their agreement to the Partition plan, did so without any intention of permitting its implementation and, further, that India is determined to undo the settlement by all means available at its disposal. In other words, Pakistan's very existence is the chief casus belli so far as India is concerned. It is this impossible position which manifests itself time and again in all of India's dealings with Pakistan, whether political, economic or

financial and unless an effective remedy is found, it is difficult to see how a direct clash can be avoided with the best will in the world.

(13) The events which took place following the announcement of the accession of Junagadh and Manavadar States to Pakistan lend further support to the contention of the Pakistan Government that the Government of India intend by all possible means at their disposal to destroy Pakistan.

In accordance with the agreed scheme of Partition and the Indian Independence Act, 1947, Indian States were under no compulsion to join either of the two Dominions. Notwithstanding this clear provision, the Government of India, by a combination of threats and cajolery, forced a number of States into acceding to the Indian Union. The Rulers of Junagadh and Manavadar were similarly threatened with dire consequences but they stood firm and exercised their right of joining Pakistan in preference to India. This was the signal for India to launch with full force her attack, using every possible weapon in order to force the States against their will, to change their affiliation. Protests were made to the Pakistan Government, pointing out that a State which had a Hindu-majority population could not accede to Pakistan, as the country had been divided on a communal basis. Another reason given was that Junagadh was not physically continuous to Pakistan and that its accession to Pakistan was calculated to cause disruption in the integrity of India. Simultaneously with these protests, the Government of India put large bodies of Indian troops on the borders of Junagadh and encouraged the neighbouring Hindu States, which had acceded to India, to do likewise. In clear violation of the Standstill Agreement, the Junagadh State was subjected to an economic blockade involving stopp age of all vital supplies, including food, cloth and coal, into the State territory. Lines of communication, including railway and telegraph, were operated in such a mannerthat it became impossible for the State or the Muslim population of Junagadh to communicate with the outside world. A strong press-campaign, calculated to destroy the morale of the State administration and to create panic among the population, was launched both inside and outside the State.

Another line of attack was adopted by setting up the so-called 'Provisional Government' with headquarters first at Bombay and later at Rajkot, which claimed the right to liberate the non-Muslim population of the Junagadh State. The so-called 'Azad Fauj' of the 'Provisional Government' was created and armed by the officers of the Indian Dominion. The 'Provisional Government' not only proceeded to seize by force State property in Rajkot, but by methods of sheer 'gangsterism' created conditions in which it became impossible for the State administration to function. At this point the Government of India sent its troops and occupied the State under the plea of an alleged 'invitation' by the Dewan. Since then an orgy of murder, arson, rape and loot has been let loose in Kathiawar by the military forces of India in exactly the same manner as in Northern India and hundreds of thousands of Muslims have had to flee from the State. According to newspaper reports, Mr Samaldas Gandhi, the head of the so-called Provisional Government, has openly thanked a member of your government for all the assistance received. All this was done in sheer disregard of the international code of conduct and ordinary neighbourly decency. In the interest of peace between the two Dominions Pakistan refrained from sending a single soldier to Junagadh. Occupations by force of Junagadh, which is Pakistan territory, is a clear act of aggression against Pakistan.

(14) In the case of Manavadar even the thin camouflage of a semblance of justification was not considered necessary and the State was taken under military occupation without the slightest explanation being given. A similar fate befell the Talukdari States of Sardargarh Bantva, Sultanabad and Mangrol. The unfortunate rulers of some of these States have been kept in detention and have been subjected to considerable pressure to wean them from their affiliation to Pakistan.

(15) This brief account of India's dealings with a friendly State can leave no doubt in the mind of any impartial person that the new India does not feel herself bound by any moral or international code of rules. The military coup d'etat by which the occupation of Junagadh and Manavadar and other States was achieved is of one piece with the general scheme of destroying the integrity and the very existence of Pakistan to which reference has been made. We have formally drawn your attention to the various acts of hostility culminating in actual seizure of Pakistan territory by the India Government in Junagadh, but have not received even the courtesy of a reply. Perhaps, now that you propose to take the case of Kashmir to the UNO, you would be good enough to let us know why in spite of our clear request you have not withdrawn from the territories of Junagadh, Manavadar and Mangrol, etc.?

In this connection it is of interest to note that the arguments advanced by India for refusing to accept the accession of Junagadh to Pakistan have been conveniently and completely ignored in connection with the accession of Kashmir to the Indian Dominion. This again is fully in keeping with the general political attitude of India towards Pakistan.

(16) These are not the only examples of aggression against Pakistan territory. Numerous raids by armed bands, assisted by the police and military, have taken place across the border into Pakistan. The Royal Indian Air Force have made repeated attacks on Pakistan territory causing damage to life and property.

(17) Another illustration of the same attitude is provided by the refusal of the India Government to implement the recent financial agreement of all outstanding cases which had been referred to the Arbitral Tribunal. The India Government is deliberately withholding the payment of rupees fifty- five crores of the cash balances which is the legal due of the Pakistan Government according to this agreement. This is the latest manifestation of their desire to strangle Pakistan financially and economically which characterized the Partition proceedings. In the case of military stores there has been a similar refusal to implement the agreement. The Supreme Commander, who was appointed as a neutral authority under the Joint Defence Council to carry into effect the partition of the armed forces and military stores, was forced, despite the protestations of the Pakistan Government, to leave by your government long before he could complete his task. At the time this was done, the Indian representatives on the Joint Defence Council pledged the word of the India Cabinet that Pakistan would receive her due share of military shares. This pledge like other similar pledges of the India Government has not been honoured and the slight trickle of military stores to Pakistan shows signs of stopping altogether.

(18) To sum up, our counter-charges against the Dominion of India are as follows :

(i) That India has never wholeheartedly accepted the Partition scheme but her leaders paid lip service to it merely in order to get the British troops out of the country;

(ii) That India is out to destroy the State of Pakistan which her leaders persistently continue to regard as part of India itself;

(iii) That the systematic sabotage against the implementation of Partition, the stoppage of such essential requirements as coal and rail transport, the deliberate withholding of Pakistan's share of funds and arms and equipment, the wholesale massacres of Muslim population are all designed towards one aim, namely, the destruction of Pakistan; and

(iv) That India's forcible occupation of Junagadh, Manavadar and other States in Kathiawar which had acceded to Pakistan, as well as the fraudulent procurement of the accession of Jammu and Kashmir State are acts of hostility against Pakistan whose destruction is India's immediate objective.

(19) I however note with pleasure your assurance that the Government of India have always desired and still earnestly desire to live on terms of friendship with Pakistan. On behalf of the Pakistan Government I fully and sincerely reciprocate this desire. I am constrained, however, to observe that the Government of India have at no stage af forded any practical proof of their desire to live on terms of friendship with Pakistan, more particularly in the case of Junagadh and Kashmir. On my side I can assure you that the earnest desire of the Government of Pakistan to live on terms of friendship with India has in many instances restrained the Government of Pakistan from taking action which would not only have been legally justifiable, but was in several instances urgently called for, and yet was not adopted in the hope that the attitude of the Government of India might even during these later stages be more favourably affected towards Pakistan. I find it more and more difficult to persuade myself to continue to entertain that hope. The course of events, very briefly set out above, would normally have been treated as a chain of aggression justifying extreme action on the p art of the aggrieved Government. Now that your letter of 22 December 1947 has indicated an intention on the part of the Government of India to invite the intervention of the United Nations, a course which the Pakistan Government has so far ineffectively suggested to the Government of India, for the resolving of their differences, I have taken this opportunity to invite your attention to the main heads of the differences between the two Governments that stand in the way of an amicable adjustment of our relations. It is my most earnest hope that these differences may be speedily composed and that our relations will thereafter ever continue to be on the most cordial, co- operative and friendly basis. I trust you will agree that the intervention of the United Nations, whatever form it is to take, should be invited in respect of all these matters, so that all pending differences may be speedily resolved.

INDIAN COMPLAINT TO THE SECURITY COUNCIL, 1 JANUARY 1948 (S/628)

The Government of India have instructed me to transmit to you the following telegraphic communication:

1. Under Article 35 of the Charter of the United Nations, any member may bring any situation whose continuance is likely to endanger the maintenance of international peace and security to the attention of Security Council. Such a situation now exists between India and Pakistan owing to the aid which invaders, consisting of nationals of Pakistan and of tribesmen from the territory immediately adjoining Pakistan on the north west, are drawing from Pakistan for operations against Jammu and Kashmir, a State which has acceded to the Dominion of India and is part of India. The circumstances of accession, the activities of the invaders which led the Government of India to take military action against them, and the assistance which the attackers have received and are still receiving from Pakistan are explained later in this memorandum. The Government of India request the Security Council to call upon Pakistan to put an end immediately to the giving of such assistance, which is an act of aggression against India. If Pakistan does not do so, the Government of India will be compelled, in self-defence, to enter Pakistan territory, in order to take military action against the invaders. The matter is therefore one of extreme urgency and calls for immediate action by Security Council for avoiding a breach of international peace.

2. From the middle of September 1947, Government of India had received reports of infiltration of armed raiders into the western parts of Jammu province of the Jammu and Kashmir State; Jammu adjoins West Punjab which is a part of the Dominion of Pakistan. These raiders had done a great deal of damage in that area and taken possession of part of the territory of the State. On 24 October, the Government of India heard of a major raid from the Frontier Province of the Dominion of Pakistan into the Valley of Kashmir. Some two thousand or more fully armed and equipped men came in motor transport, crossed over to the territory of the Jammu and Kashmir, sacked the town of Muzaffrabad, killing many people, and proceeded along the Jhelum Valley road towards Srinagar, the summer capital

of the Jammu and Kashmir State. Intermediate towns and villages were sacked and burnt, and many people killed. These raiders were stopped by Kashmir State troops near Uri, a town some fifty miles from Srinagar for some time, but the invaders got around them and burnt the power house at Mahora, which supplied electricity to the whole of Kashmir.

3. The position on the morning of 26 October, was that these raiders had been held by Kashmir State troops and part of the civil population, who had been armed at a place called Baramulla. Beyond Baramulla there was no major obstruction up to Srinagar. There was immediate danger of these raiders reaching Srinagar, destroying and massacring large number of people, both Hindu and Muslims. The State troops were spread out all over the State and most of them were deployed along the western border of Jammu province. They had been split up into small isolated groups and were incapable of offering effective resistance to the raiders. Most of the State officials had left the threatened area and the civil administration had ceased to function. All that stood between Srinagar and the fate which had over taken the places en route followed the raiders was the determination of the inhabitants of Srinagar, of all communities, and practically without arms, to defend themselves. At this time Srinagar had also a large population of Hindu and Sikh refugees who had fled there from West Punjab owing to communal disturbance in that area. There was little doubt that these refugees would be massacred if the raiders reached Srinagar.

4. Immediately after the raids into the Jammu and Kashmir State commenced, approaches were informally made to the Government of India for the accepbance of the accession of the State to the Indian Dominion. (It might be explained in parenthesis that Jammu and Kashmir form a State whose ruler, prior to transfer of power by the United Kingdom to the Dominion of India and Pakist an, had been in treaty relations with the British Crown, which controlled its foreign relations and was responsible for its defence. The treaty relations ceased with the transfer of power on 15 August last, and Jammu and Kashmir like other states acquired the right to accede to either Dominion).

5. Events moved with great rapidity, and threat to the Valley of Kashmir became grave. On 26 October, the ruler of the State, His Highness Maharaja Sir Hari Singh, appealed urgently to the Government of India for military help. He also requested that the Jammu and Kashmir State should be allowed to accede to the

Indian Dominion. An appeal for help was also simultaneously received by the Government of India from the largest popular organisation in Kashmir, the National Conference, headed by Sheikh Mohammed Abdulla. The Conference further strongly supported the request for the State's accession to the Indian Dominion. The Government of India were thus approached not only officially by the State authorities, but also on behalf of the people of Kashmir, both for military aid and for the accession of the State to India.

6. The grave threat to the life and property of innocent people in the Kashmir Valley and to the security of the State of Jammu and Kashmir that had developed as a result of the invasion of the Valley demanded immediate decision by the Government of India on both the requests. It was imperative on account of the emergency that the responsibility for the defence of Jammu and Kashmir State should be taken over by a Government capable of discharging it. But, in order to avoid any possible suggestion that India had utilised the State's immediate peril for her own political advantage, the Government of India made it clear that once the soil of the State had been cleared of the invaders and normal conditions restored, its people would be free to decide their future by the recognised democratic method of a plebiscite or referendum which, in order to ensure complete impartiality, might be held under international auspices.

7. The Government of India felt it their duty to respond to the appeal for armed assistance because:

(1) They could not allow a neighbouring and friendly State to be compelled by force to determine either its internal affairs or external relations;

(2) The accession of the Jammu and Kashmir State to the Dominion of India made India really responsible for the defence of the State.

8. The intervention of the Government of India resulted in saving Srinagar. The raiders were driven back from Baramulla to Uri and are held there by Indian troops. Nearly 19000 raiders face the Dominion forces in this area. Since operations in the Valley of Kashmir started, pressure by the raiders against the western and south-western border of the Jammu and Kashmir State has been intensified. Exact figures are not available. It is understood, however, that nearly 15000 raiders are operating against this part of the State. State troops are besieged in certain areas. Incursions by the raiders in to the State territory, involving

murder, arson, loot and the ab- duction of women, continue. The booty is collected and carried over to the tribal areas to serve as an inducement to further recruitment of the tribesmen to the ranks of the raiders. In addition to those actively participating in the raid, tribesmen and others, estimated at 10000, have been collected in different places in the districts of West Punjab bordering the Jammu and Kashmir State, and many of them are receiving military training under Pakistani nationals, including officers of the Pakistan army. They are looked after in the Pakistan territory, fed, clothed, armed and otherwise equipped, and transported to the territory of the Jammu and Kashmir State with the help, direct and indirect, of Pakistani officials, both military and civil.

9. As already stated, the raiders who entered the Kashmir Valley in October came mainly from the tribal areas to the north-west of Pakistan and, in order to reach Kashmir, passed through Pakistan territory. The raids along the south-west border of the State, which had preceded the invasion of the valley proper, had actually been conducted from Pakistan territory, and Pakistan nationals had actually taken part in them. The process of transmission across Pakistan territory and utilisation of that territory as a base of operations against the Jammu and Kashmir State continues. Recently, military operations against the western and south-western borders of the State have been intensified, and the attackers consist of nationals of Pakistan as well as tribesmen. The invaders are armed with modern weapons, including mortars and medium machine-guns, wear the battle dress of regular soldiers and, in recent engagements, have fought in regular battle formation and are using the tactics of modern warfare. Man pack radio sets are in regular use and even mark V mines have been employed. For their transport the invaders have all along used motor vehicles. They are undoubtedly being trained and to some extent being led by regular officers of the Pakistan Army. Their rations and other supplies are obtained from Pakistan territory.

10. These facts point indisputably to the conclusion:

(a) That the invaders are allowed transit across Pakistan territory;

(b) That they are allowed to use Pakistan territory as a base of operations;

(c) That they include Pakistan nationals;

(d) That they draw much of their military equipment, transportation and supplies (including petrol) from Pakistan; and

(e) That Pakistan officers are training, guiding and otherwise actively helping them.

There is no source other than Pakistan from which they could obtain such quantities of modern military equipment, training or guidance. More than once, the Government of India had asked the Pakistan Government to deny to the invaders facilities which constitute an act of aggression and hostility against India, but without any response. The last occasion in which this request was made was on 22 December, when the Prime Minister of India handed over personally to the Prime Minister of Pakistan a letter in which the various forms of aid given by Pakistan to the invaders were briefly recounted and the Government of Pakistan were asked to put an end to such aid promptly; no reply to this letter has yet been received in spite of telegraphic reminder sent on 26 December.

11. It should be clear from the foregoing recital that the Government of Pakistan are unwilling to stop the assistance in material and men which the invaders are receiving from Pakistan territory and from Pakistan nationals, including Pakistan Government personnel, both military and civil. This attitude is not only un-neutral, but constitutes active aggression against India, of which the State of Jammu and Kashmir forms a part.

12. The Government of India have exerted persuasion and exercised patience to bring about a change in the attitude of Pakistan. But they have failed, and are in consequence confronted with a situation in which their defence of the Jammu and Kashmir State is hampered and their measures to drive the invaders from the territory of the State are greatly impeded by the support which the raiders derive from Pakistan. The invaders are still on the soil of Jammu and Kashmir and the inhabitants of the State are exposed to all the atrocities of which a barbarous foe is capable. The presence, in large number of invaders in those portions of Pakistan territory which adjoins parts of Indian territory other than the Jammu and Kashmir State is a menace to the rest of India. Indefinite continuance of the present operations prolongs the agony of the people of Jammu and Kashmir, is a drain on India's resources and a constant threat to the maintenance of peace between India and Pakistan. The Government have no option, therefore, but to take more

effective military action in order to rid the Jammu and Kashmir State of the invader.

13. In order that the objective of expelling the invader from Indian territory and preventing him from launching fresh attacks should be quickly achieved, Indian troops would have to enter Pakistan territory; only thus could the invader be denied the use of bases and cut-off from his sources of supplies and reinforcements in Pakistan. Since the aid which the invaders are receiving from Pakistan is an act of aggression against India, the Government of India are entitled, under international law, to send their armed forces across Pakistan territory for dealing effectively with the invaders. However, as such action might involve armed conflict with Pakistan, the Government of India, ever anxious to proceed according to the principles and aims of the Charter of the United Nations, desire to report the situation to the Security Council under Article 35 of the Charter. They feel justified in requesting the Security Council to ask the Government of Pakistan:

(1) To prevent Pakistan Government personnel, military and civil, from participating or assisting in the invasion of the Jammu and Kashmir State;

(2) To call upon other Pakistani nationals to desist from taking any part in the fighting in the Jammu and Kashmir State; and

(3) To deny to the invaders: (a) access by any use of its territory for operations against Kashmir, (b) military and other supplies, (c) all other kinds of aid that might tend to prolong the present struggle.

14. The Government of India would stress the special urgency of the Security Council taking immediate action on their request. They desire to add that military operations in the invaded areas have, in the past few days, developing so rapidly that they must, in self-defence, reserve to themselves the freedom to take, at any time when it may become necessary, such military action as they may consider the situation requires.

15. The government of India deeply regret that a serious crisis should have been reached in their relations with Pakistan. Not only is Pakistan a neighbour but, in spite of the recent separation, India and Pakistan have many ties and many common interests. India desires nothing more earnestly than to live with her neighbour State on terms of close and lasting friendship. Peace is to the

interest of both states; indeed to the interest of the world. The Government of India's approach to the Security Council is inspired by the sincere hope that, through the prompt action of the Council, peace may be preserved.

16. The text of this reference to the Security Council is being telegraphed to the Government of Pakistan.

RESOLUTION OF THE SECURITY COUNCIL, 17 JANUARY 1948 (S/651)

The Security Council having heard statements on the situation in Kashmir from representatives of India and Pakistan;

Recognising the urgency of the situation; taking note of the telegram addressed on 6th January by its President to each of the parties and of their replies thereto; and in which they afûrmedtheir intention to conform to the Charter;

Calls upon both the Government of India and Government of Pakistan to take immediately all measures within their power (including public appeals to their people) calculated to improve the situation and to refrain from making any statements and from doing or causing to be done or permitting any acts which might aggravate the situation;

And further requests each of those Governments to inform the Council immediately of any material change in the situation which occurs or appearsto either of them to be about to occur while the matter is under consideration by the Council, and consult with the Council thereon.

RESOLUTION OF THE SECURITY COUNCIL, 20 JANUARY 1948

The Security Council,

Considering that it may investigate any dispute or any situation which might, by its continuance, endanger the maintenance of international peace and security; that, in the existing state of affairs between India and Pakistan, such an investigation is a matter of urgency.

Adopts the following Resolution:

A. A Commission of Security Council is hereby established composed of representatives of three members of the United Nations, one to be selected by India, one to be selected by Pakistan, and the third to be designated by the two so selected.

Each representative on the commission shall be entitled to select his alternates and assistants.

B. The Commission shall proceed to the spot as quickly as possible. It shall act under the authority of the Security Council and in accordance with the directions it may receive from it. It shall keep Security Council currently informed of its activities and of the development of the situation. It shall report to the Security Council regularly, submitting its conclusions and proposals.

C. The commission is invested with a dual function: (1) To investigate the facts pursuant to article 34 of the Charter; (2) to exercise, without interrupting the work of the Security Council any mediatory influence likely to smooth away difficulties, to carry out directions given to it by the Security Council, and to report how far the advice and directions, if any, of the Security Council have been carried out.

D. The Commission shall perform the functions described in clause C: (1) in regard to the situation in JAMMU and KASHMIR State set out in the letter of the Representative of India addressed to the President of the Security Council, dated 1 January 1948, and in the letter from the Minister of Foreign Affairs of Pakistan addressed to the Secretary General dated 15 January 1948; and (2) in regard to other situation set out in the letter from the Minister of Foreign Affairs of Pakistan addressed to the Secretary General, dated 15 January 1948, when the Security Council so directs.

E. The Commission shall take its decision by majority vote. It shall determine its own procedure. It may allocate among its members, alternate members, their assistants, and its personnel such duties as may have to be fulfilled for the realization of its mission and the reaching of its conclusions.

F. The Commission, its members, alternate members, their assistants and its personnel, shall be entitled to journey separately or together, wherever the necessities of their tasks may require, and, in particular, within those territories which are theatre of events of which the Security Council is seized.

G. The Secretary General of the United Nations shall furnish the Commission with such personnel and assistance as it may consider necessary.

PROCLAMATION: MAHARAJA, JAMMU AND KASHMIR, 5 MARCH 1948

In accordance with traditions of my Dynasty I have, from time to time, provided for increasing association of my people with the administration of the State with the object of realizing the goal of full responsible government at as early a date as possible and in pursuance of that object have, by the Jammu and Kashmir Constitution Act, established a constitutional government with a Council of Ministers, a Legislature with a majority of elected members and an independent Judiciary;

I have noted with gratification and pride the progress so far made and the legitimate desire of my people for the immediate establishment of a fully democratic Constitution based on adult franchise with a hereditary Ruler from my dynasty as the constitutional head of an Executive responsible to the Legislature; I have already appointed the popular leader of my people, Sheikh Mohammed Abdullah, as head of the Emergency Administration; It is now my desire to replace the Emergency Administration by a popular Interim Government and to provide for its powers, duties and functions, pending the framing of a fully democratic Constitution;

I accordingly hereby ordain as follows:

(1) My Council of Ministers shall consist of Prime Minister and such other Ministers as may be appointed on the advice of the Prime Minister. I have by Royal Warrant appointed Sheikh Mohammed Abdullah as the Prime Minister with effect from 1st day of March 1948.

(2) The Prime Minister and other Ministers shall function as a Cabinet and act on the principle of joint responsibility. A Dewan appointed by me shall also be the member of the Cabinet.

(3) I take this opportunity of giving once again solemn assurance that all sections of my people will have opportunities of service, both civil and military, solely on the basis of their merits and irrespective of their creed or community.

(4) My Council of Ministers shall take appropriate steps, as soon as restoration of normal conditions has been completed, to convene a National Assembly based upon adult suffrage, having due regard to the principle that the number of representatives from each voting area should, as far as practicable, be proportionate to the population of that area.

(5) The Constitution to be framed by the National Assembly shall provide adequate safeguards for the minorities and contain adequate provisions guaranteeing freedom of conscience, freedom of speech and freedom of assembly.

(6) The National Assembly shall, as soon as the work of framing the new Constitution is completed, submit it through the Council of Ministers for my acceptance.

(7) In conclusion I repeat the hope that the formation of a popular Interim Government and the inauguration, in the near future, of a fully democratic Constitution will ensure the contentment, happiness and the moral and material advancement of my beloved people.

RESOLUTION OF THE SECURITY COUNCIL OF 21 APRIL 1948

The Security Council,

Having considered the complaint of the Government of India concerning the dispute over the State of Jammu and Kashmir, having heard the representative of India in support of that complaint and the reply and counter complaints of representatives of Pakistan;

Being strongly of the opinion that the early restoration of peace and order in Jammu and Kashmir is essential and that India and Pakistan should do their utmost to bring about cessation of all fighting;

Noting with satisfaction that both India and Pakistan desire that the question of accession of Jammu and Kashmir to India or Pakistan should be decided through the democratic method of free and impartial plebiscite;

Considering that the continuation of the dispute is likely to endanger international peace and security;

Reaffirms the Council's Resolution of January 17th;

Resolves that the membership of the Commission established by its Resolution 39 (1948) of January 20th, 1948, shall be increased to five and shall include in addition to the membership mentioned in that Resolution, representatives of-----and------and that if the membership of the Commission has not been completed within ten days from the adoption of this Resolution, the President of the Council may designate such other member or members of the United Nations as are required to complete the membership of five;

Instructs the Commission to proceed at once to the Indian Sub Continent and there place its good offices and mediation at the disposal of the Governments of India and Pakistan with a view to facilitating the taking of necessary measures; both with respect to restoration of peace and order and to holding of a plebiscite by the two Governments, acting in cooperation with one another and with the Commission and further instructs the Commission to keep the Council informed of the action taken under the Resolution and to this end;

Recommends to the Government of India and Pakistan the following measures as those which in the opinion of the Council are appropriate to bring about the cessation of the fighting and to create proper conditions for a free and impartial plebiscite to decide whether the State of Jammu and Kashmir is to accede to India or Pakistan.

A. RESTORATION OF PEACE AND ORDER

1. The Government of Pakistan should undertake to use its best endeavours:

   (a) To secure the withdrawal from the state of Jammu and Kashmir of tribesmen and Pakistani nationals not normally resident therein who have entered the State for the purpose of fighting and to prevent any intrusion into the State of such elements and any furnishing of material aid to those fighting in the State.

   (b) To make known to all concerned that the measures indicated to this and the following paragraphs provide full freedom to all subjects of the State, regardless of creed, caste or party, to express their views and to vote on the question of the accession of the State, and that therefore they should cooperate in the maintenance of peace and order.

2. The Government of India should:

   (a) when it is established to the satisfaction of the Commission set up in accordance with the Council's Resolution of 20th January that the tribesmen are withdrawing and that arrangements for cessation of fighting have become effective, put into operation in consultation with the Commission a plan for withdrawing their forces from Jammu and Kashmir and reducing them progressively to minimum strength required for the support of civil power in the maintenance of Law and Order.

   (b) make known that the withdrawal is taking place in stages and announce the completion of each stage,

(c) when the Indian forces shall have been reduced to the minimum strength mentioned in (a) above, arrange in consultation with the Commission for the stationing of remaining forces to be carried out in accordance with the following principles:

(i) That the presence of troops should not afford any intimidation or appearance of intimidation to the inhabitants of the State,

(ii) That as small a number as possible should be retained in forward areas, and

(iii) That any reserve of troops which may be included in the total strength should be located within their present Base area.

3. The Government of India should agree that until such time as the Plebiscite Administration referred to below finds it necessary to exercise the power of direction and supervision over the State forces and police provided for in paragraph 8 they will be held in areas to be agreed upon with the Plebiscite Administration.

4. After the plan referred to in paragraph 2 (a) above has been put into operation, personnel recruited locally in each district should so far as possible be utilized for the re-establishment and maintenance of law and order with due regard to protection of minorities, subject to such additional requirements as may be specified by the Plebiscite Administration referred to in paragraph 7.

5. If these local forces should be found to be inadequate, the Commission, subject to the agreement of both the Government of India and Government of Pakistan, should arrange for the use of such forces of either Dominion as it seems effective for the purpose of paciûcation.

B. PLEBISCITE

6. The Government of India should undertake to ensure that the Government of the State invite the major political group to designate responsible representatives to share equitable and fully in the conduct of administration at the Ministerial level, while the plebiscite is being prepared and carried out.

7. The Government of India should undertake that there will be established in

Jammu and Kashmir a Plebiscite Administration to hold a plebiscite as soon as possible on the question of accession of the State to India or Pakistan.

8. The Government of India should undertake that there will be delegated by the State to the Plebiscite Administration such powers as the latter considers necessary for holding fair and impartial plebiscite including, for that purpose only, the direction and supervision of the State forces of police.

9. The Government of India should at the request of the Plebiscite Administration make available from the Indian forces such assistance as the Plebiscite Administration may require for the performance of its functions.

10. (a) The Government of India should agree that a nominee of the Secretary General of the United Nations will be appointed to be the Plebiscite Administrator.

(b) The Plebiscite Administrator, acting as an officer of the State of Jammu and Kashmir, should have authority to nominate his assistants and other subordinates and to draft regulations governing the Plebiscite. Such nominees should be formally appointed and such draft regulations should be formally promulgated by the State of Jammu and Kashmir.

(c) The Government of India should undertake that the Government of Jammu and Kashmir will appoint fully qualified persons nominated by the Plebiscite Administrator to act as special magistrates within the State judicial system to hear cases which in the opinion of the Plebiscite Administrator have a serious bearing on the preparation for and the conduct of a free and impartial plebiscite.

(d) The terms of service of the Administrator should form the subject of separate negotiation between the Secretary General of the United Nations and the Government of India. The Administrator should fix the terms of service for the Assistants and subordinates.

(e) The Administrator should have the right to communicate direct with the Government of the State and with the Commission of the Security Council and, through the Commission with the Security Council, with the Government of India and Pakistan and with their representatives with the Commission. It would be his duty to bring to the notice of any or all of the foregoing (as he in his discretion may decide) any circumstances arising which may tend, in his opinion, to interfere with the freedom of the plebiscite.

11. The Government of India should undertake to prevent and to give full support to the Administrator and his staff in preventing any threat, coercion or intimidation, bribery or other undue influence on the voters in the plebiscite, and the Government of India should publicly announce and should cause the Government of the State to announce this undertaking as an international obligation binding on all public authorities and officials in Jammu and Kashmir.

12. The Government of India should themselves and through the Government of the State declare and make known that all subjects of the State of Jammu and Kashmir, regardless of creed, caste or party, will be safe and free in expressing their views and in voting on the question of the accession of the State and that there will be freedom of the press, speech and assembly and freedom of travel in the State, including freedom of lawful entry and exit.

13. The Government of India should use and should ensure that the Government of the State also use their best endeavours to effect the withdrawal from the State of all Indian nationals other than those who are normally resident therein or who on or since 15 August 1947 have entered it for a lawful purpose.

14. The Government of India should ensure that the Government of the State release all political prisoners and take all possible steps so that:

(a) all citizens of the State who have left it on account of disturbances are invited, and are free, to return to their homes and to exercise their rights as such citizens;

(b) there is no victimization; and

(c) minorities in all parts of the State are accorded adequate protection.

15. The Commission of the Security Council should at the end of the Plebiscite certify to the Council whether the Plebiscite has or has not been really free and impartial.

C. GENERAL PROVISIONS

16. The Governments of India and Pakistan should each be invited to nominate a representative to be attached to the Commission for such assistance as it may require in the performance of its task.

17. The Commission should establish in Jammu and Kashmir such observers as it may require of any of the proceedings in pursuance of the measures indicated in the foregoing paragraphs.

18. The Security Council Commission should carry out the tasks assigned to it herein.

Adopted at the 286th meeting, Paragraph by Paragraph:

The five members of the United Nations Commission for India and Pakistan were: Czechoslovakia (nominated by India on 10February 1948); Belgium and Colombia (appointed by the Council on 23 April 1948); Argentina (nominated by Pakistan on 30 April 1948); United States of America (designated by the President of the Council on 7 May 1948, in the absence of agreement between Argentina and Czechoslovakia on the member to be designated by them).

UNCIP RESOLUTION OF AUGUST 13, 1948 (S/1100, PARA 75)

The United Nations Commission for India and Pakistan having given careful consideration to the point of view expressed by the Representatives of India and Pakistan regarding the situation in the State of Jammu and Kashmir, and

Being of the opinion that the prompt cessation of hostilities and the correction of conditions the continuance of which is likely to endanger international peace and security are essential to implementation of its endeavours to assist the Government of India and Pakistan in effecting a final settlement of the situation,

Resolves to submit simultaneously to the Governments of India and Pakistan the following proposals:

PART I

CEASE-FIRE ORDER

A. The Governments of India and Pakistan agree that their respective High Commands will issue separately and simultaneously a cease-fire order to apply to all forces under their control in the State of Jammu and Kashmir as of the earliest practicable date or dates to be mutually agreed upon within four days after these proposals have been accepted by both Governments.

B. The High Commands of the Indian and Pakistani forces agree to refrain from taking any measures that might augment the military potential of the forces under their control in the State of Jammu and Kashmir.

(For the purpose of these proposals "forces under their control" shall be considered to include all forces, organized and unorganised, fighting or participating in hostilities on their respective sides)

C. The Commander-in-Chief of forces of India and Pakistan shall promptly confer regarding any necessary local changes in present dispositions, which may facilitate the cease-fire.

D. In its discretion and as the Commission may find practicable, the Commission will appoint military observers who, under authority of the Commission and with the cooperation of both Commands, will supervise the observance of the cease-fire order.

E. The Government of India and the Government of Pakistan agree to appeal to their respective peoples to assist in creating and maintaining an atmosphere favourable to the promotion of further negotiations.

PART II

TRUCE AGREEMENT

Simultaneously with the acceptance of the proposal for the immediate cessation of hostilities as outlined in Part I, both Governments accept the following principles as a basis ofa truce agreement, the details of which shall be worked out in discussion between their Representatives and the Commission.

A

1. As the presence of troops of Pakistan in the territory of the State of Jammu and Kashmir constitutes a material change in the situation since it was represented by the Government of Pakistan before the Security Council, the Government of Pakistan agrees to withdraw its troops from that State.

2. The Government of Pakistan will use its best endeavour to secure the withdrawal from the State of Jammu and Kashmir of tribesmen and Pakistan nationals not normally resident of therein who have entered the State for the purpose of fighting.

3. Pending a final solution, the territory evacuated by the Pakistani troops will be administered by the local authorities under the surveillance of the Commission.

B

1. When the Commission shall have notified the Government of India that the tribesmen and Pakistan nationals referred to in Part II A-2 hereof have withdrawn, thereby terminating the situation which was represented by the Government of India to the Security Council as having occasioned the presence of Indian forces in the State of Jammu and Kashmir, and further, that the

Pakistani forces are being withdrawn from the State of Jammu and Kashmir, the Government of India agrees to begin to withdraw the bulk of their forces from that State in stages to be agreed upon with the Commission.

2. Pending the accept ance of the conditions for a final settlement of the situation in the State of Jammu and Kashmir, the Indian Government will maintain within the lines existing at the moment of cease-fire the minimum strength of its forces which in agreement with the Commission are considered necessary to assist local authorities in the observance of law and order. The Commission will have observers stationed where it deems necessary.

3. The Government of India will undertake to ensure that the Government of the State of Jammu and Kashmir will take all measures within its powers to make it publicly known that peace, law and order will be safeguarded and that all human and political rights will be guaranteed.

C

Upon signature, the full text of the truce agreement or a communiqué containing the principles thereof as agreed upon between the two Governments and the Commission will be made public.

PART III

The Government of India and the Government of Pakistan reaffirm their wish that the future status of the State of Jammu and Kashmir shall be determined in accordance with the will of the people and to that end, upon acceptance of the truce agreement, both the Governments agree to enter into consultations with the Commission to determine fair and equitable conditions whereby such free expression will be assured.

INDIA'S RESPONSE TO THE UNCIP RESOLUTION OF AUGUST 13, DATED AUGUST 20, 1948

New Delhi

20 August 1948

Excellency,

1. On 17 August, my colleague, the Minister without Portfolio, and I discussed with you and your colleagues of the Commission now in Delhi the Resolution which you had presented to us on the 14th instant. On the 18th, I had another discussion with you, in the course of which I tried to explain to you the doubts and difficulties which members of my Government, and representatives of the Government of Kashmir whom we consulted, had felt as the result of preliminary but careful examination of the Commission's proposals.

2. During the several conferences that we had with the Commission when it first came to Delhi, we placed before it what we considered the basic fact of the situation which had led to the conflict in Kashmir. This fact was the unwarranted aggression, at first indirect and subsequently direct, of the Pakistan Government on Indian Dominion territory in Kashmir. The Pakistan Government denied this although it was common knowledge. In recent months, very large forces of the Pakistan regular army have further entered Indian Union territory in Kashmir and opposed the Indian Army which was sent there for the defence of the State. This, we understand now, is admitted by the Pakistan Government, and yet there has been at no time any intimation to the Government of India by the Pakistan Government of this invasion; there has been a continual denial and the Pakistan Government have evaded answering repeated inquiries from the Government of India.

In accordance with the resolution of the Security Council of the United Nations adopted on January 17, 1948, the Pakistan Government should have informed the Council immediately of any material change in the situation while the matter continues to be under the consideration of the Council. The invasion of the State by large forces of the regular Pakistan Army was a very material change in the situation, and yet no information of this was given, so far as we know, to the Security Council.

The Commission will appreciate that this conduct of the Pakistan Government is not only opposed to all moral codes as well as international law and usage, but has also created a very grave situation. It is only the earnest desire of my Government to avoid any extension of the field of conflict and to restore peace, that has led us to refrain from taking any action to meet the new situation that was created by this further intrusion of the Pakistan Army into Jammu and Kashmir State. The presence of the Commission in India has naturally led us to hope that any arrangement sponsored by it would deal effectively with the present situation and prevent any recurrence of aggression.

3. Since our meeting of August 18, we have given the Commission's Resolution our most earnest thought. There are many parts of it which we should have preferred to be otherwise and more in keeping with the fundamental facts of the situation, especially the flagrant aggression of the Pakistan Government on Indian Union Territory. We recognise, however, that if a successful effort is to be made to create satisfactory conditions for a solution to the Kashmir problem without further bloodshed, we should concentrate on certain essentials only at present and seek safe guards in regard to them. It was in this spirit that I placed the following considerations before Your Excellency:

(1) That Paragraph A-3 of Part II of the Resolution should not be interpreted or applied in practice, so as:

(a) to bring into question the sovereignty of the Jammu and Kashmir Government over the portion of their territory evacuated by Pakistan troops;

(b) to afford any recognition of the so-called "Azad Kashmir Government" or

(c) to enable this territory to be consolidated in any way during the period of truce to the disadvantage of the State.

(2) That from our point of view the effective insurance of the security of the State against external aggression, from which Kashmir has suffered so

much during the last ten months, was of the most vital significance and no less important than the observance of internal law and order and that, therefore, the withdrawal of Indian troops and the strength of Indian forces maintained in Kashmir should be sufficient to ensure security against any form of external aggression as well as internal disorder.

(3) That as regard Part III, should it be decided to seek a solution of the future of the State by means of a plebiscite, Pakistan should have no part in the organisation and conduct of the plebiscite or in any other matter of internal administration in the State.

4. If I understood you correctly, A-3 of Part II of the Resolution does not envisage the creation of any of the conditions to which we have objected in paragraph 3(1) of this letter. In fact, you made it clear that the Commission was not competent to recognise the sovereignty of any authority over the evacuated areas other than that of the Jammu and Kashmir Government.

As regards paragraph 3(2), the paramount need for security is recognised by the Commission, and the time when the withdrawal of Indian forces is to begin, the stages in which it is to be carried out and the strength of Indian forces to be retained in the State, are matters of settlement between the Commission and the Government of India.

Finally, you agreed, that part III, as formulated, does not in any way recognise the right of Pakistan to have any part in a plebiscite.

5. In view of this clarification, my Government, animated by a sincere desire to promote the cause of peace, and thus to uphold the principles and prestige of the United Nations, have decided to accept the Resolution.

Accept, Excellency, the assurances of my highest consideration.

Sd.

COMMISSION'S REPLY TO INDIAN RESPONSE DATED AUGUST 25, 1948

New Delhi,
August 25, 1948

Excellency,

I have the honour to acknowledge the receipt of your communication dated August 20, 1948, regarding the terms of the Resolution of the United Nations Commission for India and Pakistan which the Commission presented to you on August 14, 1948.

The Commission requests me to convey to Your Excellency its view that the interpretation of the Resolution as expressed in paragraph 4 of your letter coincides with its own interpretation, it being understood that as regards point (1)(c) the local people of the evacuated territory will have freedom of legitimate political activity. In this connection, the term "evacuated territory" refers to those territories in the State of Jammu and Kashmir which are at present under the effective control of the Pakistan High Command.

The Commission wishes me to express to Your Excellency its sincere satisfaction that the Government of India has accepted the Resolution and appreciates the spirit in which this decision has been taken.

I wish to avail myself of this opportunity to renew to Your Excellency the assurances of my highest consideration.

Sd.

LETTER DATED 20 AUGUST 1948 FROM THE PRIME MINISTER OF INDIA TO THE CHAIRMAN UNCIP CONCERNING NORTHERN TERRITORIES

Excellency,

You will recall that in our interview with the Commission on the 17th August, I dealt at some length with the position of the sparsely populated and mountainous region of the Jammu and Kashmir State in the north. The authority of the Government of Jammu and Kashmir over this region as a whole has not been challenged or disturbed, except by roving bands of hostiles, or in some places like Skardu which have been occupied by irregulars of Pakistan troops. The Commission's resolution, as you agreed in the course of our interview on the 18th, does not deal with the problem of administration or defence in this large area. We desire that, after Pakistan troops and irregulars have withdrawn from the territory, the responsibility of administration of the evacuated areas should revert to the Government of Jammu and Kashmir and for defence to us. (The only exception that we should be prepared to accept would be Gilgit). We must be free to maintain garrisons at selected points in this area for the dual purpose of preventing the incursion of tribesmen, who obey no authority, and to guard the main trade routes from the State into Central Asia.

Accept Excellency, etc.

Jawahar Lal Nehru
Prime Minister of India

REPLY OF THE CHAIRMAN UNCIP CONCERNING NORTHERN TERRITORIES

Excellency,

I have the honour to acknowledge receipt of your letter dated 20 August 1948, relating to sparsely populated, and mountainous region of the State of Jammu and Kashmir in the north.

The Commission wishes me to confirm that, due to the peculiar conditions of this area, it did not specifically deal with the military aspect of the problem in its Resolution of 13 August 1948. It believes, however, that the question raised in your letter could be considered in the implementation of the Resolution.

Accept, Excellency, etc.

Joseph Korbil

UNCIP RESOLUTION OF JANUARY 5, 1949 (S/1430, PARA 143)

The United Nation's Commission for India and Pakistan, having received from the Governments of India and Pakistan, in communication dated December 23 and December 25, 1948, respectively, their acceptance of the following principles which are supplementary to the Commission's Resolution of August 13, 1948:

1. The question of accession of the State of Jammu and Kashmir to join India or Pakistan will be decided through the democratic method of a free and impartial plebiscite.

2. A plebiscite will be held when it shall be found by the Commission that the cease-fire and truce arrangements set forth in Parts I and II of the Commission's Resolution of August 13, 1948, have been carried out and the arrangements for the plebiscite have been completed.

3. (a) The Secretary General of the United Nations will, in agreement with the Commission, nominate a Plebiscite Administrator who shall be a personality of high international standing and commanding general confidence. He will be formally appointed to office by the Government of Jammu and Kashmir.

   (b) The Plebiscite Administrator shall derive from the S tate of Jammu and Kashmir the powers he considers necessary for organising and conducting the plebiscite and for ensuring the freedom and impartiality of the plebiscite.

   (c) The Plebiscite Administrator shall have authority to appoint such staff of assistants and observers as he may require.

4. (a) After implementation of Parts I and II of the Commission's Resolution of August 13, 1948, and when the Commission is satisfied that peaceful conditions have been restored in the State, the Commission and the Plebiscite Administrator will determine, in consultation with the Government of India, the final disposal of Indian and State armed forces, such disposal to be with due regard to the security of the State and the freedom of the plebiscite;

(b) As regards the territory referred to in A-2 of Part II of the Resolution of August 13, final disposal of the armed forces in that territory will be determined by the Commission and Plebiscite Administrator in consultation with the local authorities.

5. All civil and military authorities within the State and the principal political elements of the State will be required to co-operate with the Plebiscite Administrator in the preparation for and holding of the plebiscite.

6. (a) All citizens of the State who have left it on account of disturbances will be invited and be free to return and to exercise all their rights as such citizens. For the purpose of facilitating repatriation there shall be appointed two Commissions, one composed of nominees of India the other of nominees of Pakistan. The Commission shall operate under the direction of Plebiscite Administrator. The Governments of India and Pakistan and all authorities within the State of Jammu and Kashmir will collaborate with the Plebiscite Administrator in putting this provision into effect.

(b) All persons (other than citizens of the State) who on or since August 15, 1947, have entered it for other than lawful purposes, shall be required to leave the State.

7. All authorities within the State of Jammu and Kashmir will undertake to ensure, in collaboration with the Plebiscite Administrator, that:

(a) there is no threat, coercion or intimidation, bribery or other undue influence on the voters in the plebiscite;

(b) no restrictions are placed on legitimate political activity throughout the State. All subjects of the State, regardless of creed, caste, or party, shall be safe and free in expressing their views and in voting on the question of the accession of the State to India or Pakistan. There shall be freedom of press, speech and assembly and freedom of travel in the State, including freedom of lawful entry and exit;

(c) all political prisoners are released;

(d) minorities in all parts of the State are accorded adequate protection;

and

(e) there is no victimisation.

8. The Plebiscite Administrator may refer to the United Nations Commission for India and Pakistan problems on which he may require assistance, and the Commission in its discretion call upon the Plebiscite Administrator to carry out on its behalf any of the responsibilities with which it has been entrusted.

9. At the conclusion of the plebiscite, the Plebiscite Administrator shall report the result thereof t o the Commission and to the Government of Jammu and Kashmir. The Commission shall then certify to the Security Council whether the plebiscite has or has not been free and impartial.

10. Upon the signature of the truce agreement the details of the foregoing proposals will be elaborated in the consultations envisaged in Part III of the Commission's Resolution of August 13, 1948. The Plebiscite Administrator will be fully associated in these consultations;

Commends the Government of India and Pakistan for their prompt action in ordering a cease-fire to take effect from one minute before midnight of January 1, 1949, pursuant to the agreement arrived at as provided for by the Commission's Resolution of August 13, 1948; and

Resolves to return in the immediate future to the sub-continent to discharge the responsibilities imposed upon it by the Resolution of August 13, 1948, and by the foregoing principles.

Sd.

EXTRACT OF AGREEMENT BETWEEN MILITARY REPRESENTATIVES OF INDIA AND PAKISTAN REGARDING THE ESTABLISHMENT OF CEASE FIRE LINE IN THE STATE OF JAMMU AND KASHMIR KARACHI, 29 JULY 1949

This agreement came into being under the auspices of the Truce Sub Committee of the United Nations Commission for India and Pakistan. The members of the Indian Delegation were:

Lt Gen SM Shrinagesh

Maj Gen KS Thimayya

Brig SHFJ Manekshaw

Mr HM Patel | As Observers
Mr V Sahay |

The members of the Pakistani Delegation were:

Maj Gen WJ Cawthorn

Maj Gen Nazir Ahmad

Brig M Sher Khan

Mr M Ayub | As Observers
Mr AA Khan |

The members of the Truce Sub Committee of the United Nations Commission for India and Pakistan were as follows:

Mr Hernando Samper (Colombia), Chairman

Mr William LS Williams (US)

Lt Gen Maurice Delvoie (Military Adviser)

Mr Miguel A Marin (Legal Adviser)

This Agreement described the Cease Fire Line (CFL) in the state of Jammu and Kashmir between the Indian and Pakistani armed forces. The CFL commenced from Manawar in the south to Khor and to Glacier in the north.

The profile of the Cease-Fire Line (a UN mandated military line) has changed with the enactment of Shimla Agreement signed in the wake of 1971 war into Line of Control (a bilateral political line).

PROCLAMATION OF THE MAHARAJA OF JAMMU AND KASHMIR DATED 25 NOVEMBER 1949

Whereas with the inauguration of the new Constitution for the whole of India now being framed by the Constitution Assembly of India, the Government of India act, 1935 which now governs the constitutional relationship between this S tate and the Dominion of India will stand repealed;

And whereas, in the best interest of this State, which is closely linked with the rest of India by a community of interests in the economic, political and other fields, it is desirable that the constitutional relationship established between this State and the Dominion of India, should be continued as between this State and the contemplated Union of India; and the Constitution of India as drafted by the Constituent Assembly of India, which includes duly appointed representatives of this State, provides a suitable basis for doing so;

I now hereby declare and direct:-

That the Constitution of India shortly to be adopted by the Constituent Assembly of India in so far as it is applicable to the State of Jammu and Kashmir, govern the constitutional relationship between this State and the contemplated Union of India and shall be enforced in this S tate b y me, my heirs and successors in accordance with the tenor of its provisions;

That the provisions of the said Constitution shall, as from the date of its commencement, supersede and abrogate all other constitutional provisions inconsistent therewith which are at present in force in this State.

Karan Singh
Yuvaraj
Regent of Jammu and Kashmir

C Gansan
Deputy Secretary

TEXT OF ARTICLE 370 OF THE CONSTITUTION OF INDIA

(1) Notwithstanding any thing in this Constitution:

Temporary provisions with respect to the State of Jammu and Kashmir

(a) The provisions of Article 238 shall not apply in relation to the State of Jammu and Kashmir;

(b) The power of Parliament to make laws for the said State shall be limited to:

(i) those matters in Union List and the Concurrent List which, in consultation with the Government of the State, are declared by the President to correspond to matters specified in the Instrument of Accession governing the accession of the State to the Dominion of India as the matters with respect to which the Dominion Legislature may make laws for that State; and

(ii) such other matters in the said Lists, as, with the concurrence of the Government of the State, the President may by order specify.

Explanation—For the purposes of this Article, the Government of the State means the person for the time being recognised by the President as the Maharaja of Jammu and Kashmir acting on the advice of the Council of Ministers for the time being in office under the Maharaja's proclamation dated the fifth day of March 1948;

Declaration under Article 370(3)—In exercise of the power conferred by Article 370(3), the president has substituted the Explanation to Article 370(1) as follows:

"Explanation—For the purpose of this Article, the Government of the State means the person for the time being recognised by the President on the recommendation of the Legislative Assembly of the State as the Sadar-I-Riyasat of Jammu and Kashmir, acting on the advice of the Council of Ministers of the State for the time being in office."

(c) the provisions of Article 1 and of this Article shall apply in relation to that State;

(d) such of the other provisions of this Constitution shall apply in relation to that State subject to such exceptions and modifications as the President may by order specify:

Provided that no such order which relates to the matters specified in the Instrument of Accession of the State referred in paragraph (i) of sub clause (b) shall be issued except in consultation with the Government of the State;

Provided further that no such order which relates to matters other than those referred to in the last preceding proviso shall be issued except with the concurrence of that Government.

(2) If the concurrence of the Government of the State referred to in paragraph (ii) of sub clause (b) of clause (1) or in the second proviso to sub clause (d) of that clause be given before the Constituent Assembly for the purpose of framing the Constitution of the State is convened, it shall be placed before such Assembly for such decision as it may take thereon.

(3) Notwithstanding any thing in the foregoing provisions of this Article, the President may, by public notification, declare that this Article shall cease to be operative or shall be operative only with such exceptions and modifications and from such date as he may specify;

Provided that the recommendations of the Constituent Assembly of the State referred to in clause (2) shall be necessary before the President issues such notification.

NOTES

Cl. (1) (d): 'Modification'—

(1) The power to 'modify' includes the power to enlarge or add to an existing provision or to abrogate it, if necessary. It is co-extensive with the power to amend and is not confined to minor alterations only.

(2) Article 370 is a special provision for amending the Constitution in its application to the State of J&K. Article 368 does not curtail the power of the President under Article 370.

(3) Article 246 has been applied only with modifications to the State of J&K. As a result, the State Legislature of J&K has a residuary power of legislation over matters which may not be enumerated in the State List or the Concurrent List; the only limitation is that it must not be within the exclusive jurisdiction of Parliament.

REMARKS BY THE EDITOR

1. While other states acceded to the Indian Union as result of Instruments of Accession under the Government of India Act and were integrated in to the Union, an exception was made in case of the State of Jammu and Kashmir due to special and abnormal conditions that prevailed then and as such Article 370 was enacted as a temporary provision.

2. Article 370 limited the jurisdiction of the Union Legislature to enact laws for the State to such matters as were either specified in the Instrument of Accession or which may be added later on with the concurrence of the State Assembly. The decisions so taken were not to be final, but were subject to decisions taken in due course by the Constituent Assembly, when convened.

3. The Constitution drawn up by the Constituent Assembly dated 17 November 1956 provides for:

   - The State of Jammu and Kashmir is and shall be an integral part of the Union of India.

   - The territory of the State shall comprise all the territories, which on the 15 August 1947, were under the sovereignty/suzerainty of the Ruler of the State.

   - The executive and legislative power of the State extends to all matters except those with respect to which Parliament has the power to make laws under the Constitution of India.

   - Extensions of Provisions of Indian Constitution to Jammu and Kashmir:

1954	Customs, Central Excise, Civil Aviation, Posts & Telegraph.
1958	All-India Services; IAS, IPS and functions of Comptroller & Auditor General.
1959	Census.
1960	Powers to the Supreme Court to give Special Leave to Appeal on the decisions of the High Court of J&K. Supervision of the Election Commission on the elections to both Houses and the resolution of doubts and disputes relating to them, although they continued to be conducted according to the laws of the State Legislature.
1961	Extension of the Industries (Development and Regulation) Act, 1951.
1964	Articles 356 and 357 of the Constitution were applied to the State.
1965	Extension of Central Labour Laws.
1966	The provisions of the Constitution relating to the direct election of the representatives to Lok Sabha were applied.
1968	Entry 72 of the Union List was applied in a modified form in relation to the appeals to the Supreme Court from the decisions of the State High Court in election petitions.
1969	Article 248 and entry 97 of the Union List (relating to residuary powers of Legislature) of the Constitution were applied in a modified form and as a consequence, the Unlawful Activities (Prevention) Act, 1967, was extended.
1971	Article 226 which relates to the powers of the High Courts to issue certain writs was made applicable.
1972	Entry 60 of the Union List (sanctioning of cinematograph films) was applied.
1986	Article 249 extended.

- Article 1 pertains to the name and territory of the Union of India.
- Article 238 has been omitted by the Constitution (seventh amendment) Act 1956.
- Article 246 pertains to subject matter of laws made by Parliament and by Legislatures of States.
- Article 368 deals with the powers of the Parliament to amend the Constitution.

THE DELHI AGREEMENT, 1952

After the Constituent Assembly of the State had taken important decisions, it was deemed necessary to receive the concurrence of the Indian Government. Accordingly the representatives of Kashmir Government conferred with the representatives of the Indian Government and arrived at an arrangement. This arrangement was later known as "Delhi Agreement 1952". The salient features are as follows:

1. In view of the uniform and consistent stand taken by the Jammu and Kashmir Constituent Assembly that sovereignty in all matters other than those specified in the Instrument of Accession continues to reside in the State, the Government of India agreed that, while the residuary powers of the legislature vested in the Centre in respect of all States other than the state of Jammu and Kashmir, in the case of the latter they vested in the State itself;

2. It was agreed between the two Governments that in accordance with Article 5 of the Indian Constitution, persons who have their domicile in Jammu and Kashmir shall be regarded as citizens of India, but the State Legislature was given powers to make laws for conferring special rights and privileges on the 'State Subjects' in view of the State Subject Notification of 1927 and 1932; the State legislature was also empowered to make laws for the 'State Subjects' who had gone to Pakistan on account of communal disturbances of 1947, in the event of their return to Kashmir;

3. As the President of India commands the same respect in the State as he does in other Units of India, articles 52 to 62 of the Constitution relating to him should be applicable to the State. It was further agreed that the power to grant reprieves, pardons and remission of sentences etc., would also rest in the President of India;

4. The Union Government agreed that the State should have its own flag in addition to the Union flag, but it was agreed that the State flag will not be rival to the Union flag. It was also agreed that the Union flag will have the same respect and status in Jammu and Kashmir as in other States of the Union.

But for historical reasons connected with the freedom struggle in the State, the need for continuance of the State flag was recognised;

5. There was complete agreement with regard to the position of the Sadar- i-Riyasat, though Sadar-i-Riyasat was to be elected by the State Legislature and recognised by the President of India before installation. With regard to the powers and functions of the Sadar-i-Riyasat, the following was agreed to:

   (a) The Head of the State shall be a person recognised by the President of India on the recommendations of the State Legislature;

   (b) He shall hold office during the pleasure of the President;

   (c) He may, by writing under his hand addressed to the President, resign his office;

   (d) Subject to the above provisions, he shall hold office for a period of five years;

6. With regard to the fundamental rights, some basic principles agreed between the Parties were enunciated; it was accepted that the people of the State were to have fundamental rights. But in view of the peculiar position in which the State was placed, the whole chapter relating to the 'Fundamental Rights' of the Indian Constitution could not be made applicable to the State, the question which remained to be determined was whether the chapter on fundamental rights should form part of the State Constitution or of the Constitution of India as applicable to the State;

7. With regard to the jurisdiction of the Supreme Court of India, it was accepted that for the time being, owing to the existence of the Board of Judicial Advisers in the State, which was the highest judicial authority in the State, the Supreme Court should have only appellate jurisdiction;

8. There was divergence of view with regard to the application of article 352 empowering the President of India to proclaim general state of emergency in the State, the State Government argued that since the subject of 'Defence' is in the Union List, the Union could exercise this power in the event of war, the delegation was averse to such a proclamation on account of internal disturbances.

EXTRACT OF THE CONSTITUTION OF JAMMU & KASHMIR

PREAMBLE

We, the people of the State of Jammu and Kashmir, having solemnly resolved, in pursuance of the accession of this State to India which took place on the twenty-sixth day of October, 1947, to further define the existing relationship of the State with the Union of India as an integral part thereof, and to secure to ourselves—

JUSTICE, social, economic and political;

LIBERTY, of thought, expression, belief, faith and worship;

EQUALITY, of status and of opportunity; and to promote among us all;

FRATERNITY, assuring the dignity of the individual and the unity of the Nation;

IN OUR CONSTITUENT ASSEMBLY this seventeenth day of November, 1956, do HEREBY ADOPT, ENACT AND GIVE TO OURSELVES THIS CONSTITUTION.

PART I
PRELIMINARY

1. *Short Title and Commencement:-* (1) This Constitution may be called the Constitution of Jammu and Kashmir.

(2) This section and sections 2, 3, 4, 5, 6, 7, 8 and 158 shall come into force at once and the remaining provisions of this Constitution shall come into force on the twenty-sixth day of January, 1957, which day is referred to in this Constitution as the commencement of this Constitution.

2. *Definitions:-* 1. In this Constitution, unless the context otherwise requires:-

(a) "Constitution of India" means the Constitution of India as applicable in relation to this State;

(b) "existing law" means any law, Ordinance, order; bye-law, rule, notification or regulation passed, made or issued before the commencement of this Consitution by the Legislature or other competent authority or person having power to pass, make or issue such law, Ordinance, order; bye-law, rule, notification or regulation;

(c) "Part" means a Part of this Constitution;

(d) "Schedule" means a Schedule to this Constitution; and

(e) "Taxation" includes the imposition of any tax or impost, whether general or local or special, and "tax" shall be construed accordingly.

2. Any reference in this Constitution to Acts or laws of the State Legislature shall be construed as including a reference to an Ordinance made by the [Governor].*

†[3. Any reference in this Constitution to the Sadar-i-Riyasat shall, unless the context otherwise requires, be constured as a reference to the Governor.]

PART II
THE STATE

3. *Relationship of the State with the Union of India:-* The State of Jammu and Kashmir is and shall be an integral part of the Union of India.

4. *Territory of the State:-* The territory of the State shall comprise all the territories which on the fifteenth day of August, 1947, were under the sovereignty or suzerainty of the Ruler of the State.

5. *Extent of executive and legislative Power of the State:-* The executive and legislative power of the State extends to all matters except those with respect to which Parliament has power to make laws for the State under the provisions of the Constitution of India.

PART III
PERMANENT RESIDENTS

6. *Permanent Residents:-* (1) Every person who is, or is deemed to be, a citizen of India under the provisions of the Constitution of India shall be a permanent resident of the State, if on the fourteenth day of May, 1954:-

---

*Substituted for "Sadar-I-Riyasat" by the Constitution of Jammu and Kashmir (Sixth Amendment) Act,1965, s. 2.

†Inserted by s. 3, ibid.

(a) he was a State Subject of Class I or of Class II; or

(b) having lawfully acquired immovable property in the State, he has been ordinarily resident in the State for not less than ten years prior to that date.

(2) Any person who, before the fourteenth day of May, 1954, was a State Subject of Class I or of Class II and who having migrated after the first day of March, 1947, to the territory now included in Pakistan, returns to the State under a permit for resettlement in the State or for pemanent return issued by or under the authority of any law made by the State Legislature shall on such return be a permanent resident of the State.

(3) In this section, the expression “State Subject of Class I or of Class II” shall have the same meaning as in State Notification No. I-L/84 dated the twentieth April, 1927 read with State Notification No 13/L dated the twenty-seventh June, 1932.

7. *Construction of References to State Subjects in Existing Laws:-* Unless the context otherwise requires, all references in any existing law to hereditary State Subjects or to State Subject of Class I or of Class II or of Class III shall be construed as references to permanent residents of the State.

8. *Legislature to Define Permanent Residents:-* Nothing in the foregoing provisions of this part shall derogate from the power of the State Legislature to make any law defining the classes of persons who are, or shall be, permanent residents of the State.

9. *Special Provision for Bills Relating to Permanent Residents:-* A bill making provision for any of the following matters, namely.

(a) defining or altering the definition of the classes of persons who are, or shall be, permanent residents of the State;

(b) conferring on permanent residents any special rights or privileges;

(c) regulating or modifying any special rights or privileges enjoyed by permanent residents; shall be deemed to be passed by either House of the Legislature only if it is passed by a majority of not less than two-thirds of the total membership of that House.

10. *Rights of the Permanent Residents:-* The permanent residents of the State shall have all the rights guaranteed to them under the Constitution of India.

STATE SUBJECT DEFINITION

Notification dated the 20th April, 1927

No. I-L/84*. The following definition of the term "State Subject" has been sanctioned by His Highness the Maharaja Bahadur (vide Private Secretary's letter No 2354, dated the 31st January, 1927 to the Revenue Member of Council) and is hereby promulgated for general information.

The term State Subject means and includes :-

Class I

All persons born and residing within the State before the commencement of the reign of His Highness the late Maharaja Gulab Singh Sahib Bahadur, and also persons who settled therein before the commencement of Samvat year 1942, and have since been permanently residing therein.

Class II

All persons other than those belonging to Class I who settled within the State before the close of Samvat year 1968, and have since permanently resided and acquired immovable property therein.

Class III

All persons, other than those belonging to Classes I and II permanently residing within the State, who have acquired under a rayatnama any immovable property therein or who may hereafter acquire such property under an ijazatnama and may execute a rayatnama after ten years continuous resi- dence therein.

Class IV†

Companies which have been registered as such, within the State and which, being companies in which the Government are financially interested or as to the economic benefit to the State or to the financial stability of which the

*This Notiûcation is to be read subject to the provisions of section 6 of the Constitution of Jammu and Kashmir.

†Class IV and Note IV added vide order No. 98-H/39, published in Government Gazette dated 27th Poh, 1996. By the same order His Highness is further pleased to direct that, notwithstanding any law, rule or other order to the contrary, no disability as regards acquisition of any interest in land or other immovable property in the State shall attach to a company which is a State Subject within the meaning of Notiûcation No. I-L/84 dated 20th April, 1927, as amended.

Government are satisfied, have by a special order of His Highness been declared to be State Subjects.

Note I:- In matters of grants of the State scholarships, State lands for agricultural and house building purposes and recruitment to State service, State Subjects of Class I should receive preference over other classes and those of Class II, over Class III, subject, however, to the Order dated 31st January, 1927 of His Highness the Maharaja Bahadur regarding employment of hereditary State Subjects in Government service.

Note II:- The descendants of the persons who have secured the status of any class of the State Subjects will be entitled to become the State Subject of the same class. For example, if A is declared a State Subject of Class II his sons and grandsons will *ipso facto* acquire the status of the same Class (II) and not of Class I.

[Note III:- The wife or a widow of a State Subject of any class shall acquire the status of her husband as State Subject of the same Class as her husband, so long as she resides in the State and does not leave the State for permanent residence outside the State.]*

[Note IV:- For the purposes of the interpretation of the term 'State Subject' either with reference to any law for the time being in force or otherwise, the definition given in this Notification as amended upto date shall be read as if such amended definition existed in this Notification as originally issued.]†

---

*Note III added vide Notiûcation No. 51-L/1989 as amended by Notification No. 6-L/1990 published in Government Gazette dated 8th Baisakh, 1990 and Government Gazette dated the 23rd Bhadon, 1990 respectively.

†See footnote under Class IV.

NOTIFICATION

(Issued by order of His Highness the Maharaja Bahadur dated Srinagar, the 27th June, 1932/14th Har, 1989. Published in Government Gazette dated 24th Har, 1989)

No. 13-L/1989*:- Whereas it is necessary to determine the status of Jammu and Kashmir State Subjects in foreign territories and to inform the Governments of Foreign States as to the position of their nationals of this State; it is hereby commanded and notified for public information, as follows:-

1. That all emigrants from the Jammu and Kashmir State to foreign territories shall be considered State Subjects and also the descendants of these emigrants born abroad for two generations:

   Provided that these nationals of the Jammu and Kashmir State shall not be entitled to claim the internal rights granted to subjects of this State by the laws, unless they fulfil the conditions laid down by those laws and rules for the specific purposes mentioned therein.

2. The foreign nationals residing in the State of Jammu and Kashmir shall not acquire the nationality of the Jammu and Kashmir State until after the age of 18 on purchasing immovable property under permission of an ijazatnama and on obtaining a rayatnama after ten years continuous residence in the Jammu and Kashmir S tate as laid down in Notification No. I-L of 1984, dated 20th April, 1927.

3. Certificates of nationality of the Jammu and Kashmir State may, on application, be granted by the Minister-in-Charge of the Political Department in accordance with the provisions of section I of this Notification.

---

*This Notification is to be read subject to the provisions of section 6 of the Constitution of Jammu and Kashmir and the Jammu and Kashmir Grant of Permanent Resident Certificate (Procedure) Act, 1963 (XIII of 1963).

KASHMIR ACCORD (13 NOVEMBER 1974*)

Agreed conclusions which led to Sheikh Mohammad Abdullah's accord with Indira Gandhi, Prime Minister, and his subsequent assumption of office as Chief Minister in February 1975.

(1) The state of Jammu and Kashmir which is a constituent unit of the Union of India, shall, in its relation with the Union, continue to be governed by Article 370 of the Constitution of India.

(2) The residuary powers of legislation shall remain with the State; Parliament will continue to have the power to make laws relating to the prevention of activities directed towards disclaiming, questioning or disrupting the sovereignty and territorial integrity of India or bringing about cession of a part of the territory of India or secession of a part of the territory of India from the Union or causing insult of the Indian National Flag, the Indian National Anthem and the Constitution.

(3) Where any provision of the Constitution of India had been applied to the State of Jammu and Kashmir with adaptations and modifications, such adaptations and modifications can be altered or repealed by an order of the President under Article 370, each individual proposal in this behalf being considered on its merits; but provisions of the Constitution of India already applied to the State of Jammu and Kashmir with- out adaptation or modification are unalterable.

(4) With a view to assuring to the State of Jammu and Kashmir to have its own legislation on matters like welfare measures, cultural matters, social security, personal law and procedural law, in a manner suited to the special conditions in the State, it is agreed that the State Government can review the laws made by Parliament or extended to the State after 1953 on any matter relatable to the Concurrent List and may decide which of them, in its opinion, needs

---

*This Accord though signed in November 1974, is referred to as 1975 Accord.

†Article 254 pertains to inconsistency between laws made by the Parliament and laws made by the Legislatures of the States.

amendment or repeal. Thereafter, appropriate steps may be taken under Article 254† of the Constitution of India. The grant of President's assent to such legislation would be adopted in regard to laws to be made by Parliament in future under the Proviso to clause 2 of the Article. The State Government shall be consulted regarding the application of any such law to the State and the views of the State Government shall receive the fullest consideration.

(5) As an agreement reciprocal to what has been provided under Article 368*, a suitable modification of that Article as applied to the State should be made by the Presidential Order to the effect that no law made by the Legislature of the State of Jammu and Kashmir, seeking to make any change in or in the effect of any provision of Constitution of the State of Jammu and Kashmir relating to any of the under mentioned matters, shall take effect unless the Bill, having been reserved for the consideration of the President, receives his assent: the matters are:

(a) The appointment, powers, functions, duties, privileges and immunities of the Governor and

(b) The following matters relating to elections namely, the superintendence, direction and control of elections by the Election Commission of India, eligibility for inclusion in the electoral rolls without discrimination, adult suffrage and composition of the Legislative Council, being matters specified in sections 138, 139, 140 and 50 of the Constitution of the State of Jammu and Kashmir.

(6) No agreement was possible on the question of nomenclature of the Governor and the Chief Minister and the matter is therefore remitted to the Principals.

Mirza Mohammad Afzal Beg | G Parthasarathi
New Delhi
November 13, 1974

---

*Article 368 pertains to the powers of the Parliament to amend the Constitution.

After signing the document, Mirza Mohammad Afzal Beg wrote the acknowledgement letter to Mr G Parthasarathy on the same day, 13 November, 1974.

Camp
New Delhi
13 November, 1974

Dear Shri Parthasarathy,

I have today signed the document containing the points on which we have reached agreement.

As you may recall, in the course of discussions we had on various issues, I had proposals regarding the following matters:

(i) The provisions relating to fundamental rights to be incorporated in the State Constitution.

(ii) The superintendence, direction and control over elections to the State Legislature by the Election Commission should be removed.

(iii) Article 356 should be modified to require the consent of the State before an order is issued thereunder, or some similar safeguard should be provided.

After prolonged discussions you did not agree to these proposals.

Kindly acknowledge receipt.

Yours Sincerely,
Mirza Mohammad Afzal Beg

Shri G Parthasarthy
31 Aurengzeb Road
New Delhi

REMARKS BY THE EDITOR ON THE ISSUE OF JAMMU AND KASHMIR, POK AND NORTHERN AREAS

AREA OF J&K

• Total Area	2,22,236 sq kms
• Area under illegal occupation of Pakistan	78,114 sq kms
• Area illegally ceded to China by Pakistan	5,180 sq kms
• Area under illegal occupation of China	37,555 sq kms
• Area under effective control of India	101,387 sq kms

PAKISTAN OCCUPIED KASHMIR

Pakistan Occupied Kashmir (POK) or Azad Kashmir as Pakistan would like to call it, is supposed to be a separate and independent entity, but is kept under firm Pakistani control lest the Kashmiris (from POK) start seeking independence. It has been given the status of a country by giving it a President, a Prime Minister and a Legislature of its own.

According to Karachi Agreement, April 28, 1949 between Pakistan, POK and the Muslim Conference, Pakistan was entrusted the responsibility of Defence, Foreign Policy, Rehabilitation of refugees, negotiations with UNCIP and coordination of all affairs relating to Gilgit and Ladakh. The residual powers were kept open to interpretation which included administration and publicity with regard to its own activities like plebiscite. The Karachi Agreement institutionalised the subservience of POK to Pakistan. All that happens in Pakistan has direct repercussion on POK for furtherance of Pakistan's requirements. For example Mangla Dam in POK supplies electricity to Pakistan with no or nominal royalties.

The Constitution of POK clearly spells out a road map leading to accession of the POK to Pakistan as evident in the following clauses of the AJK (POK) Constitution:-

(a) Part 2 of section 7 states "No person or political party in AJK (POK) shall be permitted to propagate against, or take part in activities prejudicial or detrimental to the ideology of the States accession to Pakistan".

(b) Under section 5(2) vii of the AJK (POK) Legislative Assembly Election Ordinance 1970, a person would be disqualified for propagating any opinion or action in any manner prejudicial to the ideology of Pakistan,the ideology of the State's accession to Pakistan or sovereignty and integrity of Pakistan. The same rule is applicable to any one who defames or brings into ridicule the Judiciary of AJK (POK) or Pakistan or the Armed Forces of Pakistan.

(c) A Pakistani caveat exists even on the right of free speech for AJK (POK) residents while guaranteeing freedom of speech; section 9 of AJK (POK) Constitution imposes the so called reasonable restrictions in the interest of security and friendly relations with Pakistan.

(d) The oath of office for the President, Prime Minister, Minister, Speaker and MLA/MLC of AJK (POK) clearly states that "I will remain loyal to the country and the cause of accession of the State of Jammu and Kashmir to Pakistan.

(e) Under sections 31 and 56 of the Constitution, Pakistan retains all rights with regard to UNCIP resolutions, Defence, Security of AJK (POK), Currency and Issue Bills and External Affairs. Islamabad retains the right to dismiss the Government of AJK (POK) or take such actions as to enable Pakistan discharge its responsibilities under section 56 of the Constitution.

(f) Since 1974, the main executive authority rests in a Council with the Prime Minister of Pakistan in chair and AJK (POK) President as vice Chairman. The Council has 13 members out of which six are nominated by Pakistan, thus giving Pakistan a majority in a Council of 13.

It would thus be seen that Pakistan retains all vital powers in relation to POK through the Ministry of Kashmir Affairs with regard to issues mentioned above and in addition legislation, appointments, general policy relating to heavy financial commitments, public debts and loans, taxes and civil supplies.

NORTHERN AREAS

The Nothern Areas of Pakistan/POK comprise of the districts of Gilgit, Scardu, Diamir, Ghizer and Ghanche. Its area is 72495 sq kms and is inhabited by 1.5 million people. Its enthnic diversity comprises of Baltees, Shinds, Vashkuns, Mughals, Kashmiris, Pathans, Ladakhis and Turks, who speak diverse languages and dilects like Balti, Shina, Brushaski, Khawer, Wakhi, Turki, Tibeti, Pushto and

Urdu. It has a literacy rate of 14% for males and 3.5% for females. A very backward and neglected area with almost no industry, infrastructure or other elements of development. There are only two graduate level colleges and no medical or engineering colleges.

The area assumes great strategic importance as it forms a wedge between Afghanistan and Sinkiang province of China and provides land route links between Pakistan and China. The Karakoram Highway from POK and Northern Areas provide the strategic linkage between Pakistan and China particularly for clandestine transfer of military weaponry.

It is for these reasons that Pakistan does not consider Northern Areas as part of AJK (POK) as the status of the area would then be questionable and Pakistan would not have been in a position to hand over 5180 sq kms of Northern Areas to China. This is not withstanding Article 6 of Sino- Pakistan Agreement of 1963 in which this area has been considered as part of AJK/POK.

The status of Northern Areas has been kept nebulous. None of the Constitutions of Pakistan (1956,1962,1972,1973) describe Northern Areas as part of Pakistan territories. Even the 1974 Interim Constitution of AJK (POK) does not include Giligit and Baltistan as terrotories of AJK (POK). Cleverly these territories have been earmarked to be managed by Kashmir and Northern Areas Ministry (KANA) of Pakistan. A court case in AJK (POK) High court ruled in 1990 that Northern Areas are part of AJK (POK) but the order was modified by Pakistan Supreme Court. The situation is baffling—while on one hand Pakistan claims that Northern Areas are not part of AJK/POK/Kashmir, on the other hand has agreed in the Sino-Pak Agreement of 1963, in which territory of Northern Areas has been ceded to China with a proviso that once the Kashmir issue is resolved, the question of cession of territory of Northern Areas will be re opened with the country of which Kashmir will become a part. Thus, internally Pakistan does not accept Northern Areas as a part of Kashmir while in her external affairs she accepts it to be so as in the Sino-Pakistan Agreement of 1963.

Pakistan treats this area with disdain and contempt only to meet the requirement of mainland Pakistan. A large number of Northern Light Infantry (NLI) troops were employed during the Kargil conflict. O n India assuming the counter offensive to evict the Pakistani intruders, Pakistan high command left a large number of its dead from NLI unclaimed in the Indian territory. Not only that the NLI dead bodies were booby trapped to inflict casualties on Indians who tried to dispose them off with appropriate military honour. While the Indians suffered casualties while moving them to give them an honourable burial, the dead bodies were mostly blown to smithereens. Such is the concern of Pakistan for the people of Northern Areas.

Material For Further Study

The following significant correspondence between the Governments of India, Pakistan and Jammu & Kashmir State, and the Security Council Res- olutions are also relevant:

- Text of Sheikh Abdullah's Letter of September 26, 1947.
- Hari Singh's letter dated 26 October 1947 to Mountbatten; Offer of Accession.
- Government of Pakistan Communique, 30 October, 1947.
- Communique: Prime Minister of Jammu and Kashmir, 31 October, 1947.
- Speeches by Prime Ministers of India and Pakistan of 2nd and 4th November 1947, respectively.
- Pandit Nehru's speech on 25th November 1947.
- Communique of the Prime Minister of India to Pakistan on 12 December, 1947 and their reply of 16 December 1947.
- Letter of Prime Minister of India to Pakistan on 22 December 1947 and their reply on 30 December 1947.
- Resolution of the Security Council of 3rd June 1948.
- Indian Communique 1 January 1949.
- Resolution adopted by the Security Council, 30th March, 1951.
- UN letter dated September 7, 1951 addressed to the Prime Ministers of India and Pakistan, regarding Proposals for an Agreement.
- Resolution of the Security Council dated 10th November 1951.
- Proposal dated 14 February 1953 of the United Nations representative for India and Pakistan. This proposal quantifies the number of troops to be maintained by India and Pakistan on either side of the cease-fire line.
- Text of 5 Power Resolution passed by the Security Council on 24 January 1957.
- Text of 3 Power Resolution passed by the Security Council on 21February 1957.
- Text of the Jarring Report.

BRIEF ON WEST PAKISTAN–INDIA BORDER GROUND RULES

West Pakistan–India Border Ground Rules 1960

1. Ground Rules, 1960 were prepared by a Joint Sub Committee headed by Lt Gen PN Thapar, GOC-in-C Western Comd, India and Lt Gen Bakhtiar Rana, Corps Commander, Pakistan. These Ground Rules were designed for the guidance of the Border Security Forces along the Indo–West Pakistan frontier. The Ground Rules were based on the de- facto boundary as by then the boundary had not been demarcated.

2. The military aspects of the Ground Rules are as under:-

   (a) No Post/Picket or OP will be established within 150 yards of the de jure boundary.

   (b) Both sides, however can go right up to the de facto boundary in hot pursuit of an offender; send patrols within the 150 yards zone, provided both sides inform each other of the beat or any changes in the beat. It was further agreed that the patrols should comprise of not more than 11 men and should carry personal weapons only (no LMGs). No armed civilians were to be permitted in the 150 yards zone. Both sides also agreed that the existing posts/OPs could continue till the de jure boundary is established. New posts could be established within 150 yards of the border with mutual consent.

3. These rules were superseded by Border Ground Rules 1961 in so far as the Punjab (India/West Pakistan) is concerned.

West Pakistan/Punjab (India) Border Ground Rules 1961

4. With the demarcation of West Pakistan/Punjab (India) Border, and in accordance with the provisions of Indo–Pak Border Agreement dated 11 Jan 60, West Pakistan/Punjab (India) Border Ground Rules 1961 came into being. These ground rules, commonly referred to as Ground Rules 1961 superseded Ground Rules 1960 in so far as Punjab (India)/West Pakistan border is

concerned. The essential difference between the Ground Rules 1960 and 1961 is that in the new Ground Rules, there is a provision for the maintenance, repair and replacement of the boundary pillars.

5. The additional military aspects of these Ground Rules are as follows:

   (a) Within a zone extending beyond 150 yards of the boundary and up to a limit of 250 yards therefrom no Posts/Pickets or OPs more than 12 feet in height above ground level could be constructed.

   (b) Within a zone extending beyond 250 yards of the boundary and upto a limit of 1000 yards therefrom, no Posts/Pickets or OPs more than 50 feet in height above the ground level.

6. Post 1965 Indo–Pak War, during the meeting between the two Chiefs on 22 Jan 66, it was agreed that the Ground Rules of 1961 will continue to apply on India/West Pakistan Border.

7. The situation and the legal position, however, has changed with the signing of Simla Agreement in 1972 and this agreement should stand lapsed.

TASHKENT DECLARATION

The Prime Minister of India and the President of Pakistan, having met at Tashkent and having discussed the existing relations between India and Pakistan, hereby declare their firm resolve to restore normal and peaceful relations between their countries and to promote understanding and friendly relations between their peoples. They consider the attainment of these objectives of vital importance for the welfare of the 600 million people of India and Pakistan.

I

The Prime Minister of India and the President of Pakistan agree that both sides will exert all efforts to create good neighbourly relations between India and Pakistan in accordance with the United Nations Charter. They reaffirm their obligation under the Charter not to have recourse to force and to settle their disputes through peaceful means. They considered that the interests of peace in their region and particularly in the Indo–Pakistan Sub-Continent and, indeed, the interests of the peoples of India and Pakistan were not served by the continuance of tension between the two countries. It was against this background that Jammu and Kashmir was discussed, and each of the sides set forth its respective position.

II

The Prime Minister of India and the President of Pakistan have agreed that all armed personnel of the two countries shall be withdrawn not later than 25 February 1966, to the positions they held prior to 5 August 1965, and both sides shall observe the cease-fire terms on the cease-ûre line.

III

The Prime Minister of India and the President of Pakistan have agreed that relations between India and Pakistan shall be based on the principle of non-interference in the internal affairs of each other.

IV

The Prime Minister of India and President of Pakistan have agreed that both sides will discourage any propaganda directed against the other country, and will encourage propaganda which promotes the development of friendly relations between the two countries.

V

The Prime Minister of India and the President of Pakistan have agreed that the High Commissioner of India to Pakistan and High Commissioner of Pakistan to India will return to their posts and that the normal functioning of diplomatic missions of both countries will be restored. Both Governments shall observe the Vienna Convention of 1961 on Diplomatic Intercourse.

VI

The Prime Minister of India and the President of Pakistan have agreed to consider measures towards the restoration of economic and trade relations, communications, as well as cultural exchanges between India and Pakistan, and to take measures to implement the existing agreements between India and Pakistan.

VII

The Prime Minister of India and the President of Pakistan have agreed that they will give instructions to their respective authorities to carry out the repatriation of the prisoners of war.

VIII

The Prime Minister of India and the President of Pakistan have agreed that the two sides will continue the discussion of questions relating to the problems of refugees and evictions/illegal immigrations. They also agreed that both sides will create conditions which will prevent the exodus of people. They further agreed to discuss the return of the property and assets taken over by either side in connection with the conflict.

IX

The Prime Minister of India and the President of Pakistan have agreed that the sides will continue meetings both at the highest and at other levels on matters of direct concern to both countries. Both sides have recognized the need to set up joint Indian-Pakistani bodies which will report to their Governments in order to decide what further steps should be taken.

The Prime Minister of India and the President of Pakistan record their feelings of deep appreciation and gratitude to the leaders of the Soviet Union, the Soviet Government and personally to the Chairman of the Council of Ministers of U.S.S.R. for their constructive, friendly and noble part in bringing about the present meeting which has resulted in mutually satisfactory results. They also express to the Government and friendly people of Uzbekistan their sincere thankfulness for their overwhelming recep- tion and generous hospitality.

They invite the Chairman of the Council of Ministers of the U.S.S.R. to witness this Declaration.

Prime Minister of India
Lal Bahadur Shastri
Tashkent, 10 January 1966

President of Pakistan
Mohammad Ayub Khan

AGREEMENT ON WITHDRAWAL OF TROOPS FROM OCCUPIED AREAS, 1966

PART I

DISENGAGEMENT OF TROOPS AND REDUCTION OF TENSION

Phase 1

1. Both forces will withdraw 1,000 yards from the line of actual control in sectors as specified below:-

   (a) Rajasthan/Sind

   (b) Amritsar/Lahore

   (c) Jammu/Sialkot

   (d) Akhnur/Chhamb (from River Chenab NW 8061 to Mawa Wali Khad NW 7770)

2. In all other sectors including sectors divided by the 1949 cease-fire line, troops will continue to hold their respective piquets as by so doing they will be automatically separated from each other. The only exception to this will be where, in hilly terrain, opposing forces are at present considered to be too close to each other, each side will withdraw to a distance to be mutually agreed upon by the local Commanders not below the rank of Brigadier.

   (Note: In the Amritsar—Lahore sector this 1,000 yards withdrawal will be modified so that Pakistan troops who are actually on the west bank of the BRB Canal and Indian troops who are on the east bank of the BRB Canal facing each other will withdraw all armed personnel off the embankment to a distance of 200 yards on each side. Unarmed personnel may, however, live, move and work in this area. The same principle will apply in Sulaimanki-Fazilka sector, Hussainiwala sector and Khem Karan sector.)

3. After the withdrawal in this phase no new defences of any kind will be prepared in occupied territory.

4. There will be no movement of armed military, para-military or police personnel, either armed or unarmed, within the demilitarised zone and no civilian personnel will be permitted within it by either side.

5. The period for completion of this phase will be five days.

Phase 2

6. In this phase both sides will remove and nullify all defences which will include the:

   (a) Lifting of mines; and

   (b) Dismantling of all other defence works, less permanent defence structures constructed of steel and cement.

   The period for completing the phase will be 21 days which will commence immediately after the five-day period mentioned in para 5.

7. Working parties for this purpose will be formed by unarmed military personnel in uniform. No civilian or civil labour will be used for these tasks.

8. While every effort will be made to dismantle all defence works within the specified period, where owing to weather and other conditions it is not possible to complete this, the uncleared areas so left will be clearly marked and a sketch of these given to the other side.

9. There will be no firing of weapons or use of explosives within 10,000 metres of the line of actual control.

   Where explosives have to be used to dismantle defence works this will only be done under supervision as specified later, and after due intimation to the other side.

10. The present agreement affecting restriction of flights of aircraft will continue to apply.

11. To ensure that the action agreed to in Part I above is being implemented in letter and in spirit, the good offices of UNMOGIP and UNIPOM will be utilised. In the event of a disagreement, their deci sion will be final and binding to both sides.

PART II

WITHDRAWAL OF TROOPS FROM OCCUPIED AREAS

12. After the dismantling of defences has taken place, all troops, para- military forces and armed police who are now on the other side of the international border and cease-fire line, will be withdrawn. This withdrawal will be completed by 25 February 1966. If in any particular sector or part of a sector, the dismantling of defences has been completed earlier than the last date specified, withdrawal may be sector-wise if mutually agreed to.

13. During this withdrawal, there will be no follow up by civilian, armed military, para-military or police personnel until 25 February 1966. Only unarmed military personnel at a strength mutually agreed upon at the sector level may move into these unoccupied areas for normal police duties (see paragraph 16 below).

14. After troops of both sides have crossed into their own territory, the procedure which was being followed by Pakistan and India before 5 August 1965, for the security of the international border and the cease-fire line, will apply. Attention is drawn to Ground Rules, 1961 for West Pakistan/Punjab, Rajasthan and Gujerat (India).

15. It is essential that under all circumstances troops move out of occupied areas by 25 February 1966, even if the dismantling of defences and lifting of mines have not been completed.

16. For immediate settlement of any points of dispute that may arise Sector Commanders not below the rank of Major-General will be designated by name and appointment both by India and Pakistan who will meet to settle the differences. Telephone or R/T communication will be established between these designated Sector Commanders and will be permanently manned.

17. Any matter on which there is disagreement will be referred to the C- in-C, Pakistan Army, and COAS India, for their joint decision. If the issue is still not resolved by them, the good offices of Major-General Marambio will be utilised and his decision will be final and binding on both sides.

PART III

REDUCTION OF TENSION IN THE EASTERN SECTOR

18. The limit of withdrawal in the Eastern Sector will be left to local Commanders not below the rank of Major-General to mutually decide where necessary in consultation with the civil authorities concerned. Both sides will arrive at a working agreement as soon as possible.

19. Border security forces consisting of armed para-military units, police or any other irregular forces of both sides will not open fire across the border under any circumstances.

20. Any encroachments across the border will be dealt with through apprehension of personnel concerned and thereafter handing them over, to the civil authorities.

21. In any case where firing takes place on the border it will be investigated on the spot by a joint team consisting of border personnel from both sides within 24 hours of occurrence. Brigade Commanders/DIGs responsible for this investigation will be designated by name and appointment sector wise for West Bengal, Assam and Tripura by India and for the adjoining areas of East Pakistan by Pakistan.

22. Liaison between Commanders and telephone communications at various levels will be established as given in paras 12 and 13 of the Ground Rules for Indo-East Pakistan border.

23. To ensure that the above agreement is fully implemented, quarterly meetings will take place between Army and Police authorities, of India and Pakistan, to assess the extent to which the agreement is working in practice.

24. These are a supplement to the Ground Rules formulated by the Military Sub-Committee of the Indian and Pakistani delegation on 20 October 1959.

25. In order to resolve any problems that may arise in the implementation of this agreement and to further maintain friendly relations between the two countries, the C-in-C, Pakistan and the COAS, India, will meet from time to time. The meetings will be held alternately in India and Pakistan and will be initiated

by the respective Governments concerned.

26. Ground Rules to implement this withdrawal agreement in the Western Sector will be formulated by Lt. General Bakhtiar Rana—Pakistan and Lt. General Harbakhsh Singh—India, under the chairmanship of Major-General T. Marambio as early as possible.

27. This agreement comes into effect as from 0600 hours IST/0630 hours WPST, 25 January, 1966.

22 January 1966 Sd.

TREATY OF PEACE, FRIENDSHIP AND CO-OPERATION BETWEEN THE UNION OF SOVIET SOCIALIST REPUBLICS AND THE REPUBLIC OF INDIA

Wishing to expand and strengthen the existing relations of sincere friendship between them,

Considering that the further development of friendship and co- operation meets the basic national interests of both States as well as the interests of a lasting peace in Asia and throughout the world,

Being determined to contribute to strengthening world peace and security and to work tirelessly to bring about a relaxation of international tension and the final elimination of the remnants of colonialism,

Reaffirming their firm belief in the principles of peaceful co-existence and co-operation between States with different political and social systems, Convinced that in the present day world international problems can be solved only by co-operation and not through conflict,

Reaffirming their determination to follow the objectives and principles of the United Nations Charter,

The Union of Soviet Socialist Republics, on the one hand, and the Republic of India, on the other, have decided to conclude the present Treaty and with this aim in view have appointed the following plenipotentiaries:

On behalf of the Union of Soviet Socialist Republics-
the Foreign Minister of the USSR, AA Gromyko,

On behalf of the Republic of India-
the Minister of External Affairs of India, Swaran Singh,

who, upon presentation of their credentials, found in due form and proper order, agreed on the following:

Article I

The High Contracting Parties solemnly declare that there shall be a lasting peace and friendship between the two countries and their peoples. Each shall respect the independence, sovereignty and territorial integrity of the other and refrain from interfering in the internal affairs of the other Party. The High Contracting Parties shall continue to develop and strengthen the relations of sincere friendship, good neighbourliness and all-round co- operation existing between them, on the basis of the above mentioned principles as well as the principles of equality and mutual benefit.

Article II

Guided by a desire to contribute in every way towards ensuring a lasting peace and the security of their peoples, the High Contracting Parties declare their determination to continue efforts towards maintaining and strengthening peace in Asia and throughout the world, ending the arms race and achieving general and complete disarmament covering both nuclear and conventional weapons under effective international control.

Article III

Guided by their devotion to the lofty ideal of equality of all peoples and states, irrespective of race or creed, the High Contracting Parties condemn colonialism and racism in all forms and manifestations, and reaffirm their determination to strive for their final and complete abolition.

The High Contracting Parties shall cooperate with other states in achieving these aims and to support the just aspirations of the peoples in their struggle against colonialism and racial domination.

Article IV

The Union of Soviet Socialist Republics respects India's policy of non- alignment and reaffirms that this policy is an important factor for maintaining universal peace and international security and for easing tension in the world.

The Republic of India respects the peaceful policy of the Union of Soviet Socialist Republics aimed at strengthening friendship and co-operation with all peoples.

Article V

Being deeply interested in ensuring world peace and security, and attaching great importance to mutual co-operation in the international arena to achieve these aims, the High Contracting Parties shall maintain regular contacts with each other on major international problems affecting the interests of both states, through meetings and exchanges of opinion between their leading statesmen, visits by official delegations and special representatives of the two governments, and through diplomatic channels.

Article VI

Attaching great importance to economic, scientific and technical co-operation between them, the High Contracting Parties shall continue to strengthen and widen their mutually advantageous and all round cooperation in these fields and also to expand their co-operation in the fields of trade, transport and communications on the basis of principles of equality, mutual advantage and the most favoured nation principle in compliance with the existing agreements and the special agreements with neighbouring countries, as it is stipulated in the trade agreement between the Union of Soviet Socialist Republics and India of December 26, 1970.

Article VII

The High Contracting Parties shall promote the further development of relations and contacts between them in the fields of science, art, literature, education, health care, the press, radio, television, cinema, tourism and sports.

Article VIII

In accordance with the traditional friendship established between the two countries, each of the High Contracting Parties solemnly declares that it shall not enter into or participate in any military alliances directed against the other party.

Each of the High Contracting Parties undertakes to refrain from any aggression against the other party and not to allow the use of its territory for committing any act that may cause military damage on the other High Contracting Party.

Article IX

Each of the High Contracting Parties undertakes to refrain from giving any assistance to any third party taking part in an armed conflict with the other party. In the event that any of the parties is attacked or threatened with attack, the High Contracting Parties will immediately start mutual consultations with a view to eliminating this threat and taking appropriate effective measures to ensure peace and security for their countries.

Article X

Each of the High Contracting Parties solemnly declares that it shall not undertake any commitment, secret or open, with regard to one or more states, incompatible with the present Treaty. Each of the High Contracting Parties declares further that it has no commitment towards any other state or states and shall not undertake any commitments that may cause military damage to the other party.

Article XI

The present Treaty is signed for a term of twenty years and shall be prolonged automatically for every subsequent period of five years unless one of the High Contracting Parties declares its intention to terminate its operation by notifying the other High Contracting Party 12 months before the expiration of the term of the Treaty.

The Treaty is subject to ratification and shall come into force on the day the Instruments of Ratification are exchanged, which will be effected in Moscow within one month after the signing of the present Treaty.

Article XII

Any difference of interpreting any article or articles of the present Treaty that may arise between the High Contracting Parties shall be settled on a bilateral basis by peaceful means in a spirit of mutual respect and understanding.

The above-mentioned plenipotentiaries have signed the present Treaty in Russian, Hindi and English, all the texts being equally authentic, and affixed their seals thereto.

Done in New Delhi on August 9, 1971.

For the Union of Soviet Socialist Republics

AA Gromyko
Minister of Foreign Affairs

For the Republic of India

Swaran Singh
Minister of External Affairs

INSTRUMENT OF SURRENDER OF PAKISTANI FORCES DACCA, 16 DECEMBER 1971

Pakistan Eastern Command agrees to surrender all Pakistani armed forces in Bangladesh to Lieutenant General Jagjit Singh Aurora, General Officer Commanding-in-Chief of the Indian and Bangladesh forces in the eastern theatre. The surrender includes all land, air and naval forces as also all para military forces and civil armed forces. These forces will lay down their arms and surrender at the places where they are currently located to the nearest regular troops under the command of Lieutenant General Jagjit Singh Aurora.

The Pakistan Eastern Command shall come under the order of Lieutenant General Jagjit Singh Aurora as soon as this instrument has been signed. Disobedience of orders will be regarded as a breach of the surrender terms and will be dealt with in accordance with the accepted laws and usages of war. The decision of Lieutenant General Jagjit Singh Aurora will be final, should any doubt arise as to the meaning or interpretation of the surrender terms.

Lieutenant General Jagjit Singh Aurora gives a solemn assurance that personnel who surrender shall be treated with dignity and respect that soldiers are entitled to in accordance with the provisions of the Geneva Convention and guarantees the safety and well being of all Pakistani military and para military forces who surrender. Protection will be provided to foreign nationals, ethnic minorities and personnel of West Pakistan origin by the forces under the command of Lieutenant General Jagjit Singh Aurora.

Sd/-
Jagjit Singh Aurora
Lieutenant General
General Officer Commanding-in-Chief
Indian and Bangladesh Forces in the
Eastern Theatre
(Pakistan)
16 December 1971

Sd/-
Amir Abdullah Khan Niazi
Lieutenant General
Martial Law Administrator,
Zone B and Commander,
Eastern Command

16 December 1971

THE SHIMLA AGREEMENT, 2 JULY 1972

The Government of India and the Government of Pakistan are resolved that the two countries put an end to the conflictand confrontation that have hitherto marred their relations and work for promotion of a friendly and harmonious relationship and the establishment of durable peace in the subcontinent, so that both countries may henceforth devote their resources and energies to the pressing task of advancing the welfare of their peoples.

1. In order to achieve this objective, the Government of India and the Government of Pakistan have agreed as follows:

   (i) That the principles and purposes of the Charter of the United Nations shall govern the relations between the two countries.

   (ii) That the two countries are resolved to settle their differences by peaceful means through bilateral negotiations or by any other peaceful means mutually agreed upon between them. Pending the final settlement of any of the problems between the two countries, neither side shall unilaterally alter the situation and both shall prevent the organisation, assistance or encouragement of any acts detrimental to the maintenance of peaceful and harmonious relations.

   (iii) That the prerequisite for reconciliation, good neighbourliness and durable peace between them is a commitment by both the countries to peaceful co-existence, respect for each other's territorial integrity and sovereignty and non-interference in each other's internal affairs, on the basis of equality and mutual benefit.

   (iv) That the basic issues and causes of conflict which have bedevilled the relations between the two countries for the last 25 years shall be resolved by peaceful means.

   (v) That they shall always respect each other's national unity, territorial integrity, political independence and sovereign equality.

   (vi) That in accordance with the Charter of the United Nations they will refrain from the threat or use of force against the territorial integrity or political independence of each other.

2. Both Governments will take all steps within their power to prevent hostile propaganda directed against each other. Both countries will encourage the dissemination of such information as would promote the development of friendly relations between them.

3. In order progressively to restore and normalize relations between them step by step, it was agreed that:

   (i) Steps shall be taken to resume communications, postal, telegraphic, sea, land (including border posts), and air links (including overflights).

   (ii) Appropriate steps shall be taken to promote travel facilities for the nationals of the other country.

   (iii) Trade and cooperation in economic and other agreed fields will be resumed as far as possible.

   (iv) Exchange in the field of science and culture will be promoted.

   In this connection delegations from the two countries will meet from time to time to work out the necessary details.

4. In order to initiate the process of the establishment of durable peace, both the Governments agree that:

   (i) Indian and Pakistani forces will be withdrawn to their side of the international border.

   (ii) In Jammu and Kashmir, the line of control resulting from the cease fire of 17 December 1971 shall be respected by both sides without prejudice to the recognized position of either side. Neither shall seek toalter unilaterally, irrespective of mutual differences and legal interpretations. Both sides further undertake to refrain from the threat or use of force in violation of this line.

   (iii) The withdrawals shall commence upon entry into force of this agreement and shall be completed within a period of 30 days thereof.

This agreement will be subject to ratification by both countries in accordance with their respective constitutional procedures, and will come into force with effect from the date on which the instruments of ratification are exchanged.

Both Governments agree that their respective Heads will meet again at a mutually convenient time in the future and that, in the meanwhile, the representatives of the two sides will meet to discuss further the modalities and arrangements for the establishment of durable peace and normalization of relations, including the question of repatriation of the prisoners of war and civilian internees, a final settlement of Jammu and Kashmir and resumption of diplomatic relations.

Indira Gandhi
Prime Minister
Republic of India

Zulfikar Ali Bhutto
President
Islamic Republic of Pakistan

DELINEATION OF THE LINE OF CONTROL IN JAMMU AND KASHMIR RESULTING FROM THE CEASE FIRE OF DECEMBER 17, 1971, IN ACCORDANCE WITH THE SHIMLA AGREEMENT

The representatives of the Chiefs of Staff of India and Pakistan held a series of meetings alternately at Suchetgarh (India) and Wagah (Pakistan) check posts to delineate the Line of Control resulting from the Cease Fire of December 17, 1971 in accordance with paragraph 4(ii) of the Shimla Agreement signed on 2 July 1972. The following offcials represented each side:

Pakistan	**India**
Lt Gen Abdul Hameed Shah, S Pk, SQA	Lt Gen PS Bhagat, PVSM, VC
Brig SM Abbasi	Maj Gen MR Rajwade, VSM,
MC Col Mahmud Shaukat	Maj Gen IS Gill, PVSM, MC
Col Syed Refaqat, TQA	Col CM Sahni
Lt Col Afzal Khan	Lt Col MS Chehal, VSM
Lt Col Ahmad Saeed	Lt Col BM Tewari

As a result of a number of meetings, the Line of Control in Jammu and Kashmir was delineated and marked on maps duly signed by both parties, which form part of the Agreement.

DESCRIPTION OF THE LINE OF CONTROL AS DRAWN ON THE MAPS: (ALL GRID REFERENCES ARE IN YARDS)

FROM POINT 260955 ON MAP SHEET 52 B/6 TO NJ 980420 ON MAP SHEET 52 E

The Line of Control runs from 260955 (map sheet 52 B/6) NNW in a straight line to 255968 which point is marked by a stone cairn. Thence NNE in a straight line approximately 300 yards to 257972, thence eastwards in a straight line to 262978, which point is marked by a stone cairn, thence eastward in a straight line to the western bank of the Indus river at 278983 which point is marked by a stone cairn, thence NW along the western bank of the Indus river up to NJ 263005, which point is marked by a stone cairn, thence east across the Indus river to River-Nullah Junction at 266005, thence eastwards up the Nullah upto

NJ 300010, thence ENE on 86 degrees magnetic bearing in a straight line to Shangruti Point 17531 at NJ 399046, which line is marked by four stone cairns, thence NE in a straight line to the boundary line at NJ 436060, thence starting northwards along the boundary line to Chorbat La at NJ 586078, which point is marked by a stone cairn on the top of the pass, thence eastwards along the boundary line up to NJ 684080, thence NNE in a straight line to point 19820 at NJ 688096, thence NNE in a straight line to NJ 70651530, thence NE in a straight line to NJ 740180, thence northwards to NJ 739200, thence to NJ 741251, thence NNE to NJ 745258, thence NNW to NJ 730279, thence northwards to NJ 733290, thence northwards to NJ 737313 on Pakistan map and NJ 737315 on Indian map, a point in the mid stream of river Shyok, thence eastwards along the midstream of River Shyok to NJ 753308, thence NE to NJ 776329, thence eastwards following the spur to NJ 790334, thence ENE along the same spur to NJ 800343, thence eastwards to NJ 837354, thence northwards to NJ 844380, thence SE to a point on boundary at NJ 973330, thence along the boundary to NJ 980420.

Note: Wherever the Line of Control is described as running along the Nullah/ River, it will be interpreted as running through the centre of the Nullah/River unless otherwise specified.

(MR Rajwade)
Major General
Senior Staff Officer to the Indian
Senior Military Commander
11 December, 1972

(SM Abbasi)
Brigadier
Senior Staff Offcer to the Pakistan
Senior Military Commander
11 December, 1972

AGREEMENT ON THE PROHIBITION OF ATTACK AGAINST NUCLEAR INSTALLATIONS AND FACILITIES BETWEEN THE REPUBLIC OF INDIA AND THE ISLAMIC REPUBLIC OF PAKISTAN

The Government of the Republic of India and the Government of the Islamic Republic of Pakistan, hereinafter referred to as the "Contracting Parties",

Reaffirming their commitment to durable peace and the development of friendly and harmonious relations;

Conscious of the role of confidence building measures in promoting such bilateral relations based on mutual trust and good will;

Have agreed as follows:

Article I

1. Each party shall refrain from undertaking, encouraging or participating in, directly or indirectly, any action aimed at causing the destruction of, or damage to, any nuclear installation or facility in the other country.
2. The term "nuclear installation or facility" includes nuclear power and research reactors, fuel fabrication, uranium enrichment, isotopes separation and reprocessing facilities as well as any other installations with fresh or irradiated nuclear fuel and materials in any form and establishments storing significant quantities of radio-active materials.

Article II

Each Contracting Party shall inform the other on 1st January of each calendar year of the latitude and longitude of its nuclear installations and facilities and whenever there is any change.

Article III

This Agreement is subject to ratification. It shall come into force with effect from the date on which the Instruments of Ratification are exchanged.

Done at Islamabad on this Thirty-First day of December 1988, in two copies each in Hindi, Urdu and English, the English text being authentic in case of any difference or dispute of interpretation.

KPS Menon
Foreign Secretary
For the Government of the
Republic of India

Humayun Khan
Foreign Secretary
For the Government of the
Islamic Republic of Pakistan

AGREEMENT BETWEEN PAKISTAN AND INDIA ON ADVANCE NOTICE ON MILITARY EXERCISES, MANOEUVRES AND TROOP MOVEMENT, NEW DELHI 6 APRIL 1991

Whereas Pakistan and India recognise the need to jointly formulate an agreement at the Government level on giving advance notice on exercises, manoeuvres and troop movements in order to prevent any crisis situation arising due to misreading of the other side's intentions.

Therefore, the Governments of Pakistan and India jointly decide that:

1. Their Land, Naval and Air Forces will avoid holding major military manoeuvres and exercises in close proximity to each other. However if such exercises are held in within distances as prescribed in this Agreement, the strategic direction of the main force being exercised will not be towards the other side, nor will any logistic build up be carried out close to it. The following will constitute a major military manoeuvre/ exercise for the purpose of this exercise:

   (a) Land Forces:

      1. India–Pakistan International Border—Concentration of Corps level (comprising of two or more divisions) and above.

      2. Line of Control and area between Manawar Tawi and Ravi Rivers—Division level and above.

   (b) Naval Forces:

   Any exercise involving six or more ships of destroyer/frigate size and above, exercising in company and crossing into the other' s Exclusive Economic Zone (EEZ).

   (c) Air Force:

   Regional Command level and above.

2. Both sides may not conduct exercises of Land Forces at Divisional level and above within five kilometres of the areas specified at paragraph (1)a 1 and 2.

3. Both sides will provide notice regarding exercises of Land Forces as follows:

   (a) All exercises/concentrations at Divisional level in areas specified at paragraph (1)a 1 and 2.

   (b) All exercises/concentrations at Corps level within a distance of seventy five kms in areas specified at paragraph (1)a 1 and 2.

   (c) All exercises above Corps level irrespective of the distance.

4. Both sides will give fifteen days prior notice when formations with defensive roles are moved to their operational locations for periodic maintenance of their defences.

5. The schedule of major exercises with troops will be transmitted in writing to the other side through diplomatic channels in advance as follows:

   (a) Air exercises at Regional Command level and above—Fifteen days.

   (b) Divisional level exercise, and major Naval exercises involving six or more ships of destroyer/frigate size and above, exercising in company and crossing into other's EEZ—Sixty days.

   (c) Corps level exercises—Sixty days.

   (d) Army level exercises—Ninety days.

Provided that the above provisions relate to the commencement of moves of the formations and units from their permanent locations for the proposed exercises.

6. Information on the following aspects of major exercises will be intimated:

   (a) Type and level of exercises.

   (b) General area of the exercise on land, air and sea. In respect of air and sea exercises, these will be defined in latitude and longitude.

   (c) Planned duration of the activity.

   (d) Number and type of formations participating.

   (e) Any shifting of forces from other Commands/Corps/Strategic formations envisaged.

(f) The move of strategic formations, particularly armoured divisions, mechanised divisions, air assault divisions/reserve infantry formations and artillery divisions/ air artillery divisions.

Provided that in respect of major air and naval exercises, only the information at paragraphs (a) to (c) need to be intimated.

7. In case some change in exercise area/grouping of participating formations from the previously notified composition is necessitated, the country carrying out the exercise will intimate the details of changes so as to reach the other country at least thirty days in advance in respect of Corps level exercises and above, and fifteen days in advance in respect of Divisional level exercises and Naval exercises. In respect of Air exercises, if minor changes to the previously notified details are necessitated, an advance notice of seven days will be provided.

8. Any induction/concentration of additional troops of a division size force and above, within one hundred and fifty kms of areas specified at paragraph (1)a, 1 and 2 for internal security duties and/or in aid of civil power will be notified to the other side at least two days before the start of their movements, whenever possible. In case of immediate movements, information may be passed on hot line to the Army Headquarters of the other country. The force so employed will not move forward their logistic bases/installations and armour/artillery.

9. Each country will be entitled to obtain timely clarification from the country undertaking military manoeuvres/exercises concerning the assembly of formations, the extent, direction of the exercise and the duration.

10. The Naval ships and submarines belonging to the other country are not to close less than three Nautical Miles (NMs) from each other so as to avoid any accidents while operating in international waters.

11. Combat aircraft including fighter, bomber, reconnaissance, jet military trainer and armed helicopter aircraft will not fly within ten kms of each other's airspace, including the Air Defence Identification Zones (ADIZ), except when such aircrafts are operating from Jammu, Pathankot, Amritsar and Suratgarh air bases on the Indian side, as well as Pasrur, Lahore, Vehari and Rahimyar Khan air bases on the Pakistan side, in which case they will maintain a distance of five kms from each other's air space. Unarmed transport and

logistic aircraft including unarmed helicopters and Air Observations Post (AOP) aircraft will be permitted to operate up to 1000 meters from each others air space including the ADIZ.

12. Aircraft of either country will refrain from buzzing surface units and platforms of the other country in international waters.

13. This Agreement supersedes all previous understandings in so far as the above points are concerned.

14. This Agreement is subject to ratification. It shall come into force with effect from the date on which the Instruments of Ratification are exchanged.

15. Done at New Delhi on this sixth day of April, 1991.

Shaharyar M Khan
Foreign Secretary
For the Government of the
Islamic Republic of Pakistan

Muchkund Dubey
Foreign Secretary
For the Government of the
Republic of India

AGREEMENT BETWEEN PAKISTAN AND INDIA ON PREVENTION OF AIR SPACE VIOLATIONS AND FOR PERMITTING OVERFLIGHTS AND LANDINGS BY MILITARY AIRCRAFT, NEW DELHI, 6 APRIL 1991

Preamble

States parties to the present Air Agreement, recognising the fact that both the Pakistan Air Force (PAF) and Indian Air Force (IAF) aircraft operate near each other's air space.

Aware that despite best efforts by both sides, violations of each other's air space have occurred from time to time.

Desirous of promoting good neighbourly relations between the two countries.

Conscious of the fact that renewed efforts should be made to avoid unnecessary alarm

Have agreed to enter into the following Air Agreement:

Air Violations

Article 1

Henceforth, both sides will take adequate measures to ensure, that air violations of each other's air space do not take place. However, if any inadvertent violation does take place, the incident will be promptly investigated and the Headquarters (HQ) of the other Air Force informed of the results without delay, through diplomatic channels.

Article 2

Subject to articles 3, 4 and 6, the following restrictions are to be observed by military aircraft of both the forces:

(a) Combat aircraft (to include fighter, bomber, reconnaissance, jet military trainer and armed helicopter aircraft) will not fly within 10 kms of each other's air space including ADIZ. No aircraft of any side will enter the air space over the territorial waters of the other country, except by prior permission.

(b) Unarmed transport and logistic aircraft including unarmed helicopters, and Air Observation Post (AOP) aircraft, will be permitted up to 1000 meters from each other's airspace including ADIZ.

Aerial Survey, Supply Dropping, Mercy and Rescue Missions

Article 3

In the event of a country having to undertake flights less than 1000 meters from the other's air space including ADIZ, for purposes such as aerial survey, supply dropping for mercy missions and aerial rescue missions, the country concerned will give the following information in advance to their own Air Advisors for notification to the Air HQ of the other country:

(a) Type of aircraft/helicopter.

(b) Height of flight within plus/minus 1000 feet.

(c) Block number of days (normally not to exceed seven days) when flights are proposed to be undertaken.

(d) Proposed timing of fiight, where possible.

(e) Area involved (in latitude and longitude).

No formal clearance would be required as flights are being undertaken within own territory.

Air Exercises Near Border

Article 4

In order to avoid any tension being created, prior notice be given with regard to air exercises, or any special air activity proposed to be undert aken close to each other's air space including ADIZ, even though the limits as laid down in Article 2 are not likely to be infringed.

Communication Between PAF and IAF

Article 5

In matters of safety and air operations in emergency situations, the authorities designated by the respective Governments should contact each other by quickest means of communications available. The Air Advisor shall be kept informed of such contacts. Matters of flight safety and urgent air operations should promptly be brought to the notice of the other side through the authorities designated by using the telephone line established between the Army Headquarters of the two countries.

Operations from Airfields Close to the Border

Article 6

Combat aircraft (as defined in Article 2(a) above) operating from air bases specified below will maintain a distance of 5 kms from each other's airspace:

(a) Indian Side

1. Jammu
2. Pathankot
3. Amritsar
4. Suratgarh

(b) Pakistan Side

1. Pasrur
2. Lahore
3. Vehari
4. Rahim Yar Khan

Flights of Military Aircraft through each other's Air Space

Article 7

Military aircraft may fly through each other's air space with the prior permission of the other country and subject to conditions specified in Appendix A to this Agreement. *(Appendix A not attached)*

Notwithstanding paragraph 1 of this Article, each country has the sovereign right to specify further conditions, at short notice, for flights of military aircraft through its air space.

Validity of Agreement

Article 8

This Agreement supersedes all previous understandings in so far as airspace violations and overflights and landings by military aircraft are concerned.

Article 9

This Article is subject to ratification. It shall come into force with effect from the date on which the Instruments of Ratification are exchanged.

Article 10

Done at New Delhi on the sixth day of April, 1991.

Shaharyar M Khan
Foreign Secretary
For the Government of the
Islamic Republic of Pakistan

Muchkund Dubey
Foreign Secretary
For the Government of the
Republic of India

LAHORE DECLARATION
FEBRUARY 21, 1999

The Prime Ministers of the Republic of India and Islamic Republic of Pakistan:

Sharing a vision of peace and stability between their countries, and of progress and prosperity for their peoples;

Convinced that durable peace and development of harmonious relations and friendly cooperation will serve the vital interests of the two countries, enabling them to devote their energies for a better future;

Recognising that the nuclear dimension of the security environment of the two countries adds to their responsibility for avoidance of conflict between the two countries;

Committed to the principles and purposes of the Charter of the United Nations and the universally accepted principles of peaceful coexistence;

Reiterating the determination of both countries to implementing the Shimla Agreement in letter and spirit;

Committed to the objectives of universal nuclear disarmament and non-proliferation;

Convinced of the importance of the mutually agreed confidence building measures for improving the security environment;

Recalling their Agreement of 23 September, 1998, that an environment of peace and security is in the supreme national interest of both sides and that the resolution of all outstanding issues, including Jammu and Kashmir, is essential for this purpose;

Have agreed that their respective Governments:

Shall intensify their efforts to resolve all issues of Jammu and Kashmir. Shall refrain from intervention and interference in each other's internal affairs.

Shall intensify their composite and integrated dialogue process for an early and positive outcome of the agreed bilateral agenda.

Shall take immediate steps for reducing the risk of accidental or unauthorised use of nuclear weapons and discuss concepts and doctrines with a view to elaborating measures for confidence building in the nuclear and conventional fields, aimed at prevention of conflict.

Reaffirm their commitment to the goals and objectives of the SAARC Vision for the year 2000 and beyond with a view to promoting the welfare of the peoples of South Asia and to improve their quality of life through accelerated economic growth, social progress and cultural development.

Reaffirm their condemnation of terrorism in all its forms and manifestations and their determination to combat this menace.

Shall promote and protect all human rights and fundamental freedoms.

Signed at Lahore on the 21st day of February, 1999.

Sd/-	Sd/-
Atal Bihari Vajpayee	Mohammed Nawaz Sharif
Prime Minister of the	Prime Minister of the
Republic of India	Islamic Republic of Pakistan

OTHER ISSUES WITH PAKISTAN IN BRIEF

SIR CREEK DISPUTE

Originally the dispute started in 1907–08 on the border of the two principalities, Kutch and Sind. The dispute was referred to the Government of Bombay and subsequently resolved by the Government of India in 1914. It resulted in a document (Map No B 44) and implemented in the form of Map No B 74 in 1925, which became a landmark document. The award was accepted, both by the Rao of Kutch and Commissioner of Sind. In compliance with this award boundary pillars were erected along the land boundary from the head of Sir Creek towards east to a point referred to as Western Terminus and from Western Terminus at right angle towards north to Eastern Terminus generally covering the entire Rann. Thereafter the dispute remained dormant but resurfaced in 1960s as the 1914 award was questioned by Pakistan in its entirety. The matter was referred to arbitration and Indo–Pakistan Western Boundary Tribunal's Award on 19 February 1968, upheld 90 percent of India's claim to the entire Rann, conceding small sectors to Pakistan. The Award was ratified by both the countries and resulted in placement of boundary pillars. However, what the Tribunal did not do was to demarcate a small portion of the land boundary at the head of Sir Creek and the Creek itself.

Pakistan's stand has been that the boundary should run along the eastern bank of the Sir Creek, thereby claiming the entire Creek. Pakistan quotes the map accompanying the 1914 Resolution in which the boundary has been shown along the eastern bank of the Creek. Indian stand is that the boundary should run through the middle of the Creek as per the internationally recognised Thalweg principle. India also accepts the main text of the 1914 Resolution which indicates that the boundary runs along the middle of the Creek. Between the main paper and the appendix (map), internationally the main text of a document is considered more authentic.

Linked with the issue is the establishment of the maritime boundary between India and Pakistan. Once the end point of the land boundary at the mouth of Sir

Creek is decided, the maritime boundary can be drawn as per the Law of the Sea.

SIACHEN DISPUTE

Siachen Glacier is situated in North Ladakh, north of NJ 9842, the northern most delimited point of the Line of Control between India and Pakistan Occupied Kashmir (POK). The Glacier originates from a pass called Indira Col in the West and runs in southeasterly direction until its snout turns into Nubra River Valley. To its west is the Saltoro range and to its east is Karakoram range. The major passes along the Saltoro range are Sia La, Bilafond La, Gyong La and Yarma La. A number of towns are located close to the Saltoro range in the POK side and the area is comparatively better developed than on the Indian side. The Glacier is approximately 76 kilometers long with a width varying 2–8 kilometers, is one of the largest glaciers of the world. The average height of the area ranges from 20,000 to 25,000 feet, the terrain is glaciated and requires highly specialised clothing, accommodation, provisions, ammunition and equipment. Proximity wise the Glacier is strategically located between India, POK and China. There are, however, diverse views with regard to its strategic importance.

Neither the Karachi Agreement of 1949 nor the Shimla agreement of 1972 refers to the Siachen Glacier while delimiting the CFL/Line of Control between the two countries. The northern most point delimited was NJ 9842. The area north of this point was never occupied by the forces of either side till around 1983/84. When it was found that Pakistan was sending mountaineering expeditions through the area and was also preparing to occupy it, Indian troops pre empted the Pakistani move and occupied the area in 1984. Since then most bloody and expensive battle has ensued in the highest battlefield of the world. The operations in the area are extremely slow, prohibitively expensive and very high in casualties both due to combat and weather. Operations are possible only during the months of summers. Despite a number of meetings between Indian and Pakistani leaders/officials, the situation defies the solution.

TULBUL NAVIGATION PROJECT/WULAR BARRAGE DISPUTE (KASHMIR VALLEY)

The Indus Water Treaty of 1960 permits four distinct types of uses by India of the waters of the Western Rivers: domestic, irrigation, restricted use for generation of hydro electric power through a run-of-river unit and the non consumptive use.

At issue is a barrage that is to be constructed at the base of the Wular Lake in Kashmir so as to regulate the flow of the water into river Jhelum to make it navigable between Wular Lake and Baramula during the lean season between late October and mid February. During this lean season the flow of water is less than 2000 cusecs and depth two feet. To make the river navigable a discharge of 4000 cusecs and depth of four feet is the minimum requirement. The proposed Tulbul Navigation Project or Wular Barrage as Pakistan likes to refer to it involves temporary impounding of water of river Jhelum in Wular Lake in order to regulate its flow during the lean season. While India refers to it as non-consumptive use, Pakistan terms it as 'consumption' of water of river Jhelum, whose water has been assigned to Pakistan as per Indus Water Treaty, except for the purposes mentioned above. The issue can be resolved by trade off by surrendering to Pakistan equal quantity of water from the Eastern Rivers. If the two countries cannot resolve this issue bilaterally, the same could be referred to an international tribunal as per the Indus Water Treaty.

II

INDIA–CHINA–TIBET–OTHERS

TIBET

The geological plateau of Tibet lies between the altitude of 4000 mtrs in the west to 2000 mtrs in the east and covers an area of 469294 sq miles. Much of the vast area is rugged, traversed by more than twenty mountain chains with peaks as high as 6000 mtrs. Great mountain ranges border Tibet on three sides with Himalayas in the south, Kun Lun and Nan Shan in the north and Karakoram in the west. Northern Tibet is a desolate wasteland. Southern Tibet is well inhabited and contains the cities of Lhasa, Gyantse and Shigatse. Eastern Tibet has good grazing land and forests. Tibet is the source of great rivers of India; Indus, Sutlej and Brahamputra. Besides, the sacred Mt Kailash and Mansarover lake are situated here.

TIBETAN GLOSSARY

Amban	Imperial envoy from the Manchu Dynasty to the Dalai Lama and was a resident in Lhasa during the period 1727–1913
Bon	Pre-Buddhist Shamanist religion of Tibet
Dharma	The Way, according to Buddhist religion
Drapa	Monk
Gelukpa	Yellow Hat sect
Gyalpo	King
Han	Chinese
Karma	Sum of deeds that determines next life
Lama	Tibetan Buddhist priest
Mantra	Sacred text
Rimpoche	High incarnate lama
Sangha	Religious community
Tantra	Occult writing
Thanka	Buddhist painted scroll
Tisri	Imperial chaplain (high Lama)
Tulkus	Reincarnate lamas

IMPORTANT POST 1949 CHRONOLOGY OF EVENTS IN TIBET

7 October 50	The Chinese People's Liberation Army invades Tibet.
11 November 50	Tibetan Government seeks UN help to stop the invasion.
23 May 51	The Tibetan delegates coerced to sign the 17-Point Agreement on Measures for the Peaceful Liberation of Tibet.
25 April 56	China sets up Preparatory Committee for Tibet Autonomous Region in Lhasa.
16 June 58	Voluntary National Defence Army, also commonly known as *Chushi Gangdruk* was formed under the leadership of Andruk Gompo Tashi in Lhoka. This marked the culmination of Khampa revolts that began in 1956–57 in Kham and Amdo.
10 March 59	Tibetan uprising in Lhasa.
17 March 59	The Dalai Lama flees Lhasa.
29 March 59	The UN General Assembly Resolution 1353 (XIV) passed on Tibet.
24 October 60	The Dalai Lama and his entourage move to Dharamshala and set up their 'Government in Exile'.
2 September 60	Representatives of the Tibetan people and Lamas from various sects meet in Dharamshala as the Tibetan Constituent Assembly. This day is celebrated every year by Tibetan exiles as Democracy Day.
10 October 61	The Tibetan Constitution is promulgated by the Dalai Lama.
20 December 61	The UN General Assembly passes Resolution 1723

	(XVI) on Tibet. Tibet's right to self-determination figured for the first time in it.
9 September 65	China establishes 'Tibet Autonomous Region (TAR)'.
18 December 65	The UN General Assembly passes Resolution 2079 (XX) on Tibet.
May 1966– January 1969	The period of the Proletarian Cultural Revolution, during which the Red Guards destroyed nearly 95 percent of Tibet's monastries and temples.
12 September 83	Beijing decides on population transfer to Tibet as a policy 'Hanisation of Tibet'.
21 September 87	The Dalai Lama addresses the US Congressional Human Rights Caucus, outlining his Five-Point Peace Plan for Tibet, which in part, is a reply to Chinese Five-Point Plan for the Dalai Lama's return to China.
22 September 87	The US Congress passes H.Con.Res.191 welcoming the Dalai Lama's peace initiative.
27 September 87	Pro-independence demonstration in Lhasa.
14 October 87	The European Parliament at Strasbourg passes resolution on Tibet.
15 October 87	The West German Bundestag at Bonn passes resolution on Tibet.
22 December 87	US Public law 100-204 'Foreign Relations Authorization Act fiscal years 1988 and 1989' is passed, condemning human rights violations in Tibet and sanctioning assistance to Tibetan refugees.
15 June 88	The Dalai Lama makes his 'Strasbourg Statement' before the European Parliament, conceding defence and foreign affairs to China but demanding genuine and complete autonomy for Tibet.
16 September 88	The US Congress passes S.Con.Res.129, supporting

	the Dalai Lama's peace intiative as outlined in his Stasbourg Statement.
28 January 89	The Panchen Lama passes away in Shigatse.
6 March 89	Beijing imposes martial law in Tibet.
10 December 89	The Dalai Lama is awarded the Nobel Peace Prize.
25 March 91	Voice of America starts a Tibetan language service.
16 April 91	President George Bush receive the Dalai Lama at the White House.
18 April 91	The US Public Law passes Resolution 102-138 (h.r. 1415) on Foreign Relation Authorization Act for fiscal years 1992 and 1993, which declares that 'Tibet including those areas incorporated into the Chinese provinces of Sichaung, Yunnan, Gansu and Qinghai, is an occupied country under the established principles of international law.'
6 June 91	The Australian Parliament (Canberra) passes resolution on Tibet.
6–7 September 91	The Liberal International Congress at Luzern passes resolution on Tibet.
28 October 91	The above-mentioned law [102-138 (1415)] is enacted by the Senate and House of Representatives of the US Congress.
30 January 94	A group of overseas Chinese intellectuals, including prominent dissidents release a draft 'Constitution of the Federal Republic of China' in San Francisco. This draft Constitution grants Autonomous statehood to Tibet, and largely meets the Dalai Lama's demands made in 1987 (Washington DC) and in 1988 (Strasbourg).
18–20 March 94	World Parliamentarians Convention on Tibet is held in New Delhi.

TIBETAN CALENDAR

The Tibetan calendar repeats itself in a cycle of sixty years called Rub-byun in Tibetan, Prabhava in Sanskrit and Sexagenary in English. Each cycle of sixty years is formed by combining the names of five elements (iron, water, wood, fire and earth) and twelve animals (monkey, hen, dog, pig, mouse, ox, tiger, hare, dragon, serpent, horse and sheep). A complete cycle starts with Fire-Hare and ends with Fire-Tiger. A typical Tibetan calendar starting from 1944 to 2000 (not a full cycle) is given below:

EnglishYear	Name of the Year	EnglishYear	Name of the Year
1944	Wood Monkey	1973	Water Bull
1945	Wood Bird	1974	Wood Tiger
1946	Fire Dog	1975	Wood Hare
1947	Fire Boar	1976	Fire Dragon
1948	Earth Mouse	1977	Fire Serpent
1949	Earth Bull	1978	Earth Horse
1950	Iron Tiger	1979	Earth Sheep
1951	Iron Hare	1980	Iron Monkey
1952	Water Dragon	1981	Iron Bird
1953	Water Snake	1982	Water Dog
1954	Wood Horse	1983	Water Pig
1955	Wood Sheep	1984	Wood Mouse
1956	Fire Monkey	1985	Wood Bull
1957	Fire Bird	1986	Fire Tiger
1958	Earth Dog	1987	Fire Rabbit
1959	Earth Boar	1988	Earth Dragon
1960	Iron Mouse	1989	Earth Snake
1961	Iron Bull	1990	Iron Horse
1962	Water Tiger	1991	Iron Sheep
1963	Water Horse	1992	Water Monkey
1964	Wood Dragon	1993	Water Bird
1965	Wood Snake	1994	Wood Dog
1966	Fire Horse	1995	Wood Pig
1967	Fire Sheep	1996	Fire Mouse
1968	Earth Monkey	1997	Fire Bull
1969	Earth Bird	1998	Earth Tiger
1970	Iron Dog	1999	Earth Rabbit
1971	Iron Boar	2000	Iron Dragon
1972	Water Mouse		

TREATY BETWEEN TIBET AND CHINA A.D. 821–822

(*Translation from the tibetan text*)

The Great King of Tibet, the Miraculous Divine Lord, and the Great King of China, the Chinese Ruler Hwang-ti, being in the relationship of nephew and uncle, have conferred together for the alliance of their kingdoms. They have made and ratified a great agreement. Gods and men all know it and bear witness so that it may never be changed; and an account of the agreement has been engraved on this stone pillar to inform future ages and generations.

The Miraculous Divine Lord Thri-tsug De-tsen and the Chinese King Wen Wu Hsia-te Hwang-ti, nephew and uncle, seeking in their far reaching wisdom to prevent all causes of harm to the welfare of their countries now or in the future, have extended their benevolence imp artially over all. With the single desire of acting for the peace and benefitof all their subjects they have on the high purpose of ensuring lasting good; and they have made this great treaty in order to fulfil their decision to restore the former ancient friendship and mutual regard and the old relationship of friendly neighbourliness.

Tibet and China shall abide by the frontiers of which they are now in occupation. All to the east is the country of Great China; and all to the west is, without question, the country of Great Tibet. Henceforth on neither side shall there be waging of war, nor seizing of territory. If any person incurs suspicion he shall be arrested; his business shall be inquired into and he shall be escorted back.

Now that the two kingdoms have been allied by this great treaty, it is necessary that messengers should once again be sent by the old route to maintain communications and carry the exchange of friendly messages regarding the harmonious relations between the Nephew and Uncle. According to the old custom, horses shall be changed at the foot of the Chiang Chun pass, the frontier between Tibet and China. At the Suiyung barrier the Chinese shall meet Tibetan envoys and provide them with all facilities from there onwards. At Ching-shui the Tibetans shall meet Chinese envoys and provide all facilities. On the sides they shall be treated with customary honour and respect in conformity with the friendly relations between Nephew and Uncle.

Between the two countries no smoke nor dust shall be seen. There shall be no sudden alarms and the very word 'enemy' shall not be spoken. Even the frontier guards shall have no anxiety, nor fear and shall enjoy land and bed at their ease. All shall live in peace and share the blessing of happiness for ten thousand years. The fame of this shall extend to all places reached by the sun and the moon.

This solemn agreement has established a great epoch when Tibetans shall be happy in the land of Tibet, and Chinese in the land of China. So that it may never be changed, the Three Precious Jewels of Religion, the Assembly of Saints, the Sun and Moon, Planets and Stars have been invoked as witnesses. An oath has been taken with solemn words and with the sacrifice of animals; and the agreement has been ratified.

If the parties do not act in accordance with this agreement or if they violate it, whichever it be, Tibet or China, nothing that the other party may do by way of relation shall be considered a breach of the treaty on their part.

The Kings and Ministers of Tibet and China have taken the prescribed oath to this effect and the agreement has been written in detail. The two Kings have affixed their seals. The Ministers specially empowered to execute the agreement have inscribed their signatures and copies have been deposited in the royal records of each party.

The treaty is carved in Tibetan and Chinese on one side of a stone pillar near the Jokhang, the Cathedral of Lhasa. On another side is a historical introduction in Tibetan only; and on the other two sides are bilingual lists of the names of the ministers who witnessed it. The texts have been edited in Ancient Historical Edict at Lhasa. (H.E.Richardson Vol XIX of the Prize Publication Fund of the Royal Asiatic Society).

The king of Tibet named in the treaty is better known as Ralpachen (815–841); and the Chinese Emperor is Mu Tsung of T'sang dynasty (821–825).

Two translations of the Chinese text of the treaty can be seen in G Timkowsky's Travels of the Russian Mission through China, etc. London 1827 and one by S.W. Bushell in JRAS 1880.

EXTRACT OF TREATY BETWEEN TIBET AND BASHAHR, 1681

Professor L. Petech gives the best available information about this in his valuable article on 'The Tibetan–Ladakhi–Moghul War of 1681–1683' in the Indian Historical Quarterly, Vol. XXIII, September 1947. At the time of that war there was an alliance and a brief general agreement about friendly relations and the exchange of envoys between Raja Kehari Singh of Bashahr and the Government of the Vth Dalai Lama.

EXTRACT OF TREATY BETWEEN TIBET AND LADAKH, 1683

This treaty terminated the war mentioned above. Its conditions are summarized by Professor Petech and included the cession to Tibet of the Province of Ngari, commercial stipulations mainly connected with the important trade in wool, and the dispatch to Lhasa every second year of a sort of tribute mission. This liability was taken over by Kashmir when that State annexed Ladakh in 1842, and continued to be discharged down to 1950. The mission was known as the Lopchak. The frontier between Ladakh and Tibet was fixed at 'the Lhari stream at Demchok'.

TREATY BETWEEN TIBET AND LADAKH, 1842

(translation)

As on this auspicious day, the 2nd of Assuj, Sambhat 1899 [16th or 17th September A.D. 1842], we the officers of the Lhasa Government Kalon of Sokan and Bakshi Shajpuh, Commander of the Forces, and two officers on behalf of the most resplendent Sri Khalsa ji Sahib, the asylum of the world, King Sher Singh ji and Sri Maharaj Sahib Raja-i Rajagan Raja Sahib Bahadur RajaGulab Singh ji, the Mukhtar-ud-Daula Diwan Hari Chand and the asylum of vizirs, Vizir Ratnun, in a meeting called together for the promotion of peace and unity, and by professions and vows of friendship, unity and sincerity of heart and by taking oaths like those of Kunjak Sahib, have arranged and agreed that relations of peace, friendship and unity between Sri Khalsa ji and Sri Maharaj Sahib Bahadur Raja Gulab Singh ji and the Emperor of China and the Lama Guru of Lhasa will henceforward remain firmly established forever; and we declare in the presence of the Kunjak Sahib that on no account whatsoever will there be any deviation, difference or departure [from this agreement]. We shall neither at present nor in future have anything to do or interfere at all with the boundaries of Ladakh and its surroundings as fixed from ancient times and will allow the annual export of wool, shawls and tea by way of Ladakh according to old established custom.

Should any of the opponents of Sri Khalsa ji and Sri Raja Sahib Bahadur at any time enter our territories, we shall not pay any heed to his words or allow him to remain in our country.

We shall offer no hindrance to traders of Ladakh who visit our territories. We shall not, even to the extent of a hair's breadth, act in contravention of the term that we have agreed to above regarding firm friendship, unity and fixed boundaries of Ladakh and the keeping open of the route for wool, shawls and tea. We call Kunjak Sahib, Kairi, Lassi, Zhoh Mahan, and Khushal Choh as witnesses to this treaty.

The agreement is quoted in Aitchison's Treaties. The veracity of this treaty will need further analysis as by this time, the Raja of Jammu was virtually independent of Sikhs to the extent that the Dogras did not even support the Sikhs in their fight against the British. Participations by Chinese is also suspect.

TREATY BETWEEN TIBET AND NEPAL, 1856

(translation)

Treaty of Peace, consisting of ten Articles, between the States of Gurkha and Tibet (Bhote), settled and concluded by us, the Chief Sardars, Bharadars, and Lamas of both the Governments, whose signatures and seals are attached below. May God bear witness to it. We further agree that both States pay respect as always before to the Emperor of China and that the two States are to treat each other like brothers, for so long as their actions correspond with the spirit of this Treaty. May God not allow that State to prosper which may make war upon the other, unless the other acts contrary to this Treaty, in which case the State that declares war upon the other shall be exempt from all blame.

1. The Tibetan Government agrees to pay the sum of ten thousand Rupees annually in cash to the Gurkha Government.

2. The States of Gurkha and of Tibet have both respected the Emperor of China up to the present time. The country of Tibet is merely the shrine or place of worship of the Lama, for which reason the Gurkha Government will in future give all the assistance that may be in its power to the Government of Tibet, if the troops of any other 'Raja' invade that country.

3. The Government of Tibet agrees to discontinue the collection of all duties that have hitherto been levied upon subjects of the Gurkha State, merchants and other trading with its country.

4. The Government of Tibet agrees to give up to the Gurkha Government all the Sikh prisoners now in captivity within its territories, and all the Gurkha Sipahis, and officers, and women who were captured in the war, also all the guns that were taken; and the Gurkha Government agrees to give up to the Government of Tibet all the Sipahis, also the ryots of Kerong, Kuti, Junga, Tagla Khar and Chewur Gumba, and all the arms and Yaks [chowrie cows] belonging to that country now in its possession, and on the final completion of this Treaty it will restore Tagla Khar, Chewur Gumba, Kerong, Junga, Kuti and Dhakling and will withdraw all the troops that may be on this side of the Bhairab Langar

range.

5. A Bharadar on the part of the Gurkha Government (not merely a Naikia) will for the future reside at Lhasa.

6. The Gurkha Government, with the free consent of the Government of Tibet, will establish a trading factory at Lhasa, for the sale of all kinds of merchandise, from jewellery etc. to articles of clothing and of food.

7. The Gurkha Bharadar residing at Lhasa will not interfere in the disputes of the subjects, merchants, traders, etc. of the Government of Tibet, neither will the Tibetan Government interfere in any disputes between subjects of the Gurkha Government, Kashmiris of Nepal etc, who may be residing within the jurisdiction of Lhasa, but whenever quarrels may occur between Gurkha and Tibetan subjects, the authorities of the two States will sit together and jointly adjudicate them; and all Amdani [fines etc.] will, if paid by subjects of Tibet, be taken by that Government, and if paid by Gurkha subjects, Kashmiris of Nepal etc., will be appropriated by the Gurkha Government.

8. Should any Gurkha subject commit a murder within the jurisdiction of that Government and take refuge in Tibet, he shall be surrendered by that country, and if any Tibetan subject who may have committed a murder there take refuge in the Gurkha country, he shall in like manner be given up to the Government of Tibet.

9. If the property of any Gurkha subjects and merchants be plundered by any subject of the Tibetan Government, the party who has stolen it shall be compelled by the Tibetan Government to restore it; should he not be able to do so at once, he shall be obliged by the Tibetan Bharadar to make some arrangement, and will be allowed a reasonable time to make it good. In like manner, if the property of any Tibetan subjects or merchants be plundered by any subject of the Gurkha authorities to restore it; should he not be able to do so at once, he shall be obliged by the Gurkha Government to make some arrangement and will be allowed a reasonable time to make it good.

10. All subjects of Tibet who may have joined the Gurkha cause during the war, and all subjects of the Gurkha Government who may have taken part with the Tibetan Government, shall, after the completion of this Treaty be respected

both in person and property, and shall not be injured by either Government.

Dated Sambhat 1912 Chaitra Badi 3rd (2nd day) Sombar; corresponding with 24th March 1856.

The treaty, translated from the Nepalese text, is given in Aitchison's Treaties, Vol. XIV, pp. 49–50. A translation from the Tibetan is also given in the "Tibet: Past and Present" by Sir Charles Bell.

EXTRACT OF THE CONVENTION OF CHEFOO BETWEEN THE BRITISH GOVERNMENT AND THE GOVERNMENT OF CHINA, 1876

Her Majesty's Government having it in contemplation to send a mission of exploration next year, by way of Peking, through Kansuh and Kokonor, or by way of Szechuen to Thibet, and thence to India, the Tsungli Yamen, having due regard to the circumstances, will, when the time arrives, issue the necessary passports, and will address letters to the High Provincial Authorities and the Residents in Thibet. If the Mission should not be sent by these routes but should be proceeding across the Indian frontier to Thibet, the Tsungli Yamen, on receipt of a communication to that effect from the British Minister, will write to the Chinese Resident in Thibet, and the Resident, with due regard to the circumstances, will send officers to take care of the Mission, and passports for the Mission will be issued by the Tsungli Yamen, that its passage be not obstructed.

(*The above is a separate article. The main body of the Convention did not concern Tibet*)

EXTRACT OF CONVENTION RELATING TO BURMAH AND THIBET, JULY 24TH 1886, BETWEEN THE BRITISH GOVERNMENT AND GOVERNMENT OF CHINA

In as much as inquiry into the circumstances, by the Chinese Government, has shown the existence of many obstacles to the Mission to Thibet provided for in the separate article of the Chefoo Agreement, England consents to countermand the Mission forthwith. With regard to the desire of the British Government to consider arrangements for frontier trade between India and Thibet, it will be the duty of the Chinese Government, after careful inquiry into the circumstances, to adopt measures to exhort and encourage the people with a view to the promotion and development of trade. Should it be practicable, the Chinese Government shall then proceed carefully to consider trade regulations; but if insuperable obstacles should be found to exist, the British Government will not press the matter unduly.

(*The remainder of the Convention was concerned with the recognition of British supremacy in Burma.*)

CONVENTION OF MARCH 17TH 1890 BETWEEN GREAT BRITAIN AND CHINA RELATING TO SIKKIM AND TIBET

(*Ratifications Exchanged at London, August 27th, 1890*) [*English Text*] (*British and Foreign State Papers, 1889–1890, Vol. LXXXII, pp.9-11*)

WHEREAS Her Majesty the Queen of the United Kingdom of Great Britain and Ireland, Empress of India, and His Majesty the Emperor of China, are sincerely desirous to maintain and perpetuate the relations of friendship and good understanding which now exist between their respective Empires; and whereas recent occurrences have tended towards a disturbance of the said relations, and it is desirable to clearly define and permanently settle certain matters connected with the boundary between Sikkim and Tibet, Her Britannic Majesty and His Majesty the Emperor of China have resolved to conclude a Convention on this subject, and have, for this purpose, named Plenipotentiaries, that is to say:

Her Majesty the Queen of Great Britain and Ireland, His Excellency the Most Honourable Henry Charles Keith Petty Fitzmaurice, G.M.S.I., G.C.M.G., G.M.I.E., Marquess of Lansdowne, Viceroy and Governor-General of India;

And His Majesty the Emperor of China, His Excellency Sheng Tai, Imperial Associate Resident in Tibet, Military Deputy Lieutenant-Governor;

Who, having met and communicated to each other their full powers, and finding these to be in proper form, have agreed upon the following Convention in eight Articles:-

I. The boundary of Sikkim and Tibet shall be the crest of the mountain range separating the waters flowing into the Sikkim Teesta and its affluents from the waters flowing into the Tibetan Mochu and northwards into other rivers of Tibet. The line commences at Mount Gipmochi on the Bhutan frontier, and follows the above-mentioned water parting to the point where it meets Nepal territory.

II. It is admitted that the British Government, whose Protectorate over the Sikkim State is hereby recognized, has direct and exclusive control over the internal administration and foreign relations of that State, and except through and with the permission of the British Government neither the Ruler of the State nor any of its officers shall have official relations of any kind, formal or informal, with any other country.

III. The Government of Great Britain and Ireland and the Government of China engage reciprocally to respect the boundary as defined in Article I, and to prevent acts of aggression from their respective sides of the frontier.

IV. The question of providing increased facilities for trade across the Sikkim–Tibet frontier will hereafter be discussed with a view to a mutually satisfactory arrangement by the High Contracting Powers.

V. The question of pasturage on the Sikkim side of the frontier is reserved for further examination and future adjustment.

VI. The High Contracting Powers reserve for discussion and arrangement the method in which official communications between the British authorities in India and the authorities in Tibet shall be conducted.

VII. Two joint Commissioners shall, within six months from the ratification of this Convention, be appointed, one by the British Government in India, the other by Chinese Resident in Tibet. The said Commissioners shall meet and discuss the questions which, by the last three preceding Articles, have been reserved.

VIII. The present Convention shall be ratified, and the Ratifications shall be exchanged in London as soon as possible after the date of the signature thereof.

In witness whereof the respective negotiators have signed the same, and affixed thereunto the seals of their arms.

Done in quadruplicate at Calcutta, this 17th day of March, in the year of our Lord 1890, corresponding with the Chinese date, the 27th day of the second moon of the 16th year of Kuang Hsu.

LANDSDOWNE. (Signature of the Chinese Plenipotentiary)

(*The convention was signed at Calcutta. No Tibetan representative was present or took part in the negotiations*)

REGULATIONS REGARDING TRADE, COMMUNICATION AND PASTURAGE, TO BE APPENDED TO THE CONVENTION BETWEEN GREAT BRITAIN AND CHINA OF MARCH 17, 1890, RELATIVE TO SIKKIM AND TIBET

(*British and Foreign State Papers, 1892–1893, Vol. LXXXV*)

1. A trade mart shall be established at Yatung on the Tibetan side of the frontier, and shall be open to all British subjects for purposes of trade from the 1st day of May, 1894. The Government of India shall be free to send officers to reside at Yatung to watch the conditions of British trade at that mart.

2. British subjects trading at Yatung shall be at liberty to travel freely to and fro between the frontier and Yatung, to reside at Yatung, and to rent houses and godowns for their own accommodation, and the storage of their goods. The Chinese Government undertakes that suitable buildings for the above purposes shall be provided for British subjects, and also that a special and fitting residence shall be provided for the officer or officers appointed by the Government of India under Regulation I to reside at Yatung. British subjects shall be at liberty to sell their goods to whom so ever they please, to purchase native commodities in kind or in money, to hire transport of any kind, and in general to conduct their business transactions in conformity with local usage, and without any vexatious restrictions. Such British subjects shall receive efficient protection for their persons and property. At Lang-jo and Ta-chun, between the frontier and Yatung, where rest-houses have been built by the Tibetan authorities, British subjects can break their journey in consideration of a daily rent.

3. Import and export trade in the following articles:- arms, ammunition, military stores, salt, liquors, and intoxicating or narcotic drugs, may, at the option of either Government, be entirely prohibited, or permitted only on such conditions as either Government, on their own side, may think fit to impose.

4. Goods, other than goods of the descriptions enumerated in Regulation 3, entering Tibet from British India, across the Sikkim–Tibet frontier, or vice versa,

whatever their origin, shall be exempt from duty for a period of five years, commencing from the date of the opening of Yatung to trade; but after the expiration of this term, if found desirable, a tariff may be mutually agreed upon and enforced. Indian tea may be imported into Tibet at a rate of duty not exceeding that at which Chinese tea is imported into England, but trade in Indian tea shall not be engaged in during the five years for which other commodities are exempt.

5. All goods on arrival at Yatung, whether from British India or from Tibet, must be reported at the Custom Station there for examination, and the report must give full particulars of the description, quantity, and value of the goods.

6. In the event of trade disputes arising between British and Chinese or Tibetan subjects in Tibet, they shall be inquired into and settled in personal conference by the Political Officer for Sikkim and the Chinese Frontier Officer. The object of personal conference being to ascertain facts and do justice, where there is a divergence of views, the law of the country to which the defendant belongs shall guide.

7. Despatches from the Government of India to the Chinese Imperial Resident in Tibet shall be handed over by the Political Officer for Sikkim to the Chinese Frontier Officer, who will forward them by special courier. Despatches from the Chinese Imperial Resident in Tibet to the Government of India will be handed over by the Chinese Frontier Officer to the Political Officer for Sikkim, who will forward them as quickly as possible.

8. Despatches between the Chinese and Indian officials must be treated with due respect, and couriers will be assisted in passing to and fro by the officers of each Government.

9. After the expiration of one year from the date of the opening of Yatung, such Tibetans as continue to graze their cattle in Sikkim will be subject to such Regulations as the British Government may from time to time enact for the general conduct of grazing in Sikkim. Due notice will be given of such Regulations.

General Articles

1. In the event of disagreement between the Political Officer for Sikkim and the Chinese Frontier Officer, each official shall report the matter to his immediate superior, who in turn, if a settlement is not arrived at between them, shall refer such matter to their respective Governments for disposal.

2. After the lap se of five years from the date on which these Regulations shall come into force, and on six months' notice given by either party, these Regulations shall be subject to revision by Commissioners appointed on both sides for purpose, who shall be empowered to decide on and adopt such amendments and extensions as experience shall prove to be desirable.

3. It having been stipulated that Joint Commissioners should be appointed by the British and Chinese Governments under Article VII of the Sikkim–Tibet Convention to meet and discuss, with a view to the final settlement of the questions reserved under Articles IV, V, and VI of the said Convention; and the Commissioners thus appointed having met and discussed the questions referred to, namely, trade, communication, and pasturage, have been further appointed to sign the Agreement in nine Regulations and three General Articles now arrived at, and to declare that the said nine Regulations and the three General Articles form part of the Convention itself.

In witness whereof the respective Commissioners have hereto subscribed their names.

Done in quadruplicate at Darjeeling, this 5th day of December, in the year 1893, corresponding with the Chinese date, the 28th day of the 10th moon of the 19th year of Kuang Hsu.

AW PAUL,
British Commissioner.

Ho CHANG-JUNG,
JAMES H. HART,
Chinese Commissioners.

(*A Tibetan Minister was present at the negotiations in Darjeeling but took no active part and did not sign the Regulations*).

CONVENTION BETWEEN GREAT BRITAIN AND TIBET SEPTEMBER 7TH 1904

(*British and Foreign State Papers, 1904–1905, Vol. XCVIII, PP. 148–151*)

WHEREAS doubts and difficulties have arisen as to the meaning and validity of the Anglo-Chinese Convention of 1890, and the Trade Regulations of 1893, and as to the liabilities of the Tibetan Government under these Agreements; and whereas recent occurrences have tended towards a disturbance of the relations of friendship and good understanding which have existed between the British Government and the Government of Thibet; and whereas it is desirable to restore peace and amicable relations, and to resolve and determine the doubts and difficulties as aforesaid, the said Governments have resolved to conclude a Convention with these objects, and the following Articles have been agreed upon by Colonel F.E. Younghusband, C.I.E., in virtue of full of powers vested in him by His Britannic Majesty's Government, and on behalf of that said Government, and Lo- sang Gyal-Tsen, the Ga-den Ti-Rimpoche, and the representatives of the Council, of the three monasteries Se-ra, Dre-pung, and Ga-den, and of the ecclesiastical and lay officials of the National Assembly on behalf of the Government of Thibet:-

I. The Government of Thibet to engage to respect the Anglo-Chinese Convention of 1890, and to recognize the frontier between Sikkim and Thibet, as defined in Article I of the said Convention, and to erect boundary pillars accordingly.

II. The Thibetan Government undertakes to open forthwith trade marts to which all British and Thibetan subjects shall have free right of access at Gyangtse and Gartok, as well as Yatung.

The regulations applicable to the trade mart at Yatung, under the Anglo-Chinese Agreement of 1893, shall, subject to such amendments as may hereafter be agreed upon by common consent between the British and Thibetan Governments, apply to the marts above mentioned.

In addition to establishing trade marts at the places mentioned, the Thibetan

Government undertakes to place no restrictions on the trade by existing routes, and to consider the question of establishing fresh trade marts under similar conditions if development of trade requires it.

III. The question of the amendment of the Regulations of 1893 is reserved for separate consideration, and the Thibetan Government undertakes to appoint fully authorized delegates to negotiate with representatives of the British Government as to the details of the amendments required.

IV. The Thibetan Government undertakes to levy no dues of any kind other than those provided for in the tariff to be mutually agreed upon.

V. The Thibetan Government undertakes to keep the roads to Gyangtse and Gartok from the frontier clear of all obstruction and in a state of repair suited to the needs of the trade, and to establish at Yatung, Gyangtse, and Gartok, and at each of the other trade marts that may hereafter be established, a Thibetan Agent who shall receive from the British Agent appointed to watch over British trade at the marts in question any letter which the latter may desire to send to the Thibetan or the Chinese authorities. The Thibetan Agent shall also be responsible for the due delivery of such communications and for the transmission of the replies.

VI. As an indemnity to the British Government for the expense incurred in the despatch of armed troops to Lhasa, to exact reparation for breaches of Treaty obligations, and for the insults offered to and attacks upon the British Commissioner and his following and escort, the Thibetan Government engages to pay a sum of 500,000!—equivalent to 75 lakhs of rupees to the British Government. The indemnity shall be payable at such place as the British Government may from time to time, after due notice, indicate, whether in Thibet or in the British districts of Darjeeling or Jalpaiguri, in seventy-five annual instalments of one lakh of rupees each on the 1st January in each year, beginning from the 1st January, 1906.

VII. As security for the payment of the above-mentioned indemnity, and for the fulfilment of the provisions relative to trade marts specified in Articles II, III, IV, and V, the British Government shall continue to occupy the Chumbi Valley until the indemnity has been paid, and until the trade marts have been effectively opened for three years, whichever date may be the later.

VIII. The Thibetan Government agrees to raze all forts and fortifications and remove all armaments which might impede the course of free communication between the British frontier and the towns of Gyangtse and Lhasa.

IX. The Government of Thibet engages that, without the previous consent of the British Government-

(a) No portion of Thibetan territory shall be ceded, sold, leased, mortgaged or otherwise given for occupation, to any Foreign Power;

(b) No such Power shall be permitted to intervene in Thibetan affairs;

(c) No Representative or agents of any Foreign power shall be admitted to Thibet.

(d) No concession for railways, roads, telegraphs, mining or other rights, shall be granted to any Foreign Power, or the subject of any Foreign Power. In the event of consent to such Concessions being granted, similar or equivalent Concessions shall be granted to the British Government;

(e) No Thibetan revenues, whether in kind or in cash, shall be pledged or assigned to any Foreign Power, or to the subject of any foreign power.

X. In witness whereof the negotiators have signed the same, and affixed there unto the seals of their arms.

Done in quintuplicate at Lhasa, this 7th day of September, in the year of our Lord, 1904, corresponding with the Thibetan date, the 27th of the seventh month of the Wood Dragon year.

(Thibet Frontier Commission)

F.E. YOUNGHUSBAND,
Colonel,
British Commissioner.

(Seal of Dalai Lama affixed by the Ga-den Ti-Rimpoche.)

(Seal of British Commissioner.)

(Seal of Council.) (Seal of Dre-pung Monastery) (Seal of Sera Monastery) (Seal of Ga-den Monastery) (seal of National Assembly)

In proceeding to the signature of the Convention, dated this day, the representatives of Great Britain and Thibet declare that the English text shall be binding.

(Thibet Frontier Commission)

F.E. YOUNGHUSBAND,
Colonel,
British Commissioner.

(Seal of Dalai Lama affixed by the Ga-den Ti-Rimpoche.)

(Seal of Council.) (Seal of Dre-pung Monastery) (Seal of Sera Monastery) (Seal of Ga-den Monastery) (seal of National Assembly)

AMPTHILL,
Viceroy and Governor-General of India.

The convention was ratified by the Viceroy and Governor-General of India in council at Simla on the 11th day of November, 1904, subject to reduction of the indemnity to Rs. 25,00,000 and a declaration that British occupation of the Chumbi valley would cease after payment of three annual instalments of the indemnity, provided that the Tibetans had complied with the terms of the convention in all other respects.

This was the first direct treaty between Great Britain and Tibet. The Chinese Ambassador at Lhasa was present at the negotiations and signing, but did not sign.

CONVENTION BETWEEN GREAT BRITAIN AND CHINA RESPECTING TIBET, APRIL 27, 1906

(*Ratifications exchanged in London July 23 1906*)

(*British and Foreign State Papers, Vol XCIX, pp. 171–173*)

WHEREAS His Majesty of Great Britain and Ireland and of the British Dominions beyond the Seas, Emperor of India, and His Majesty the Emperor of China are sincerely desirous to maintain and perpetuate the relations of friendship and good understanding which now exists between their respective Empires;

And whereas the refusal of Tibet to recognise the validity of or to carry into full effect the provisions of the Anglo-Chinese Convention of March 17, 1890, and Regulations of December 5, 1893, placed the British Government under the necessity of taking steps to secure their rights and interests under the said Convention and Regulations;

And whereas a Convention of ten articles was signed at Lhasa on September 7, 1904, on behalf of Great Britain and Tibet, and was ratified by the Viceroy and Governor-General of India on behalf of Great Britain on November 11, 1904, a declaration on behalf of Great Britain modifying its terms under certain conditions being appended thereto;

His Britannic Majesty and His Majesty the Emperor of China have resolved to conclude a Convention on this subject and have for this purpose named Plenipotentiaries, that is to say:-

His Majesty the King of Great Britain and Ireland:

Sir Ernest Mason Satow, Knight Grand Cross of the Most Distinguished Order of Saint Michael and Saint George, His said Majesty's Envoy Extraordinary and Minister Plenipotentiary to His Majesty the Emperor of China;

And His Majesty the Emperor of China:

His Excellency Tong Shoa-yi, His said Majesty's High Commissioner Plenipotentiary and a Vice-President of the Board of Foreign Affairs; who having communicated to each other their respective full powers and finding them to be in good and true form have agreed upon and concluded the following Convention in six articles:-

I. The Convention concluded on September 7, 1904, by Great Britain and Tibet, the texts of which in English and Chinese are attached to the present Convention as an annexe, is hereby confirmed, subject to the modification stated in the declaration appended thereto, and both of the High Contracting Parties engage to take at all times such steps as may be necessary to secure the due fulfilment of the terms specified therein.

II. The Government of Great Britain engages not to annex Tibetan territory or to interfere in the administration ofTibet. The Government of China also undertakes not to permit any other foreign state to interfere with the territory or internal administration of Tibet.

III. The Concessions which are mentioned in Article IX(d) of the Convention concluded on September 7th, 1904 by Great Britain and Tibet are denied to any state or to the subject of any state other than China, but it has been arranged with China that at the trade marts specified in Article II of the aforesaid Convention Great Britain shall be entitled to lay down telegraph lines connecting with India.

IV. The provisions of the Anglo-Chinese Convention of 1890 and Regulations of 1893 shall, subject to the terms of this present Convention and annexe thereto, remain in full force.

V. The English and Chinese texts of the present Convention have been carefully compared and found to correspond, but in the event of there being any difference of meaning between them the English text shall be authoritative.

VI. This Convention shall be ratified by the Sovereigns of both countries and ratifications shall be exchanged in London within three months after the date of signature by the Plenipotentiaries of both Powers.

In token whereof the respective Plenipotentiaries have signed and sealed this Convention, four copies in English and four in Chinese.

Done at Peking this twenty-seventh day ofApril, one thousand nine hundred and six, being the fourth day of the fourth month of the thirty- second year of the reign of Kuang-Hsu.

ERNEST SATOW.

(Signature and Seal of the Chinese Plenipotentiary)

Notes were also exchanged by which the Chinese undertook not to employ any foreigners in Tibet. The Tibetans took no part in this Convention and its terms were never formally communicated to them

CONVENTION BETWEEN GREAT BRITAIN AND RUSSIA RELATING TO PERSIA, AFGHANISTAN AND TIBET, AUGUST 31, 1907

(*As related to Tibet*)

His Majesty the King of the United Kingdom of Great Britain and Ireland and of the British Dominions beyond the Seas, Emperor of India, and His Majesty the Emperor of All the Russias, animated by the sincere desire to settle by mutual agreement different questions concerning the interests of their States on the Continent of Asia, have determined to conclude Agreements destined to prevent all cause of misunderstanding between Great Britain and Russia in regard to the questions referred to, and have nominated for this purpose their respective Plenipotentiaries, to wit:

His Majesty the King of the United Kingdom of Great Britain and Ireland and of the British Dominions beyond the Seas, Emperor of India, the Right Honourable Sir Arthur Nicholson, His Majesty's Ambassador Extra- ordinary and Plenipotentiary to His Majesty the Emperor of All the Russias;

His Majesty the Emperor of All the Russias, the Master of his Court Alexander Iswolsky, Minister of Foreign Affairs;

Who, having communicated to each other their full powers, found in good and due form, have agreed on the following:-

ARRANGEMENT CONCERNING THIBET

The Governments of Great Britain and Russia recognising the suzerain rights of China in Thibet, and considering the fact that Great Britain, by reason of her geographical position, has a special interest in the maintenance of the status quo in the external relations of Thibet, have made the following arrangement:-

Article I

The two High Contracting Parties engage to respect the territorial integrity of Thibet and to abstain from all interference in the internal administration.

Article II

In conformity with the admitted principle of the suzerainty of China over Thibet, Great Britain and Russia engage not to enter into negotiations with Thibet except through the intermediary of the Chinese Government. This engagement does not exclude the direct relations between British Commercial Agents and the Thibetan authorities provided for in Article V of the Convention between Great Britain and Thibet of the 7th September 1904, and confirmed by the Convention between Great Britain and China of the 27th April 1906; nor does it modify the engagements entered into by Great Britain and China in Article I of the said Convention of 1906.

It is clearly understood that Buddhists, subjects of Great Britain or of Russia, may enter into direct relations on strictly religious matters with the Dalai Lama and the other representatives of Buddhism in Thibet; the Governments of Great Britain and Russia engage, as far as they are concerned, not to allow those relations to infringe the stipulations of the present arrangement.

Article III

The British and Russian Governments respectively engage not to send Representatives to Lhasa.

Article IV

The two High Contracting Parties engage neither to seek nor to obtain, whether for themselves or their subjects, any concessions for railways, roads, telegraphs, and mines, or other rights in Thibet.

Article V

The two Governments agree that no part of the revenues of Thibet, whether in kind or in cash, shall be pledged or assigned to Great Britain or Russia or to any of their subjects.

ANNEXE TO THE ARRANGEMENT BETWEEN GREAT BRITAIN AND RUSSIA CONCERNING THIBET

Great Britain reaffirms the declaration, signed by His Excellency the Viceroy and Governor-General of India and appended to the Ratification of the Convention of the 7th September 1904, to the effect the occupation of the Chumbi Valley by British forces shall cease after the payment of three annual instalments of the indemnity of 25,00,000 rupees, provided that the trade marts mentioned in Article II of that Convention have been effectively opened for three years, and that in the meantime the Thibetan authorities have faithfully complied in all respects with the terms of the said Convention of 1904. It is clearly understood that if the occupation of the Chumbi Valley by the British forces has, for any reason, not been terminated at the time anticipated in the above Declaration, the British and Russian Governments will enter upon a friendly exchange of views on this subject.

The present Convention shall be ratified, and the ratification exchanged at St. Petersburgh as soon as possible.

In witness whereof the respective Plenipotentiaries have signed the present Convention and affixed thereto their seals.

Done in duplicate at St. Petersburgh, the 18th (31st) August 1907.

sd

The Tibetans were never informed about the provisions of this treaty.

AGREEMENT BETWEEN GREAT BRITAIN, CHINA AND TIBET AMENDING TRADE REGULATIONS IN TIBET, OF DECEMBER 5, 1893

(*ratifications exchanged at Peking, October 14, 1908*)

(*British and Foreign State Papers, 1907–1908, Vol. CI, pp. 170–175*)

PREAMBLE

WHEREAS by Article I of the Convention between Great Britain and China on the 27th April, 1906, that is the 4th day of the 4th moon of the 32nd year of Kwang Hsu, it was provided that both the High Contracting Parties should engage to take at all times such steps as might be necessary to secure the due fulfilment of the terms specified in the Lhasa Convention of the 7th September, 1904, between Great Britain and Tibet, the text of which in English and Chinese was attached as an Annexe to the above-named Convention;

And whereas it was stipulated in Article III of the said Lhasa Convention that the question of the amendment of the Tibet Trade Regulations which were signed by the British and Chinese Commissioners on the 5th day of Decembe r, 1893 should be reserved for separate consideration, and whereas the amendment of these Regulations is now necessary;

His Majesty the King of the United Kingdom of Great Britain and Ireland and of the British Dominions beyond the Seas, Emperor of India, and His Majesty the Emperor of the Chinese Empire have for this purpose named as their Plenipotentiaries, that is to say:

His Majesty the King of Great Britain and Ireland and of the British Dominions beyond the Seas, Emperor of India: Mr. E. C. Wilton, C. M. G.;

His Majesty Emperor of the Chinese Empire: His Majesty's Special Commissioner Chang Yin Tang;

And the High Authorities of Tibet have named as their fully authorized representative to act under the directions of Chang Tachen and take part in the negotiations, the Tsarong Shape, Wang Chuk Gyalpo.

And whereas Mr. E. C. Wilton and Chang Tachen have communicated to each other their respective full powers and have found them to be in good and true form and have found the authorization of the Tibetan Delegate to be also in good and true form, the following amended Regulations have been agreed upon:-

1. The Trade Regulations of 1893 shall remain in force in so far as they are not inconsistent with these Regulations.

2. The following places shall form, and be included within, the boundaries of the Gyantse mart:-

(a) The line begins at the Chumig Dangsang (Chhu-Mig-Dangs-Sangs) north-east of the Gyantse Fort, and thence it runs in a curved line, passing behind the Pekor Chode (Dpal-Hkhor-Choos-Sde), down to Chag- Dong-Gang (Phyag-Gdong-Sgang); thence passing straight over the Nyan Chu, it reaches the Zamsa (Zam-Srag).

(b) From the Zamsa the line continues to run, in a south-eastern direction, round to Lachi-To (Gla-Dkyii-Stod), embracing all the farms on its way, viz., the Lahong, the Hogtso (Hog-Mtsho), the Tong-Chung-Shi (Grong-Chhung-Gshis), and the Rabgang (Rab-Sgang), & so on.

(c) From Lachi-To the line runs to the Yutog (Gyu-Thog), and thence runs straight, passing through the whole area of Gamkar-Shi (Ragal- Mkhar-Gshis), to Chumig Dangsang.

As difficulty is experienced in obtaining suitable houses and godowns at some of the marts, it is agreed that British subjects may also lease lands for the building of houses and godowns at the marts, the locality for such building sites to be marked out specially at each mart by the Chinese and Tibetan authorities in consultation with the British Trade Agent. The British Trade Agents and British subjects shall not build houses and godowns except in such localities, and this arrangement shall not be held to prejudice in any way the administration of the Chinese and Tibetan local authorities over such localities, or the right of British subjects to rent houses and godowns outside such localities for their own accommodation and the storage of their goods. British subjects desiring to lease building sites shall apply through the British Trade Agent to the Municipal Office at the mart for a permit to lease. The amount of rent, or the period or conditions of the lease, shall then be settled in a friendly way by the lessee and the owner themselves. In the event of a disagreement between the owner and lessee as to the amount of rent or the period or condition or the lease, the case will be settled by the Chinese and Tibetan Authorities, in consultation with the British Trade Agent. After the lease is settled, the sites shall be verified by the Chinese and Tibetan Officers of the Municipal Office conjointly with the British Trade Agent. No building is to be commenced by the lessee on a site before the municipal office has issued him a permit to build, but it i s agreed that there shall be no vexatious delays in the issue of such permit.

3. The administration of the trade marts shall remain with the Tibetan Officers, under the Chinese Officers' supervision and directions.

The Trade Agents at the marts and Frontier Officers shall be of suitable rank, and shall hold personal intercourse and correspondence one with another on terms of mutual respect and friendly treatment. Questions which cannot be decided by agreement between the Trade Agents and the Local Authorities shall be referred for settlement to the Government of India and the T ibetan High Authorities at Lhasa. The purport of a reference by the Government of India will be communicated to the Chinese Imperial Resident at Lhasa. Questions which cannot be decided by agreement between the Government of India and the Tibetan High Authorities at Lhasa shall, in accordance with the terms of Article I of the Peking Convention of 1906, be referred for settlement to the Government s of Great Britain and China.

4. In the event of disputes arising at the marts between British subjects and persons of Chinese and Tibetan nationalities, they shall be inquired into and settled in personal conferences between the British Trade Agent at the nearest mart and the Chinese and Tibetan Authorities of the Judicial Court at the mart, the object of personal conference being to ascertain facts and to do justice. Where there is a divergence of view the law of the country to which the defendant belongs shall guide. In any of such mixed cases, the Oficer or Officers of the defendant's nationality shall preside at the trial, the Officer or Officers of the plaintiff's country merely attending to watch the course of the trial.

All questions in regard to rights, whether of property or person, arising between British subjects, shall be subject to the jurisdiction of the British Authorities.

British subjects who may commit any crime at the marts or on the routes to the marts shall be handed over by the local authorities to the British Trade Agent at the mart nearest to the scene of offence, to be tried and punished according to the laws of India, but such British subjects shall not be subjected by the local authorities to any ill-usage in excess of necessary restraint.

Chinese and Tibetan subjects, who may be guilty of any criminal act towards British subjects at the marts or on the routes thereto, shall be arrested and punished by the Chinese and Tibetan Authorities according to law.

Justice shall be equitably and impartially administered on both sides. Should it happen that Chinese or Tibetan subjects bring a criminal complaint against a British subject before the British Trade Agent, the Chinese or Tibetan Authorities shall have the right to send a representative, or representatives, to watch the course of trial in the British Trade Agent's Court. Similarly, in cases in which a British subject has reason to complain of a Chinese or Tibetan subject in the Judicial Court at the mart, the British Trade Agent shall have the right to send a representative to the Judicial Court to watch the course of trial.

5. The Tibetan Authorities, in obedience to the instructions of the Peking Government, having a strong desire to reform the judicial system of Tibet, and to bring it into accord with that of Western nations, Great Britain agrees to relinquish her rights of extraterritoriality in Tibet, when ever such rights are relinquished in China, and when she is satisfied that the state of the Tibetan laws and the arrangements for their administration and other considerations warrant her in so doing.

6. After the withdrawal of the British troops, all the rest-houses, eleven in number, built by Great Britain upon the routes leading from the Indian frontier to Gyantse, shall be taken over at original cost by China and rented to the Government of India at a fair rate. One-half of each rest-house will be reserved for the use of the British officials employed on the inspection and maintenance of the telegraph lines from the marts to the Indian frontier and for the storage of their materials, but the rest-houses shall otherwise be available for occupation by British, Chinese, and Tibetan officers of respectability who may proceed to and from the marts.

Great Britain is prepared to consider the transfer to China of the telegraph lines from the Indian frontier to Gyantse when telegraph lines from China reach that mart, and in the meantime Chinese and Tibetan messages will be duly received and transmitted by the line constructed by the Government of India.

In the meantime China shall be responsible for the due protection of the telegraph lines from the marts to the Indian frontier, and it is agreed that all persons damaging the lines or interfering in any way with them or with the officials engaged in the inspection or maintenance thereof shall at once be severely punished by the local authorities.

7. In law suits involving cases of debt on account of loans, commercial failure, and bankruptcy, the authorities concerned shall grant a hearing and take steps necessary to enforce payment; but, if the debtor plead poverty and be without means, the authorities concerned shall not be held responsible for the said debts, nor shall any public or official property be distrained upon in order to satisfy these debts.

8. The British Trade Agents at the various trade marts now or hereafter to be established in Tibet may make arrangements for the carriage and transmission of their posts to and from the frontier of India. The couriers employed in conveying these posts shall receive all possible assistance from the local authorities whose districts they traverse and shall be accorded the same protection as the persons employed in carrying the despatches of the Tibetan Authorities. When efficient arrangements have been made by China in Tibet for a postal service, the question of the abolition of the Trade Agents' couriers will be taken into consideration by Great Britain and China. No restrictions whatever shall be placed on the employment by British officers and traders of Chinese and Tibetan subjects in any lawful capacity. The persons so employed shall not be exposed to any kind of molestation or suffer any loss of civil rights to which they may be entitled as Tibetan subjects, but they shall not be exempted from all lawful taxation. If they be guilty of any criminal act, they shall be dealt with by the local authorities according to law without any attempt on the part of their employer to screen or conceal them.

9. British officers and subjects, as well as goods, proceeding to the trade marts, must adhere to the trade routes from the frontier of India. They shall not, without permission, proceed beyond the marts, or to Gartok from Yatung and Gyantse, or from Gartok to Yatung and Gyantse, by any route through the interior of Tibet, but natives of the Indian frontier, who have already by usage traded and

resided in Tibet, elsewhere than at the marts shall be at liberty to continue their trade, in accordance with the existing practice, but when so trading or residing they shall remain, as heretofore, amenable to the local jurisdiction.

10. In cases where officials or traders, en route to and from India or Tibet, are robbed of treasure or merchandise, public or private, they shall forthwith report to the Police officers,who shall take immediate measures to arrest the robbers and hand them to the Local Authorities. The Local Authorities shall bring them to instant trial,and shall also recover and restore the stolen property. But if the robbers flee to places out of the jurisdiction and influence of Tibet,and cannot be arrested,the Police and the Local Authorities shall not be held responsible for such losses.

11. For public safety, tanks or stores of kerosene oil or any other combustible or dangerous articles in bulk must be placed far away from inhabited places at the marts.

British or Indian merchants wishing to build such tanks or stores may not do so until, as provided in Regulation 2, they have made application for a suitable site.

12. British subjects shall be at liberty to deal in kind or in money, to sell their goods to whomsoever they please, to purchase native commodities from whomsoever they please, to hire transport of any kind, and to conduct in general their business transactions in conformity with local usage and without any vexatious restrictions or oppressive exactions whatever.

It being the duty of the Police and Local Authorities to afford efficient protection at all times to the persons and property of the British subjects at the marts, and along the routes to the marts, China engages to arrange effective police measures at the marts and along the routes to the marts. On due fulfilment of these arrangements,Great Britain undertakes to withdraw the Trade Agents' guards at the marts and to station no troops in Tibet,so as to remove all cause for suspicion and disturbance among the inhabitants. The Chinese Authorities will not prevent the British Trade Agents holding personal intercourse and correspondence with the Tibetan officers and people. Tibetan subjects trading, travelling, or residing in India shall receive equal advantages to those accorded by this Regulation to British subjects in Tibet.

13. The present Regulations shall be in force for a period of ten years reckoned from the date of signature by the two Plenipotentiaries as well as by the Tibetan Delegate; but if no demand for revision be made by either side within six months after the end of the first ten years, then the Regulations shall remain in force for another ten years from the end of the first ten years; and so it shall be at the end of each successive ten years.

14. The English, Chinese, and Tibetan texts of the present Regulations have been carefully compared, and in the event of any question arising as to the interpretation of these Regulations, the sense as expressed in the English text shall be held to be the correct sense.

15. The ratifications of the present Regulations under the hand of His Majesty the King of Great Britain and Ireland, and of His Majesty the Emperor of the Chinese Empire, respectively, shall be exchanged at London and Peking within six months from the date of signature.

In witness whereof the two Plenipotentiaries and the T ibetan Delegate have signed and sealed the present Regulations.

Done in quadruplicate at Calcutta this 20th day of April, in the year of our Lord 1908, corresponding with the Chinese date, the 20th day of the 3rd moon of the 34th year of Kuang-Hsu.

E. C. WILTON
British Commissioner.

CHANG YIN TANG,
Chinese Special Commissioner.

WANG CHUK GYALPO,
Tibetan Delegate.

In spite of the intention expressed in Article II of the 1904 Convention, the new Regulations were in fact negotiated by the Chinese Commissioner. The Tibetan representative took no active part but merely signed the regulations.

TREATY BETWEEN TIBET AND MONGOLIA

(said to have been signed at Urga in January 1913)

Whereas Mongolia and Tibet, having fired themselves from the Manchu dynasty and separated themselves from China, have become independent States, and whereas the two States have always professed one and the same religion, and to the end that their ancient mutual friendships may be strengthened: on the part of the Government of the Sovereign of the Mongolian people—Nikta Biliktu Da Lama Rabdan, acting Minister of Foreign Affairs and Assistant Minister—General and Manlai Caatyr Bei Tzu Damdinsurun; on the part of the Dalai Lama, Ruler of Tibet—Gujir Tsanshib Kanchen Lubsan-Agwan, Donir Agwan Choinzin Tschchantso, Manager ofthe bank, and Gendurm-Galsan, secretary, have agreed on the following:-

Article 1

The Dalai Lama, Sovereign of Tibet, approves of and acknowledges the formation of an independent Mongolian State, and the proclamation on the 9th day of the 2nd month of the year of the Pig, of the master of the Yellow Faith Jetsum Dampa Lama as the Sovereign of the land.

Article 2

The Sovereign of the Mongolian people Je-tsun Dampa Lama approves and acknowledges the formation of an independent State and the proclamation of the Dalai Lama as Sovereign of Tibet.

Article 3

Both States shall take measures, after mutual consideration, for the prosperity of the Buddhist faith.

Article 4

Both States, the Mongolian and the Tibetan, shall henceforth, for all time, afford each other aid against dangers from without and from within.

Article 5

Both States, each on its own territory, shall afford mutual aid to their subjects, travelling officially and privately on religious or on State business.

Article 6

Both States, the Mongolian and the Tibetan, shall, as formerly, carry on mutual trade in the produce of their lands—in goods, cattle & so on, and likewise open industrial institutions.

Article 7

Henceforth transactions on credit shall be allowed only with the knowledge and permission of official institutions; without such permission no claims shall be examined by Government Institutions. Should such agreements have been entered into before the conclusion of the present treaty, and should the parties thereto be unable to settle matters amicably, while the loss suffered is great, the payment of such debts may be enforced by the said institutions, but in no case shall the debts concern the Shabinars* and Hoshuns†.

Article 8

Should it be necessary to supplement the articles of this treaty, the Mongolian and Tibetan Governments shall appoint special Plenipotentiaries, who shall come to an Agreement according to the circumstances then existing.

Article 9

The present treaty shall come into force on the date of the signature thereof.

Plenipotentiaries of the Mongolian Government: Acting Ministers of Foreign Affairs Biliktu Da Lama Rabdan and Assistant Minister—General and Manlai Caatyr Bei Tzu Damdinsurun.

Plenipotentiaries of the Dalai Lama, Sovereign of Tibet: Gujir Tsanshib Kanchen Lubsan Agwan, Donir Agwan Choinzin Tschichamtso, Manager of the Bank of Tibet, and Gendum-Galsan, secretary.

According to the Mongolian chronology, on the 4th day of the 12th month of the second year of 'Him who is exalted by all'.

According to the chronology of Tibet, in the year of the Water-Mouse, on the same month and day.

The validity of the above agreement was never clearly established. See Bell, *Tibet: Past and Present*, pp. 150, 151.
*Shabinars—people who depended on the court of Hu-tuk-tu and paid taxes to the Court.
†Hoshun—principality.

INDIA–TIBET FRONTIER—EXCHANGE OF NOTES BETWEEN THE BRITISH AND TIBETAN PLENIPOTENTIARIES

To

Lonchen Shatra, Tibetan Plenipotentiary

In February last you accepted the India–Tibet frontier from the Isu Razi Pass to the Bhutan frontier, as given in the map (two sheets)*, of which two copies are herewith attached, subject to the confirmation of your government and the following conditions:-

(a) The Tibetan ownership in private estates on the British side of the frontier will not be disturbed.

(b) If the sacred places of Tso Karpo and Tsari Sarpa fall within a day's march of the British side of the frontier, they will be included in Tibetan territory and the frontier modified accordingly.

I understand that your Government have now agreed to this frontier subject to the above two conditions. I shall be glad to learn definitely from you that this is the case.

You wished to know whether certain dues now collected by the Tibetan Government at Tsona Jong and in Kongbu and Kham from the Monpas and Lopas for articles sold may still be collected. Mr. Bell has informed you that such details will be settled in a friendly spirit, when you have furnished him the further information, which you have promised.

The final settlement of this India–Tibet frontier will help to prevent causes of future dispute and thus cannot fail to be of great advantage to both Governments.

A.H. McMAHON

Delhi, 24th March 1914 British Plenipotentiary.

---

*Map not attached in this book.

To

Sir Henry McMahon,

British Plenipotentiary to the China–Tibet Conference.

As it was feared that there might be friction in future unless the boundary between India and Tibet is clearly defined, I submitted the map, which you sent to me in February last, to the Tibetan Government at Lhasa for orders. I have now received orders from Lhasa, and I accordingly agree to the boundary as marked in red in the two copies of the maps* signed by you subject to the condition mentioned in your letter, dated 24th March, sent to me through Mr. Bell. I have signed and sealed the two copies of the maps. I have kept one copy here and return herewith the other.

Sent on the 29th day of the 1st month of the Wood-Tiger year (25th March 1914) by Lonchen Shatra, the Tibetan Plenipotentiary.

Seal of Lonchen Shatra.

---

* Map not attached

CONVENTION BETWEEN GREAT BRITAIN, CHINA AND TIBET, SIMLA, 1914

His Majesty the King of the United Kingdom of Great Britain and Ireland and of the British Dominions beyond the Seas, Emperor of India, His Excellency the President of Republic of China, and His Holiness the Dalai Lama of Tibet, being sincerely desirous to settle by mutual agreement various questions concerning the interests of their several States in the Continent of Asia, and further to regulate the relations of their several Governments, have resolved to conclude a Convention on this subject and have nominated for this purpose their respective Plenipotentiaries, that is to say:

His Majesty the King of the United Kingdom of Great Britain and Ireland and of the British Dominions beyond the Seas, Emperor of India, Sir Arthur Henry McMahon, Knight Grand Cross of the Royal Victorian Order, Knight Commander of the Most Eminent Order of the Indian Empire, Companion of the Most Exalted Order of the Star of India, Secretary to the Government of India, Foreign and Political Department;

His Excellency the President of the Republic of China, Monsieur Ivan Chen, Officer of the Order of the Chia Ho;

His Holiness the Dalai Lama of Tibet, Lonchen Ga-den Shatra Pal-jor Dorje; who having communicated to each other their respective full powers and finding them to be in good and due form have agreed upon and concluded the following Convention in eleven Articles:-

Article 1

The Convention specified in the Schedule to the present Convention shall, except in so far as they may have been modified by, or may be inconsistent with or repugnant to, any of the provisions of the present Convention, continue to be binding upon the High Contracting Parties.

Article 2

The Government of Great Britain and China recognising that Tibet is under the suzerainty of China, and recognising also the autonomy of Outer Tibet, engage to respect the territorial integrity of the country, and to abstain from interference in the administration of Outer Tibet (including the selection and installation of the Dalai Lama), which shall remain in the hands of the Tibetan Government at Lhasa.

The Government of China engages not to convert Tibet into a Chinese province. The Government of Great Britain engages not to annex Tibet or any portion of it.

Article 3

Recognising the special interest of Great Britain, in virtue of the geographical position of Tibet, in the existence of an effective Tibetan Government, and in the maintenance of peace and order in the neighbourhood of the frontiers of India and adjoining States, the Government of China engages, except as provided in Article 4 of this Convention, not to send troops into Outer Tibet, nor to station civil or military officers, nor to establish Chinese colonies in the country. Should any such troops or officials remain in Outer Tibet at the date of the signature of this Convention, they shall be withdrawn within a period not exceeding three months.

The Government of Great Britain engages not to station military or civil officers in Tibet (except as provided in the Convention of September 7, 1904, between Great Britain and Tibet) nor troops (except the Agents' escorts), nor to establish colonies in that country.

Article 4

The foregoing Article shall not be held to preclude the continuance of the arrangement by which, in the past, a Chinese high official with suitable escort has been maintained at Lhasa, but it is hereby provided that the said escort shall in no circumstances exceed 300 men.

Article 5

The Governments of China and Tibet engage that they will not enter into any negotiations or agreements regarding Tibet with one another, or with any other Power, excepting such negotiations and agreements between Great Britain and Tibet as are provided for by the Convention of September 7, 1904, between Great Britain and Tibet and the Convention of April

27, 1906, between Great Britain and China.

Article 6

Article III of the Convention of April 27, 1906, between Great Britain and China is hereby cancelled, and it is understood that in Article IX(d) of the Convention of September 7, 1904, between Great Britain and Tibet the term 'Foreign Power' does not include China.

Not less favourable treatment shall be accorded to British commerce than to the commerce of China or the most favoured nation.

Article 7

(a) The Tibet Trade Regulations of 1893 and 1908 are hereby cancelled.

(b) The Tibetan Government engages to negotiate with the British Government new Trade Regulations for Outer Tibet to give effect to Articles II, IV and V of the Convention of September 7, 1904, between Great Britain and Tibet without delay; provided always that such Regulations shall in no way modify the present Convention except with the consent of the Chinese Government.

Article 8

The British Agent who resides at Gyantse may visit Lhasa with his escort whenever it is necessary to consult with the Tibetan Government regarding matters arising out of the Convention of September 7, 1904, between Great Britain and Tibet, which it has been found impossible to settle at Gyantse by correspondence or otherwise.

Article 9

For the purpose of the present Convention the borders of Tibet, and the boundary between Outer and Inner Tibet, shall be as shown in red and blue respectively on the map attached hereto.*

(Whereas the Simla Convention itself after being initialled by the Chinese Plenipotentiary was not signed or ratified by the Chinese Government, it was accepted as binding by the two other parties as between themselves).

*Map not attached in this book.

Nothing in the present Convention shall be held to prejudice the existing rights of the Tibetan Government in Inner Tibet, which include the power to select and appoint the high priests of monasteries and to retain full control in all matters affecting religious institutions.

Article 10

The English, Chinese and Tibetan texts of the present Convention have been carefully examined and found to correspond, but in the event of there being any difference of meaning between them the English text shall be authoritative.

Article 11

The present Convention will take effect from the date of signature.

In token whereof the respective Plenipotentiaries have signed and sealed this Convention, three copies in English, three in Chinese and three in Tibetan.

Done at Simla this third day of July, A.D., one thousand nine hundred and fourteen, corresponding with the Chinese date, the third day of the seventh month of the third year of the Republic, and the Tibetan date, the tenth day of the fifth month of the Wood-Tiger year.

Initial of the Lonchen Shatra.
Seal of the Lonchen Shatra.

(Initialled) A.H.M.
Seal of the
BritishPlenipotentiary.

Schedule

1. Convention between Great Britain and China relating to Sikkim and Tibet, signed at Calcutta the 17th March 1890.

2. Convention between Great Britain and Tibet, signed at Lhasa the 7th September 1904.

3. Convention between Great Britain and China respecting Tibet, signed at Peking the 27th April 1906.

The notes exchanged are to the following effect:-

1. It is understood by the High Contracting Parties that Tibet forms part of Chinese territory.

2. After the selection and installation of the Dalai Lama by the Tibetan Government, the latter will notify the installation to the Chinese Government whose representative at Lhasa will then formally communicate to His Holiness the titles consistent with his dignity, which have been conferred by the Chinese Government.

3. It is also understood that the selection and appointment of all officers in Outer Tibet will rest with the Tibetan Government.

4. Outer Tibet shall not be represented in the Chinese Parliament or in any other similar body.

5. It is understood that the escorts attached to the British Trade Agencies in Tibet shall not exceed seventy-five per centum of the escort of the Chinese Representative at Lhasa.

6. The Government of China is hereby released from its engagements under Article III of the Convention of March 17, 1890, between Great Britain and China to prevent acts of aggression from the Tibetan side of the Tibet–Sikkim frontier.

7. The Chinese high official referred to in Article 4 will be free to enter Tibet as soon as the terms of Article 3 have been fulfilled to the satisfaction of representatives of the three signatories to this Convention, who will investigate

and report without delay.

Initial of the Lonchen Shatra.*
Seal of the Lonchen Shatra.

(Initialof A.H.M.)
Seal of the
BritishPlenipotentiary.

On the withdrawal of the Chinese, a Declaration was signed by the plenipotentiaries of Britain and Tibet declaring that the Convention was to be binding on the Governments of Britain and Tibet and agreeing that so long as the Chinese Government withheld its signature it would be debarred from the enjoyment of privileges accruing thereunder.

*Owing to the impossibility of writing initials in Tibetan, the mark of the Lonchen at this place is his signature.

ANGLO–TIBETAN TRADE REGULATIONS—JULY 1914

Whereas by Article 7 of the Convention concluded between the Governments of Great Britain, China and Tibet on the third day of July, A.D. 1914, the Trade Regulations of 1893 and 1908 were cancelled and the Tibetan Government engaged to negotiate with the British Government new Trade Regulations for Outer Tibet to give effect to Articles II, IV and V of the Convention of 1904;

His Majesty the King of United Kingdom of Great Britain and Ireland, and of the British Dominions beyond the Seas, Emperor of India, and His Holiness the Dalai Lama of Tibet have for this purpose named as their Plenipotentiaries, that is to say:

His Majesty the King of Great Britain and Ireland and of the British Dominions beyond the Seas, Emperor of India; Sir A.H.McMahon, G.C.V.O., K.C.I.E., C.S.I.;

His Holiness the Dalai Lama of Tibet; Lonchen Ga-den Shatra Pal-jor Dorje;

And whereas Sir A.H.McMahon and Lonchen Ga-den Shatra Pal-jor Dorje have communicated to each other since their respective full powers and have found them to be in good and true form, the following Regulations have been agreed upon:-

I. The area falling within a radius of three miles from the British Trade Agency site will be considered as the area of such Trade Mart. It is agreed that British subjects may lease lands for the building of houses and godowns at Marts. This arrangement shall not be held to prejudice the right of British subjects to rent houses and godowns outside the Marts for their own accommodation and the storage of their goods. British subjects desiring to lease building sites shall apply through the British Trade Agent to the Tibetan Trade Agent. In consultation with the British Trade Agent the Tibetan Trade Agent will assign such or other suitable building sites without unnecessary delay. They shall fix the terms of the leases in conformity with the existing laws and rates.

II. The administration of the Trade Marts shall remain with the Tibetan Authorities, with the exception of the British Trade Agency sites and compounds of the rest-houses, which will be under the exclusive control of the British Trade Agents.

The Trade Agents at the Marts and Frontier Officers shall be of suitable rank, and shall hold personal intercourse and correspondence with one another on terms of mutual respect and friendly treatment.

III. In the event of disputes arising at the Marts or on the routes to the Marts between British and subjects of other nationalities, they shall be enquired into and settled in personal conference between the British and Tibetan Trade Agents at the nearest Mart. Where there is a divergence of view the law of the country to which the defendant belongs shall guide.

All questions in regard to rights, whether of property or person, arising between British subjects, shall be subject to the jurisdiction of the British Authorities.

British subjects, who may commit any crime at the Marts or on the routes to the Marts, shall be handed over by the Local Authorities to the British Trade Agent at the Mart nearest to the scene of the offence, to be tried and punished according to the laws of India; but such British subjects shall not be subjected by the Local Authorities to any ill-usage in excess of necessary restraint.

Tibetan subjects, who may be guilty of any criminal act towards British subjects, shall be arrested and punished by the Tibetan Authorities according to law.

Should it happen that a Tibetan subject or subjects bring a criminal complaint against a British subject or subjects before the British Trade Agent, the Tibetan Authorities shall have the right to send a representative or representatives of suitable rank to attend the trial in the British Trade Agent's Court. Similarly in cases in which a British subject or subjects have reason to complain against a Tibetan subject or subjects, the British Trade Agent shall have the right to send a representative or representatives to the Tibetan Trade Agent's Court to attend the trial.

IV. The Government of India shall retain the right to maintain the telegraph lines from the Indian frontier to the Marts. Tibetan messages will be duly received and transmitted by these lines. The Tibetan Authorities shall be responsible for the due protection of the telegraph lines from the Marts to the Indian frontier, and it is agreed that all persons damaging the lines or interfering with them in any way or with the officials engaged in the inspection or maintenance thereof shall at once be severely punished.

V. The British Trade Agents at the various Trade Marts now or hereafter to be established in Tibet may make arrangements for the carriage and transport of their posts to and from the frontier of India. The couriers employed in conveying these posts shall receive all possible assistance from the Local Authorities whose districts they traverse, and shall be accorded the same protection and facilities as the persons employed in carrying the despatches of the Tibetan Government. No restrictions whatever shall be placed on the employment by British officers and traders of Tibetan subjects in any lawful capacity. The persons so employed shall not be exposed to any kind of molestation or suffer any loss of civil rights, to which they may be entitled as Tibetan subjects, but they shall not be exempted from lawful taxation. If they be guilty of any criminal act, they shall be dealt with by the Local Authorities according to law without any attempt on the part of their employer to screen them.

VI. No rights of monopoly as regards commerce or industry shall be granted to any official or private company, institution, or individual in Tibet. It is of course understood that companies and individuals, who have already received such monopolies from the Tibetan Government previous to the conclusions of this agreement, shall retain their rights and privileges until the expiry of the period fixed.

VII. British subjects shall be at liberty to deal in kind or in money, to sell their goods to whomsoever they please, to hire transport of any kind, and to conduct in general their business transactions in conformity with local usage and without any vexations, restrictions or oppressive exactions whatever. The Tibetan Authorities will not hinder the British Trade Agents or other British subjects from holding personal intercourse or correspondence with the inhabitants of the country.

It being the duty of the Police and the Local Authorities to afford efficient protection at all times to the persons and property of the British subjects at the Marts and along the routes to the Marts, Tibet engages to arrange effective

Police measures at the Marts and along the routes to the Marts.

VIII. Import and export in the following Articles:-

arms, ammunition, military stores, liquors and intoxicating or narcotic drug may at the option of either Government be entirely prohibited, or permitted only on such conditions as either Government on their own side may think fit to impose.

IX. The present Regulations shall be in force for a period of ten years reckoned from the date of signature by the two Plenipotentiaries; but, if no demand for revision be made on either side within six months after the end of the first ten years the Regulations shall remain in force for another ten years from the end of the first ten years; and so it shall be at the end of each successive ten years.

X. The English and Tibetan texts of the present Regulations have been carefully compared, but in the event of there being any difference of meaning between them the English text shall be authoritative.

XI. The present Regulations shall come into force from the date of signature.

Done at Simla this third day of July, A.D. one thousand nine hundred and fourteen, corresponding with the Tibetan date, the tenth day of the fifth month of the Wood-Tiger year.

Seal of the DALAI LAMA

A HENRY McMAHON,
British Plenipotentiary

Signature of the
Lonchen Shatra.

Seal of British Plenipotentiary

Seal of the
Lonchen Shatra.

Seal of the
Drepung
Monastery

Seal of the
Sera Monastery

Seal of the
Gaden Monastery

Seal of the
National
Assembly

AGREEMENT ON MEASURES FOR THE PEACEFUL LIBERATION OF TIBET, 1951

The Tibetan nationality is one of the nationalities with a long history within the boundaries of China and like many other nationalities, it has done its glorious duty in the course of the creation and development of the great Motherland. But, over the last 100 years or more, imperialist forces penetrated into China and in consequence also penetrated into the Tibetan region and carried out all kinds of deceptions and provocations. Like previous reactionary Governments, the Kuomintang reactionary government continued to carry out policy of oppression and sowing dissension among the nationalities, causing division and disunity among the Tibetan people. The local government of Tibet did not oppose the imperialist deception and provocation and adopted an unpatriotic attitude towards the great Motherland. Under such conditions the Tibetan nationality and people were plunged into the depths of enslavement and sufferings. In 1949 basic victory was achieved on a nation-wide scale in the Chinese people's war of liberation; the common domestic enemy of all nationalities—the Kuomintang reactionary Government—was overthrown and the common foreign enemy of all nationalities—the aggressive imperialist forces—was driven out. On this basis the founding of the People' s Republic of China (CPR) and of the Chinese People's Government (CPG) was announced.

In accordance with the Common Programme passed by the Chinese People's Political Consultative Conference (CPPCC), the CPG declared that all nationalities within the boundaries of the CPR are equal and that they shall establish unity and mutual aid and oppose imperialism and their own public enemies, so that the CPR will become a big family of fraternity and co-operation, composed of all its nationalities. Within the big family of all nationalities of the CPR, national regional autonomy shall be exercised in areas where national minorities are concentrated and all national minorities shall have freedom to develop their spoken and written languages and to preserve or reform their customs, habits and religious beliefs, and the CPG shall assist all national minorities to develop their political, economic, cultural and educational construction work. Since then, all nationalities within the country—with the exception of those in the areas of Tibet and Taiwan— have gained liberation. Under the unified leadership of the

CPG and the direct leadership of higher levels of people's governments, all national minorities have fully enjoyed the right of national equality and have exercised, or are exercising, national regional autonomy.

In order that the influences of aggressive imperialist forces in Tibet might be successfully eliminated, the unification of the territory and sovereignty of the CPR accomplished, and national defence safeguarded; in order that the Tibetan nationality and people might be freed and return to the big family of the CPR to enjoy the same rights of national equality as all other nationalities in the country and develop their political, economic, cultural and educational work. The CPG, when it ordered the People's Liberation Army (PLA) to march into Tibet, notified the local government of Tibet to send delegates to the central authorities to conduct talks for the conclusion of an agreement on measures for the peaceful liberation of Tibet. In the latter part of April 1951 the delegates with full powers of the local government of Tibet arrived in Peking. The CPG appointed representatives with full powers to conduct talks on a friendly basis with delegates with full powers of the local government of Tibet. As a result of the talks both parties agreed to establish this agreement and ensure that it be carried into effect.

(1) The Tibetan people shall unite and drive out imperialist aggressive forces from Tibet; the Tibetan people shall return to the big family of the Motherland—the People's Republic of China.

(2) The local government of Tibet shall actively assist the PLA to enter Tibet and consolidate the national defences.

(3) In accordance with the policy towards nationalities laid down in the Common Programme of the CPPCC, the Tibetan people have the right of exercising national regional autonomy under the unified leadership of the CPG.

(4) The central authorities will not alter the existing political system in Tibet. The central authorities also will not alter the established status, functions and powers of the Dalai Lama. Officials of various ranks shall hold office as usual.

(5) The established status, functions and powers of the Panchen Ngoerhtehni shall be maintained.

(6) By the established status, functions and powers of the Dalai Lama and of the

Panchen Ngoerhtehni are meant the status,functions and powers of the thirteenth Dalai Lama and of the ninth Panchen Ngoerhtehni when they were in friendly and amicable relations with each other.

(7) The policy of freedom ofreligious belief laid down in the Common Programme of the CPPCC shall be carried out. The religious beliefs, customs and habits of the Tibetan people shall be respected and lama monasteries shall be protected. The central authorities will not effect a change in the income of the monasteries.

(8) Tibetan troops shall be reorganised step by step into the PLA and become a part of the national defence forces of the CPR.

(9) The spoken and written language and school education of the Tibetan nationality shall be developed step by step in accordance with the actual conditions in Tibet.

(10) Tibetan agriculture, livestock-raising, industry and commerce shall be developed step by step and the people's livelihood shall be improved step by step in accordance with the actual conditions in Tibet.

(11) In matters related to various reforms in Tibet, there will be no compulsion on the part of the central authorities. The local government of Tibet should carry out reforms of its own accord, and, when the people raise demands for reform, they shall be settled by means of consultation with the leading personnel of Tibet.

(12) In so far as former pro-imperialist and pro-Kuomintang officials resolutely severe relations with imperialism and the Kuomintang and do not engage in sabotage or resistance, they may continue to hold office irrespective of their past.

(13) The PLA entering Tibet shall abide by all the above-mentioned policies and shall also be fair in all buying and selling and shall not arbitrarily take a needle or thread from the people.

(14) The CPG shall have centralised handling of all external affairs of the area of Tibet; and there will be peaceful co-existence with neighbouring countries and establishment and development of fair commercial and trading relations

with them on the basis of equality, mutual benefit and mutual respect for territory and sovereignty.

(15) In order to ensure the implementation of this agreement, the CPG shall set up a Military and Administrative Committee and a Military Area HQ in Tibet and—apart from the personnel sent there by the CPG—shall absorb as many local Tibetan personnel as possible to take part in the work. Local Tibetan personnel taking part in the Military and Administrative Committee may include patriotic elements from the local government of Tibet, various districts and various principal monasteries; the name-list shall be set forth after consultation between the representatives designated by the CPG and various quarters concerned and shall be submitted to the CPG for appointment.

(16) Funds needed by the Military and Administrative Committee, the Military Area HQ and the PLA entering Tibet shall be provided by the CPG. The local government of Tibet should assist the PLA in the purchase and transport of food, fodder and other daily necessities.

(17) This agreement shall come into force immediately after signature and seals are affixed to it.

Signed and sealed by delegates of the CPG with full powers: Chief Delegate—Li Wei-Han (Chairman of the Commission of NationalitiesAffairs); Delegates—Chang Ching-wu, Chang Kuo-hua, Sun Chih-yuan. Delegates with full powers of the local government of Tibet: Chief Delegate—Kaloon Ngabou Ngawang Jigme (Ngabo Shape); Delegates— Dazasak Khemey Sonam Wangdi, Khentrung Thupten Tenthar, Khenchung Thupten Lekmuun, Rimshi Samposey Tenzin Thundup.

Peking, 23rd May, 1951. Sd.

AGREEMENT BETWEEN THE REPUBLIC OF INDIA AND THE PEOPLE'S REPUBLIC OF CHINA ON TRADE AND INTERCOURSE BETWEEN TIBET REGION OF CHINA AND INDIA, 29 APRIL 1954

The Government of the Republic of India and the Central People's Government of the People's Republic of China.

Being desirous of promoting trade and cultural intercourse between Tibet Region of China and India and of facilitating pilgrimage and travel by the peoples of China and India.

Have resolved to enter into the present Agreement based on the following principles:

(1) mutual respect for each other's territorial integrity and sovereignty,

(2) mutual non-aggression,

(3) mutual non-interference in each other's internal affairs,

(4) equality and mutual benefit, and

(5) peaceful coexistence.

And for this purpose have appointed as their respective Plenipotentiaries:

The Government of the Republic of India, H.E. Nedyam Raghavan, Ambassador Extraordinary and Plenipotentiary of India accredited to the People's Republic of China;

The Central People's Government of the People's Republic of China, H.E. Chang Han-fu, Vice-Minister of Foreign Affairs of the Central People's Government, who, having examined each other's credentials and finding them in good and due form, have agreed upon the following:-

Article I

The High Contracting Parties mutually agree to establish Trade Agencies:

(1) The Government of India agrees that the Government of China may establish Trade Agencies at New Delhi, Calcutta and Kalimpong.

(2) The Government of China agrees that the Government of India may establish Trade Agencies at Yatung, Gyantse and Gartok.

The Trade Agencies of both Parties shall be accorded the same status and same treatment. The Trade Agents of both Parties shall enjoy freedom from arrest while exercising their functions, and shall enjoy in respect of themselves, their wives and children who are dependenton them for livelihood freedom from search.

The Trade Agencies of both Parties shall enjoy the privileges and immunities for couriers, mail bags and communications in code.

Article II

The High Contracting Parties agree that traders of both countries known to be customarily and specifically engaged in trade between Tibet Region of China and India may trade at the following places:

(1) The Government of China agrees to specify (1) Yatung, (2) Gyantse and (3) Phari as markets for trade. The Government of India agrees that trade may be carried on in India, including places like (1) Kalimpong, (2) Siliguri and (3) Calcutta, according to customary practice.

(2) The Government of China agrees to specify (1) Gartok, (2) Pulanchung (Taklakot), (3) Gyanima-Khargo, (4) Gyanima-Chakra, (5) Ramura, (6) Dongbra, (7) Puling-Sumdo, (8) Nabra, (9) Shangtse and (10) Tashigong as markets for trade; the Government of India agrees that in future, when in accordance with the development and need of trade between the Ari District of Tibet Region of China and India, it has become necessary to specify markets for trade in the corresponding district in India adjacent to the Ari District of Tibet Region of China, it will be prepared to consider on the basis of equality and reciprocity to do so.

Article III

The High Contracting Parties agree that pilgrimage by religious believers of the two countries shall be carried on in accordance with the following provisions:-

(1) Pilgrims from India of Lamaist, Hindu and Buddhist faiths may visit Kang Rimpoche (Kailas) and Mavam Tso (Manasarovar) in Tibet Region of China in accordance with custom.

(2) Pilgrims from Tibet Region of China of Lamaist and Buddhist faiths may visit Banaras, Sarnath, Gaya and Sanchi in India in accordance with custom.

(3) Pilgrims customarily visiting Lhasa may continue to do so in accordance with custom.

Article IV

Traders and pilgrims of both countries may travel by the following passes and route:

(1) Shipki La pass, (2) Mana pass, (3) Niti pass, (4) Kungri Bingri pass, (5) Darma pass, and (6) Lipu Lekh pass.

Also, the customary route leading to Tashigong along the valley of the Shangatsangpu (Indus) River may continue to be traversed in accordance with custom.

Article V

For travelling across the border, the High Contracting Parties agree that diplomatic personnel, officials and nationals of the two countries shall hold passports issued by their own respective countries and visaed by the other Party except as provided in Paragraphs 1, 2, 3 and 4 of this Article.

(1) Traders of both countries known to be customarily and specifically engaged in trade between Tibet Region of China and India, their wives and children who are dependent on them for livelihood and their attendants will be allowed entry for purposes of trade into India or Tibet Region of China, as the case may be, in accordance with custom on the production of certificates duly issued by the local government of their own country or by its duly authorised agents and examined by the border check-posts of the other Party.

(2) Inhabitants of the border districts of the two countries who cross the border to carry on petty trade or to visit friends and relatives may proceed to the border districts of the other Party as they have customarily done heretofore

and need not be restricted to the passes and route specified in Article IV above and shall not be required to hold passports, visas or permits.

(3) Porters and mule-team drivers of the two countries who cross the border to perform necessary transportation services need not hold passports issued by their own country, but shall only hold certificates good for a definite period of time (three months, half a year or one year) duly issued by the local government of their own country or by its duly authorised agents and produce them for registration at the border check posts of the other Party.

(4) Pilgrims of both countries need not carry documents of certification but shall register at the border check posts of the other Party and receive a permit for pilgrimage.

(5) Notwithstanding the provisions of the foregoing paragraphs of this Article, either Government may refuse entry to any particular person.

(6) Persons who enter the territory of the other Party in accordance with the foregoing paragraphs of this Article may stay within its territory only after complying with the procedures specified by the other Party.

Article VI

The present Agreement shall come into effect upon ratification by both Governments and shall remain in force for eight (8) years. Extension of the present Agreement may be negotiated by the two Parties if either Party requests for it six (6) months prior to the expiry of the Agreement and the request is agreed to by the other Party.

Done in duplicate in Peking on the twenty-ninth day of April, 1954, in the Hindi, Chinese and English languages, all texts being equally valid.

(Sd.) NEDYAM RAGHAVAN,
Plenipotentiary of the
Government of the Republic
of India

(Sd.) CHANG HAN-FU,
Plenipotentiary of the Central People's
Government, People's Republic of
China.

NOTES EXCHANGED

Peking
April 29, 1954

Your Excellency Mr. Vice-Foreign Minister,

In the course of our discussions regarding the Agreement on Trade and Intercourse Between the Tibet Region of China and India, which has been happily concluded today, the Delegation of the Government of Republic of India and the Delegation of the Government of the People's Republic of China agreed that certain matters be regulated by an exchange of Notes. In pursuance of this understanding, it is hereby agreed between the two Governments as follows:-

(1) The Government of India will be pleased to withdraw completely within six (6) months from date of exchange of the present notes the military escorts now stationed at Yatung and Gyantse in Tibet Region of China. The Government of China will render facilities and assistance in such withdrawal.

(2) The Government of India will be pleased to hand over to the Government of China at reasonable price the postal, telegraph and public telephone services together with their equipment operated by the Government of India in Tibet Region of China. The concrete measures in this regard will be decided upon through further negotiations between the Indian Embassy in China and the Foreign Ministry of China, which shall start immediately after the exchange of the present notes.

(3) The Government of India will be pleased to hand over to the Government of China at a reasonable price the twelve (12) rest houses of the Government of India in Tibet Region of China. The concrete measures in this regard will be decided upon through further negotiations between the Indian Embassy in China and the Foreign Ministry of China, which shall start immediately after the exchange of the present notes. The Government of China agrees that they shall continue as rest houses.

(4) The Government of China agrees that all buildings within the compound walls of the Trade Agencies of the Government of India at Yatung and Gyantse in Tibet Region of China may be retained by the Government of India. The

Government of India may continue to lease the land within its Agency compound walls from the Chinese side. And the Government of India agrees that the Trade Agencies of the Government of China at Kalimpong and Calcutta may lease lands from the Indian side for the use of the Agencies and construct buildings thereon. The Government of China will render every possible assistance for housing the Indian Trade Agency at Gartok. The Government of India will also render every possible assistance for housing the Chinese Trade Agency at New Delhi.

(5) The Government of India will be pleased to return to the Government of China all lands used o r occupied by the Government of India other than the lands within its Trade Agency compound walls at Yatung.

If there are godowns and buildings of the Government of India on the above mentioned lands used or occupied and to be returned by the Government of India and if Indian traders have stores, godowns or buildings on the above mentioned lands so that there is need to continue leasing lands, the Government of China agrees to sign contracts with the Government of India or Indian traders, as the case may be, for leasing to them those parts of the land occupied by the said godowns, buildings or stores and pertaining thereto.

(6) The T rade Agents of both Parties may , in accordance with the laws and regulations of the local governments, have access to their nationals involved in civil or criminal cases.

(7) The Trade Agents and traders of both countries may hire employees in the locality.

(8) The hospitals of the India Trade Agencies at Gyantse and Yatung will continue to serve personnel of the Indian Trade Agencies.

(9) Each Government shall protect the person and property of the traders and pilgrims of the other country.

(10) The Government of China agrees, so far as possible, to construct rest houses for the use of pilgrims along the route from Pulan-chung (Tak- lakot) to Kang Rimpoche (Kailas) and Mavam Tso (Manasarovar); and the Government of India agrees to place all possible facilities in India at the disposal of pilgrims.

(11) Traders and pilgrims of both countries shall have the facility of hiring means of transportation at normal and reasonable rates.

(12) The three Trade Agencies of each Party may function throughout the year.

(13) Traders of each country may rent buildings and godowns in accordance with local regulations in places under the jurisdiction of the other Party.

(14) Traders of both countries may carry on normal trade in accordance with local regulations at places as provided in Article II of the Agreement.

(15) Disputes between traders of both countries over debts and claims shall be handled in accordance with local laws and regulations.

On behalf of the Government of the Republic of India, I hereby agree that the present Note along with Your Excellency's reply shall become an agreement between our two Governments which shall come into force upon the exchange of the present notes.

I avail myself of this opportunity to express to Your Excellency Mr. Vice-Foreign Minister, the assurances of my highest consideration.

CHANG HAN-FU,
Vice-Minister of Foreign Affairs,
Central People's Government,
People's Republic of China.

N RAGHAVAN
Ambassador Extraordinary
and Plenipotentiary of
the Republic of India.

TRADE AGREEMENT (BETWEEN THE REPUBLIC OF INDIA AND THE PEOPLE'S REPUBLIC OF CHINA, 14 OCTOBER 1954

The Government of the Republic of India and the Central People's Government of the People's Republic of China, animated by the common desire to develop trade between the two countries and to strengthen further the friendship that already exists between the Governments and the peoples of India and China have, on the basis of equality and mutual benefit, reached agreements as follows:-

Article I

The two contracting parties being desirous of adopting all appropriate measures for the expansion of trade between the two countries agree to give the fullest consideration to all suggestions for the promotion of such trade.

Article II

The two contracting parties agree that all commercial transactions between the two countries shall be carried out in accordance with the Import, Export and Foreign Exchange Regulations in force from time to time in their respective countries.

Article III

The two contracting parties agree to accord, subject to the laws and regulations of the two countries for the time being in force, facilities for the import and export of the commodities mentioned in the attached Schedules 'A' and 'B'*.

Article IV

The present Agreement will not preclude the two contracting parties from facilitating trade in commodities not mentioned in the attached Schedules 'A' and 'B'.

---

*Schedules of Goods for Import and Export not reproduced in this book.

Article V

The Trade between the Republic of India and the Tibet Region of the People's Republic of China will be conducted in accordance with the provisions of the Agreement between the Republic of India and the People's Republic of China on Trade and Intercourse between India and the Tibet Region of China signed in Peking on the 29th April 1954.

Article VI

The Government of the Republic of India agree that on request by the Government of the People's Republic of China, they will subject to the regulations in force, accord reasonable facilities for the entry into the Port of Calcutta and subsequent movement to the Tibet Region of the People's Republic of China, of such commercial goods as cannot be obtained in India. These facilities will be accorded only to goods of Chinese origin.

Article VII

All commercial and non-commercial payments between the Republic of India and the People's Republic of China may be effected in Indian rupees or in pounds sterling as may be mutually convenient. For the purpose of facilitating such payments, the People's Bank of China will open one or more account(s) with one or more commercial bank(s) in India authorised to deal in Foreign Exchange to be called account(s) 'A'. In addition, the People's Bank of China will, if necessary, open another account with the Reserve Bank of India to be called account 'B'. All payments between the two countries will be made through account(s) 'A'. Account 'B' will be used only for replenishing the balance(s) in account(s) 'A' whenever necessary. Payments to be made by residents of India to residents of the People's Republic of China will be effected by crediting the amounts of such payments to the above-mentioned account(s) 'A'. Payments to be made to residents of India by residents of the People's Republic of China will be effected by debiting the said account(s) 'A'. The account(s) 'A' will be replenished as and when necessary by one of the following methods, namely:-

(i) By transfer of funds from another account 'A' of the People's Bank of China with another commercial bank, or from account 'B' with the Reserve Bank of India;

(ii) By sale of sterling to the bank concerned. Account 'B' will be replenished by either sale of sterling to the Reserve Bank of India or by transfer of funds from account(s) 'A'.

2. Article VII of this Agreement covers the following payments:-

(i) Payments for the commodities imported or exported under the present Agreement;

(ii) Payments connected with commercial transactions and covering insurance, freight (in case of shipments of goods by the ships of either country), port charges, storage and forwarding expenses and bunkering;

(iii) Payments for distribution of films, for incomes and expenses of cultural performances and other exhibitions;

(iv) Payments of expenses on account of tours of delegations of commercial, cultural, social or official nature;

(v) Payments for the maintenance of the Embassy, Consulates and Trade Agencies of the Republic of India in China and for the maintenance of the Embassy, Consulates and Trade Agencies of the People's Republic of China in India;

(vi) Other non-commercial payments on which agreement is reached between the Reserve Bank of India and the People's Bank of China.

3. Any balances on the credit side of the account(s) 'A' or account 'B' maintained by the People's Bank of China will be convertible on demand into sterling at any time at the usual Banks' selling rate of sterling as fixed from time to time by the Indian Exchange Banks' Association. The above-mentioned balances will be convertible into sterling even after the expiry of this Agreement.

4. Payments for Border Trade between the Republic of India and the People's Republic of China, however, will be settled according to the customary practice.

Article VIII

The two contracting parties agree to consult with each other on questions that may arise in the course of the implementation of the present Agreement.

Article IX

This Agreement will come into force from the date of its signature and will remain valid for a period of two years.

This Agreement can be extended or renewed by negotiation between the two contracting parties to be commenced three months prior to its expiry.

Done in duplicate in New Delhi on the fourteenth Day of October 1954, in the Hindi, Chinese and English languages, all texts being equally authentic.

(Sd.) KUNG YUAN,
On behalf of the Government of
the People's Republic of China

(Sd.) HVR IENGAR
On behalf of the Government
of the Republic of India

UNITED NATIONS GENERAL ASSEMBLY 14TH SESSION, 834TH PLENARY MEETING, 1959 PERTAINING TO HUMAN RIGHTS IN TIBET

The Question of Tibet: Draft Resolution submitted by the Federation of Malaya and Ireland.

The General Assembly,

Recalling the principles regarding fundamental human rights and freedoms set out in the Charter of the United Nations and in the Universal Declaration of Human Rights adopted by the General Assembly on December 10th 1948,

Considering that the fundamental human rights and freedoms to which the Tibetan people, like all others, are entitled include the right to civil and religious liberty for all without distinction,

Mindful also of the distinctive cultural and religious heritage of the people of Tibet and of the autonomy, which they have traditionally enjoyed,

Gravely concerned at reports, including the official statements of His Holiness the Dalai Lama, to the effect that the fundamental human rights and freedoms of the people of Tibet have been forcibly denied to them,

Deploring the effect of these events in increasing international tensions and embittering relations between peoples at a time when earnest and positive efforts are being made by responsible leaders to reduce tension and improve international relations.

1. Affirms its belief that respect for the principles of the Charter and of the Universal Declaration of Human Rights is essential for the evolution of a peaceful world order based on the rule of law,

2. Calls for respect for the fundamental human rights of the Tibetan people and for their distinctive cultural and religious life.

Voting by roll call:

In favour:	Federation of Malaya, Greece, Guatemala, Haiti, Honduras, Iceland, Iran, Israel, Italy, Japan, Jordan, Laos, Liberia, Luxembourg, Mexico, Netherlands, New Zealand, Nicaragua, Norway, Pakistan,Panama, Paraguay, Peru, Philippines, Sweden, Thailand, Tunisia, Turkey, United States of America, Uruguay, Venezuela, Argentina, Australia, Austria, Bolivia, Brazil, Canada, Chile, China, Colombia, Cuba, Denmark, Ecuador, El Salvador.
Against:	Hungary, Poland, Romania, Ukrainian Soviet Socialist Republic, Union of Soviet Socialist Republics, Albania, Bulgaria, Byelorussian S.S.R., Czechoslovakia.
Abstaining:	Finland, France, Ghana, India, Indonesia, Iraq, Lebanon, Libya, Morocco, Nepal, Portugal, Saudi Arabia, Spain, Sudan, Union of South Africa, United Arab Republic, United Kingdom of Great Britain and Northern Ireland, Yemen, Yugoslavia, Afghanistan, Belgium, Burma, Cambodia, Ceylon, Dominican Republic, Ethiopia.

The draft resolution was adopted by 45 votes to 9 with 26 abstentions. The vote of Costa Rica, whose delegate was absent, was later recorded in favour of the resolution.

SINO-NEPALESE TREATY OF PEACE AND FRIENDSHIP, KATHMANDU, APRIL 28, 1960

The Chairman of the People's Republic of China and the His Majesty the King of Nepal, desiring to maintain and further develop peace and friendship between the People's Republic of China and the Kingdom of Nepal.

Convinced that the strengthening of good neighbourly relations and friendly co-operation between the People's Republic of China and the Kingdom of Nepal is in accordance with the fundamental interests of the people's of the two countries and conducive to the consolidation of peace in Asia and the world.

Have decided for this purpose to conclude the present Treaty in accordance with the Five Principles of peaceful co-existence jointly affirmed by the two countries, and have appointed as their respective plenipotentiaries:

The Chairman of the People's Republic of China:
Premier Chou En-lai of the State Council,
His Majesty the King of Nepal:
Prime Minister Bishweshwer Prasad Koirala.
The above-mentioned Plenipotentiaries,

Having examined each other's credentials and found them in good and due form,

Have agreed upon the following:

Article 1

The Contracting Parties recognise and respect the independence, sovereignty and territorial integrity of each other.

Article 2

The Contracting Parties will maintain and develop peaceful and friendly relations between the People's Republic of China and the Kingdom of Nepal. They undertake to settle all disputes between them by means of peaceful negotiation.

Article 3

The Contracting Parties agree to develop and further strengthen the economic and cultural ties between the two countries in a spirit of friendship and co-operation, in accordance with the principles of equality and mutual benefit and non-interference in each other's internal affairs.

Article 4

Any difference o r dispute arising out of the interpretation or application of the present Treaty shall be settled by negotiation through normal diplomatic channel.

Article 5

The present Treaty is subject to ratification and the instruments of ratification will be exchanged in Peking as soon as possible.

The present Treaty will come in to force immediately on the exchange of the instruments of ratification and will remain in force for a period of ten years.

Unless either of the Contracting Parties gives to the other notice in writing to terminate the Treaty at least one year before the expiration of this period, it will remain in force without any specific time limit, subject to the right of either Contracting Parties to terminate it by giving to the other in writing a year's notice of its intention to do so.

Done in duplicate in Kathmandu on the twenty-eighth day of April 1960, in the Chinese, Nepali and English languages, all texts being equally authentic.

Plenipotentiary of the People's Republic of China	Plenipotentiary of the Kingdom of Nepal
Sd. Chou En-lai	Sd. BP Koirala

PROPOSALS OF THE CONFERENCE OF SIX NON-ALIGNED NATIONS HELD AT COLOMBO, 10 TH TO 12 TH DECEMBER, 1962 ON INDIA–CHINA CONFLICT

1. The Conference considers that the existing de facto cease-fire period is a good starting point for a peaceful settlement of the Indian Chinese conflict.

2. (a) With regard to the Western Sector, the Conference would like to make an appeal to the Chinese Government to carry out their 20 kilometers withdrawal of their military posts as has been proposed in the letter of Prime Minister Chou En-lai to Prime Minister Nehru of November 21 and November 28, 1962.

   (b) The Conference would make an appeal to the Indian Government to keep their existing military position.

   (c) Pending a final solution of the border dispute, the area vacated by the Chinese military withdrawals will be demilitarized zone to be administered by civilian posts of both sides to be agreed upon, without prejudice to the rights of the previous presence of both India and China in that area.

3. With regard to the Eastern Sector, the Conference considers that the line of actual control in the areas recognized by both the Governments could serve as a cease-fire line to their respective positions. Remaining areas in this sector can be settled in their future discussions.

4. With regard to the problems of the Middle Sector, the Conference suggests that they will be solved by peaceful means, without resorting to force.

5. The Conference believes that these proposals, which could help in consolidating the cease-fire, once implemented, should pave the way for discussions between representatives of both parties for the purpose of solving problems entailed in the cease-fire position.

6. The Conference would like to make it clear that a positive response for the proposed appeal will not prejudice the position of either of the two Governments as regards its conception of the final alignment of the boundaries.

CLARIFICATIONS GIVEN BY THE REPRESENTATIVES OF THE COLOMBO POWERS TO THE GOVERNMENT OF INDIA, 13 JANUARY 1963

Upon request from the Government of India, the following clarifications of paragraphs 2, 3 and 4 of the Colombo Conference proposals were given by the Delegations of Ceylon, U.A.R. and Ghana:

Western Sector

(i) The withdrawal of Chinese forces proposed by the Colombo Conference will be 20 kilometers as proposed by Prime Minister Chou En-lai to Prime Minister Nehru in the statement of the Chinese Government dated 21st November and in Prime Minister Chou En-lai's letter of 28th November, 1962, i.e., from the line of actual control between the two sides as of November 7, 1959, as defined in maps III and V circulated by the Government of China.

(ii) The existing military posts which the forces of the Government of India will keep will be on and upto the line indicated in (i) above.

(iii) The demilitarized zone of 2 0 kilometers created by Chinese military withdrawals will be administered by civilian posts of both sides. This is a substantive part of the Colombo Conference proposals. It is as to the location, the number of posts and their composition that there has to be an agreement between the two Governments of India and China.

Eastern Sector

The Indian forces can, in accordance with the Colombo Conference proposals, move right upto the south of the line of actual control, i.e. the McMahon Line except for the two areas on which there is difference of opinion between the Governments of India and China. The Chinese forces similarly can move upto the north of McMahon Line except for these two areas. The two areas referred to as the remaining areas in the Colombo Conference proposals, arrangements in regard to which are to be settled between the Governments of India and China, according to the Colombo Conference proposals, are Chedong or the Thagla ridge area and the Longju area, in which cases there is a difference of opinion as to the line of actual control between the two Governments.

Middle Sector

The Colombo Conference desired that the status quo in this sector should be maintained and neither side should do anything to disturb the status quo.

THE BOUNDARY AGREEMENT BETWEEN CHINA AND PAKISTAN, 1963

The Government of thePeople's Republic of China and the Government of Pakistan;

Having agreed, with a view to ensuring the prevailing peace and tranquillity on the border, to formally delimit and demarcate the boundary between China's Sinkiang and the contiguous areas the defence of which is under the actual control of Pakistan, in a spirit of fairness, reasonableness, mutual understanding and mutual accommodation, and on the basis of the ten principles as enunciated in the Bandung Conference;

Being convinced that this would not only give full expression to the desire of the peoples of China and Pakistan for the development of good neighbourly and friendly relations, but also help safeguard Asian and world peace.

Have resolved for this purpose to conclude the present agreement and have appointed as their respective plenipotentiaries the following:

For the Government of the People's Republic of China; Chen Y i, Minister of Foreign Affairs;

For the Government of Pakistan; Mr. Zulfikar Ali Bhutto, Minister of External Affairs;

Who, having mutually examined their full powers and found them to be in good and due form, have agreed upon the following:

Article I

In view of the fact that the boundary between China's Sinkiang and contiguous areas the defence of which i s under the actual control of Pakistan has never been formally delimited, two parties agree to delimit it on the basis of the traditional customary boundary line including natural features and in a spirit of equality, mutual benefit and friendly co-operation.

Article 2

(One) In accordance with the principle expounded in Article 1 of the present agreement, the two parties have fixed, as follows the alignment of the entire boundary line between China's Sinkiang and the contiguous areas the defence of which is under the actual control of Pakistan:

(1) Commencing from its north-western extremity at height 5630 metres (a peak, the reference co-ordinates of which are approximately longitude 74 degrees 34 minutes east and latitude 37 degrees 03 minutes north), the boundary line runs generally eastward and then southeastward strictly along the main watershed between the tributaries of the Tashkurgan river of the Tarim river system on the one hand and tributaries of the Hunza river of the Indus river system on the other hand, passing through the Kalik Daban (Dawan), the Mintake Daban (pass), the Kharchanai Daban (named on the Chinese map only), the Mutsjilga Daban (named on the Chinese map only), and the Parpik Pass (named on the Pakistan map only), and reaches the Khunjerab (Yutr) Daban (Pass).

(2) After passing through the Khunjerab (Yutr) Daban (pass), the boundary line runs generally southward along the above mentioned main watershed up to a mountain-top south of this Daban (pass), where it leaves the main watershed to follow the crest of a spur lying generally in a southeasterly direction, which is the watershed between the Akjilga river (a nameless corresponding river on the Pakistan map) on the one hand, and the Taghumbash (Oprang) river and the Koliman Su (Oprang Jilga) on the other hand.

According to the map of the Chinese side, the boundary line, after leaving the southeastern extremity of this spur, runs along a small section of the middle line of the bed of the Keliman Su to reach its confluence with the Kelechin river. According to the map of the Pakistan side, the boundary line, after leaving the southeastern extremity of the spur, reaches the sharp bend of the Shaksgam or Muztagh River.

(3) From the aforesaid point, the boundary line runs up the Kelechin river (Shaksgam or Mistagh river) along the middle line of its bed to its confluence (reference co-ordinates approximately longitude 76 degrees 02 minutes east and latitude 36 degrees 26 minutes north) with the Snor- bulak Daria (Shimshal river or Braldu river).

(4) From the confluence of the aforesaid two rivers, the boundary line, according to the map ofthe Chinese side, ascends the crest of a spur and runs along it to join the Karakoram range main watershed at a mountain-top (reference co-ordinates approximately longitude 75 degrees 54 minutes east and latitude 36 degrees 15 minutes north) which on this map is shown as belonging to the Shorgulak mountain. According to the map of the Pakistan side, the boundary line from the confluence of the above-mentioned two rivers ascends the crest of a corresponding spur and runs along it, passing through height 6520 metres (21,390 feet) till it joins the Karakoram range main watershed at a peak (reference co-ordinates approximately longitude 75 degrees 57 minutes east and latitude 36 degrees 03 minutes north).

(5) Thence, the boundary line, running generally southward and then east- ward, strictly follows the Karakoram range main watershed which separates the Tarim river drainage system from the Indus river drainage system, passing through the east Mustagh pass (Muztagh pass), the top of the Chogri peak (K-2), the top of the broad peak, the top of the Gasher- brum mountain 8068, the Indirakoli pass (names on the Chinese maps only) and the top of the Teram Kankri peak, and reaches its southeastern extremity at the Karakoram pass.

(Two) The alignment of the entire boundary line as described in section one of this article, has been drawn on the one million scale map of the Chinese side in Chinese and the one million scale map of the Pakistan side in English which are signed and attached to the present agreement. (*Not attached in this book*)

(Three) In view of the fact that the maps of the two sides are not fully identical in their representation of the topographical features the two parties have agreed that the actual features on the ground shall prevail, so far as the location and alignment of the boundary described in Section one is concerned, and that they will be determined as far as possible by joint survey on the ground.

Article 3

The two parties have agreed that:

Wherever the boundary follows a river, the middle line of the river bed shall be the boundary line; and that

Wherever the boundary passes through Daban (pass), the water-parting line thereof shall be the boundary line.

Article 4

I. The two parties have agreed to set up, as soon as possible, a joint boundary demarcation commission. Each side will appoint a chairman, one or more members and a certain number of advisers and technical staff. The joint boundary demarcation commission is charged with the responsibility, in accordance with the provisions of the present agreement, to hold concrete discussions on and carry out the following tasks jointly:

(1) To conduct necessary surveys of the boundary area on the ground, as stated in Article 2 of the present agreement, so as to set up boundary markers at places considered to be appropriate by the two parties and to delineate the boundary line of the jointly prepared accurate maps.

(2) To draft a protocol setting forth in detail the alignment of the entire boundary line and the location of all the boundary markers and prepare and get printed detailed maps, to be attached to the protocol, with the boundary line and the location of the boundary markers shown on them.

II. The aforesaid protocol, upon being signed by the representatives of the Governments of the two countries, shall become an annex to the present agreement, and the detailed maps shall replace the maps attached to the present agreement.

III. Upon the conclusion of the above-mentioned protocol, the tasks of the joint boundary demarcation commission shall be terminated.

Article 5

The two Parties have agreed that any dispute concerning the boundary, which may arise after the delimitation of the boundary line actually existing between the two countries shall be settled peacefully by the two parties through friendly consultations.

Article 6

The two Parties have agreed that after the settlement of the Kashmir dispute between Pakistan and India, the sovereign authority concerned will reopen negotiations with the Government of the People's Republic of China, on the boundary, as described in Article Two of the present Agreement, so as to sign a formal Boundary Treaty to replace the present agreement:

Provided that in the event of that sovereign authority being Pakist an, the provisions of this agreement and the aforesaid Protocol shall be maintained in the formal Boundary Treaty to be signed between the People's Republic of China and Pakistan.

Article 7

The present agreement shall come into force on the date of its signature.

Done in duplicate in Peking on the second day of March, 1963, in the Chinese and English language, both texts being equally authentic.

Marshal Chen Yi,
Plenipotentiary of the
Government of the
People's Republic of China

Zulfikar Ali Bhutto,
Plenipotentiary of the
Government of Pakistan

REMARKS BY THE EDITOR

The Government of India agitated to the Government of Pakistan through a note dated 10 May 1963 and warned Pakistan of serious consequences since the territory ceded to China belonged to India and was under illegal and temporary occupation of Pakistan. Pakistan vide their note dated 9 August 1962 rejected the contents of the Indian note dated 10 May 1963 alleging that India has not fulfilled their commitment of plebiscite in Kashmir. A note dated 31 December 1963 was also forwarded to China by India alleging aggressive and expansionist move by the Government of China.

AGREEMENT ON THE MAINTENANCE OF PEACE AND TRANQUILLITY ALONG THE LINE OF ACTUAL CONTROL IN THE INDIA–CHINA BORDER AREAS, 1993, BEIJING

The Government of the Republic of India and the Government of the People's Republic of China (hereinafter referred to as the two sides), have entered into the present agreement in accordance with the five Principles of mutual respect for sovereignty and territorial integrity, mutual non- aggression, non-interference in each others internal affairs, equality and mutual benefit and peaceful coexistence and with a view to maintaining peace and tranquillity in areas along the actual line of control in the India–China border areas.

1. The two sides are of the view that the India–China boundary question shall be resolved through peaceful and friendly consultations. Neither side shall use or threaten to use force against the other by any means. Pending an ultimate solution to the boundary question between the two countries, the two sides shall strictly respect and observe the line of actual control between the two sides. No activities of either side shall overstep the actual line of control. In case of personnel of one side cross the line of actual control, upon being cautioned by the other side, they shall immediately pull back to their own side of the line of actual control. When necessary, the two sides shall jointly check and determine the segments of the actual line of control where they have different views as to its alignment.

2. Each side will keep its military forces in the areas along the line of actual control to a minimum level compatible with the friendly and good neighbourly relations between the two countries. The two sides agree to reduce their military forces along the line of actual control in conformity with the requirements of the principle of mutual and equal security to ceilings to be mutually agreed. The extent, depth, timing and nature of the reduction of the military forces along the line of actual control shall be determined through mutual consultations between the two countries. The reduction of military forces shall be carried out by stages in mutually agreed geographical locations sector-wise within the areas along the line of actual control.

3. Both sides shall workout through consultations effective confidence building measures in the areas along the line of actual control. Neither side will undertake specified levels of military exercises in mutually identified zones. Each side shall give the other prior notification of military exercises of specified levels near the line of actual control permitted under this Agreement.

4. In case of contingencies or other problems arising in the area along the line of actual control, the two sides shall deal with them through meetings and friendly consultations between border personnel of the two countries. The form of such meetings and channels of communication between the border personnel shall be mutually agreed upon by the two sides.

5. The two sides agree to take adequate measures to ensure that air intrusions across the line of actual control do not take place and shall under take mutual consultations should intrusions occur. Both sides shall also consult on possible restrictions on air exercises in areas to be mutually agreed near the line of actual control.

6. The two sides agree that references to the line of actual control in this Agreement do not prejudice their respective positions on the boundary questions.

7. The two sides shall agree through consultations on the form, method, scale and content of effective verification measures and supervision required for the reduction of military forces and the maintenance of peace and tranquillity in the areas along the line of actual control under this Agreement.

8. Each side of the India–China Joint Working Group on the boundary question shall appoint diplomatic and military experts to formulate, through mutual consultations, implementation measures for the present Agreement. The experts shall advise the Joint Working Group on the resolution of differences between the two sides on the alignment of the line of actual control and address issues relating to redeployment with a view to reduction of military forces in the areas along the line of actual control. The experts shall also assist the Joint Working Group in supervision of the implementation of the Agreement, and settlement of differences that may arise in that process, based on the principle of good faith and mutual confidence.

9. The present Agreement shall come into effect as of the date of signature and is subject to amendments and addition by agreement of the two sides.

Signed in duplicate at Beijing on the Seventh day of September 1993 in the Hindi, Chinese and English languages, all three texts having equal validity.

Tang Jiaxuan	R.L. Bhatia
Vice-Foreign Minister	Minister of State for External Affairs
People's Republic of China	Republic of India

AGREEMENT BETWEEN INDIA AND CHINA ON CONFIDENCE BUILDING MEASURES IN THE MILITARY FIELD ALONG THE LINE OF ACTUAL CONTROL IN THE INDIA–CHINA BORDER AREAS, 1996 NEW DELHI

The Government of the Republic of India and the Government of the People's Republic of China (hereafter referred to as two sides),

Believing that it served the fundamental interest of the people of India and China to foster a long term good neighbourly relationship in accordance with the five principles of mutual respect for sovereignty and territorial integrity, mutual non-aggression, non-interference in each others internal affairs, equality and mutual benefit and peaceful coexistence,

Convinced that the maintenance of peace and tranquillity along the line of actual control in the India–China border areas accords with the fundament al interests of the two peoples and will also contribute to the ultimate resolution of the boundary question,

Reaffirming that neither side shall use or threaten to use force against the other by any means or seek unilateral military superiority,

Pursuant to the agreement between the Government of Republic of India and the Government of the People's Republic of China on the maintenance of peace and tranquillity along the line of actual control in the India–China border areas, signed on 7th September 1993,

Recognizing the need for effective confidence building measures in the military field along the line of actual control in the border areas between the two sides,

Noting the utility of confidence building measures already in place along the line of actual control in the India–China border areas,

Committed to enhancing mutual confidence and transparency in the military field have agreed as follows:

Article 1

Neither side shall use its military capability against the other side. No armed forces deployed by either side in the border areas along the line of actual control as part of the respective military strength shall be used to attack the other side, or engage in military activities that threaten the other side or undermine peace, tranquillity and stability in the India–China border areas.

Article II

The two sides reiterate their determination to seek a fair, reasonable and mutually acceptable settlement of the boundary question. Pending an ultimate solution to the boundary question, the two sides reaffirm their commitment to strictly respect and observe the line of actual control in the India–China border areas. No activities of either side shall overstep the line of actual control.

Article III

The two sides agree to take the following measures to reduce or limit their respective military forces within mutually agreed geographic zones along the line of actual control in India–China border areas:

1. The two sides reaffirm that they shall reduce or limit their respective military forces within mutually agreed geographical zones along the line of actual control in the India–China border areas to minimum levels compatible with the friendly and good neighbourly relations between the two countries and consistent with the principle of mutual and equal security.

2. The two sides shall reduce or limit the number of field armies, border defence forces, paramilitary forces and any other mutually agreed category of armed force deployed in mutually agreed geographical zones along the line of control to be mutually agreed upon. The major categories of armaments to be reduced, or limited are as follows: combat tanks, infantry combat vehicles, guns (including howitzers) with 75 mm or bigger calibre, mortars with 120 mm or bigger calibre, surface to surface missiles, surface to air missiles and any other weapon system mutually agreed upon.

3. The two sides shall exchange data on the military forces and armaments to be reduced or limited and decide on ceilings on military forces

and armaments to be kept by each side within mutually agreed geographical zones along the line of actual control in the India–China border areas. The ceilings shall be determined in conformity with the requirement of the principle of mutual and equal security with due consideration being given to parameters such as nature of terrain, road communication and other infrastructure and time taken to induct/de- induct troops and armaments.

Article IV

In order to maintain peace and tranquillity along the line of actual control in the India–China border areas and to prevent any tension in the border areas due to misreading by either side of the other side's intensions:

1. Both sides shall avoid holding large scale military exercises involving more than one Division (approximately 15,000 troops) in close proximity of the line of actual control in the India–China border areas. However, if such exercises are to be conducted, the strategic direction of the main force involved shall not be towards the other side.

2. If either side conducts a major military exercise involving more than one Brigade Group (approximately 5000 troops) in close proximity of the line of actual control in the India–China border areas, it shall give the other side prior notification with regard to type, level, planned duration and area of exercise as well as the number and type of formations participating in the exercise.

3. The date of completion and de-induction of troops from the area of exercise shall be intimated to the other side within five days of completion or de-induction.

4. Each side shall be entitled to obtain timely clarification from the side undertaking the exercise in respect of data specified in Paragraph 2 of the present article.

Article V

With a view to preventing air intrusions across the line of actual control in the India–China border areas and facilitating overflights and landings by military aircraft:

1. Both sides shall take adequate measures to ensure that air intrusions across the line of actual control do not take place. However, if an intrusion does take place, it should cease as soon as detected and the incident shall be promptly investigated by the side operating the aircraft. The results of the investigation shall be immediately communicated, through diplomatic channels or at border personnel meetings, to the other side.

2. Subject to paragraph 3 and 5 of this Article, combat aircraft (to include fighter, bomber, reconnaissance, military trainer, armed helicopter and other armed aircrafts) shall not fly within ten kilometers of the line of actual control.

3. If either side is required to undertake flights of combat aircraft within ten kilometers of the line of actual control, it shall give the following information in advance to the other side, through diplomatic channels:

(a) Type and number of combat aircraft;

(b) Height of proposed flight (in meters);

(c) Proposed duration of flight (normally not to exceed ten days);

(d) Proposed timings of flights; and

(e) Area of operation defined in latitude and longitude.

4. Unarmed transport aircraft, survey aircraft and helicopters shall be permitted to fly up to the line of actual control.

5. No military aircraft of either side shall fly across the line of actual control, except by prior permission. Military aircraft of either side may fly across the line of actual control or over fly the other sides airspace or land on the other side only after obtaining the latter's prior permission, after providing the latter with detailed information of the flight in accordance with the international practice in this regard.

Notwithstanding the above stipulation, each side has the sovereign right to specify additional conditions, including at short notice, for flights or landings of military aircrafts of the other side on its side of the line of actual control or through its air space.

6. In order to ensure flight safety in emergency situations, the authorities designated by the two sides may contact each other by the quickest means of communication available.

Article VI

With a view to preventing dangerous military activities along the line of actual control in the India–China border areas, the two sides agree as follows:

(1) Neither side shall open fire, cause bio-degradation, use hazardous chemicals, conduct blast operations or hunt with guns or explosives within two kilometers from the line of actual control. The prohibition shall not apply to routine firing activities in small arms firing ranges.

(2) If there is a need to conduct blast operations within two kilometers of the line of actual control as part of developmental activities, the other side shall be informed through diplomatic channels or by convening a border personnel meeting, preferably five days in advance.

(3) While conducting exercises with live ammunition in areas close to the line of control, precautions shall be taken to ensure that a bullet or a missile does not accidentally fall on the other side across the line of actual control and causes harm to personnel or property of the other side.

(4) If the border personnel of both sides come face to face situation due to differences on the alignment of the line of actual control or any other reason, they shall exercise self-restrain and take all necessary steps to avoid an escalation of the situation. Both sides shall also enter into immediate consultations through diplomatic and/or other available channelsto review the situation and prevent escalation of the tension.

Article VII

In order to strengthen exchanges and co-operation between the military personnel and establishments in the border areas along the line of actual control, the two sides agree:

(a) To maintain and expand the regime of scheduled and flag meetings between their border representatives at designated places along the line of actual control;

(b) To maintain and expand telecommunication links between the border meeting points at designated places along the line of actual control;

(c) To establish step by step medium and high level contacts between the border authorities of the two sides.

Article VIII

1. Should the personnel of one side cross the line of actual control and enter the other side because of unavoidable circumstances like natural disasters, the other side shall extend all possible assistance to them and inform their side, as soon as possible regarding the forced or inadvertent entry across the line of actual control. The modalities of the return of the concerned personnel to their own side shall be settled through mutual consultations.

2. The two sides shall provide each other, at the earliest possible, with information pertaining to natural disasters and epidemic diseases in contiguous border areas which might affect the other side. The exchange of information shall take place through diplomatic channels or at border personnel meetings.

Article IX

In case a doubtful situation develops in the border region, or in case one of the sides has some questions or doubts regarding the manner in which the other side is observing this agreement, either side has the right to seek a clarification from the other side. The clarification sought and replies to them shall be conveyed through diplomatic channels.

Article X

1. Recognising that the full implementation of some of the provisions of the present Agreement will depend on the two sides arriving at a common understanding of the alignment of the line of actual control in the India–China border areas, the two sides agree to speed up the process of clarification and confirmation of the line of actual control. As an initial step in this process, they are clarifying the alignment of the line of actual control in those segments where they have different perceptions. They also agree to exchange maps

indicating their respective perceptions of the entire alignment of the line of actual control as soon as possible.

2. Pending the completion of the process of clarifiation and confirmation of the line of actual control, the two sides shall work out modalities for implementation of the confidence building measures envisaged under this Agreement on an interim basis, without prejudice to their respective positions on the alignment of the line of actual control as well as on the boundary question.

Article XI

Detailed implementation measures required under Article I to X of this Agreement shall be decided through mutual consultations in the India–China Joint Working Group on the Boundary question. The India–China Diplomatic and Milit ary Expert Group shall assist the India–China Joint W orking Group in devising implementation measures under the Agreement.

Article XII

This Agreement is subject to ratification and shall enter into force on the date of exchange of Instruments of Ratification. It shall remain in effect until either side decides to terminate it after giving six months notice in writing. It shall become invalid six months after the notification.

This Agreement is subject to amendment and addition by mutual agreement in writing between the two sides.

Signed in duplicate in New Delhi on 29 November 1996 in the Hindi, Chinese and English languages, all three texts being equally authentic. In case of divergence, the English text shall prevail.

Sd.

REMARKS BY THE EDITOR

The resolution of the International Boundary dispute seems far away Some pockets have been jointly identified as disputed, their resolution is the first step. The second and contiguous step is to mutually agree on the alignment of the Line of Actual Control. The last step is to decide on the International Boundary by a process of give and take. The dialogue is on but the progress is painfully slow.

The ground position is that after the Chinese unilateral withdrawal, post 1962, the LAC came in to being only in the western sector . This LAC extends approximately 320 km from Daulat Beg Oldi (DBO) to Demchok in Ladakh with a demilitrised zone of 20 km.

In the eastern sector, the Chinese do not recognize the Mcmahon Line, consider it illegal and claim another 90,000 km of the Indian territory in the Indian state of Arunachal Pradesh.

Consequent to the Peace and Tranquility Agreement, both sides have agreed to define the entire 4056 km border as LAC. By implication the McMahon Line ceases to exist.

McMahon Line was drawn during theTripartite Agreement between British, China and Tibet in 1914 which the Chinese declined to ratify . Thus the Agreement became binding between British India and Tibet only. On India having recognized PRC and Tibet being part of China, legally the Chinese view point seems to prevail. McMahon Line becomes null and void.

III

INDIA–NEIGHBOURING COUNTRIES–OTHERS

TREATY OF SEGOWLEE BETWEEN NEPAL AND EAST INDIA COMPANY, 2 DECEMBER 1815

Treaty of Peace between the Honourable East India Company and Maha Rajah Bikram Sah, Rajah of Nipal, settled between Lieutenant-Colonel Bradshaw on the part of the Honourable Company, in virtue of the full powers vested in him by his Excellency, the Right Honourable Francis, Earl of Moira, Knight of the Most Noble Order of the Garter, one of His Majesty's Most Honourable Privy Council, appointed by the Court of Directors of the said Honourable Company to direct and control all the affairs in the East Indies, and by Sree Gooroo Gujraj Misser and Chunder Seekur Opedeea on the part of Maha Rajah Girmaun Jode Bikram Shah Bauder, Shumsheer Jung, in virtue of the powers to that effect vested in them by the said Rajah of Nipal,—2nd December 1815. WHEREAS war has arisen between the Honourable East India Company and the Rajah of Nipal, and WHEREAS the parties are mutually disposed to restore the relations of peace and amity which, previously to the occurrence of the late differences, had long subsisted between the two States, the following terms of peace have been agreed upon.

Article 1st

There shall be perpetual peace and friendship between the Honourable East India Company and the Rajah of Nipal.

Article 2nd

The Rajah of Nipal renounces all claim to the lands which were the subject of discussion between the two States before the war; and acknowledges the right of the Honourable Company to the sovereignty of those lands.

Article 3rd

The Rajah of Nipal hereby cedes to the Honourable East India Company in perpetuity all the under-mentioned territories, viz—

Firstly

The whole of the low lands between the Rivers Kali and Rapti.

Secondly

The whole of the low lands (with the exception of Bootwul Khass) lying between the Rapti and the Gunduck.

Thirdly

The whole of the low lands between the Gunduck and Coosah, in which the authority of the British government has been introduced, or is in actual course of introduction.

Fourthly

All the low lands between the Rivers Mitchee and the Teestah.

Fifthly

All the territories within the hills eastward of the River Mitchee including the fort and lands of Nagree and the Pass of Nagarcote leading from Morung into the hills, together with the territory lying between that Pass and Nagree. The aforesaid territory shall be evacuated by the Gurkah troops within forty days from this date.

Article 4th

With a view to indemnify the Chiefs and Barahdars of the State of Nipal, whose interests still suffer by the alienation of the lands ceded by the fore going Article, the British Government agrees to settle pensions to the aggregate amount of two lakhs of rupees per annum on such Chiefs as may be selected by the Rajah of Nipal, and in the proportions which the Rajah may fix. As soon as the selection is made, Sunnuds shall be granted under the seal and signature of the Governor-General for the pensions respectively.

Article 5th

The Rajah of Nipal renounces for himself, his heirs, and successors, all claim to or connexion with the countries lying to the west of the River Kali and engages never to have any concern with those countries or the inhabitants thereof.

Article 6th

The Rajah of Nipal engages never to molest or disturb the Rajah of Sikkim in the possession of his territories; but agrees, if any differences shall arise between the State of Nipal and the Rajah of Sikkim or the subjects of either, that such differences shall be referred to the arbitration of the British Government by whose award the Rajah of Nipal engages to abide.

Article 7th

The Rajah of Nipal hereby engages never to take or retain in his service any British subject, nor the subject of any European and American State, without the consent of the British Government.

Article 8th

In order to secure and improve the relations of amity and peace hereby established between the two States, it is agreed that accredited Ministers from each shall reside at the Court of the other.

Article 9th

This treaty, consisting of nine Articles, shall be ratified by the Rajah of Nipal within fifteen days from this date, and the ratification shall be delivered to lieut.-Colonel Bradshaw, who engages to obtain and deliver to the Rajah the ratification of the Governor-General within twenty days, or sooner, if practicable.

DONE at Segowlee, on the 2nd day of December,1815.

PARIS BRADSHAW, LT.-COL.,P.A.

TREATY BETWEEN BRITISH AND NEPAL, NOVEMBER 1, 1860

During the disturbances which followed the mutiny of the Native army of Bengal in 1857, the Maharajah of Nipal not only faithfully maintained the relations of peace and friendship established between the British Government and the State of Nipal by the Treaty of Segowlee, but freely placed troops at the disposal of the British authorities for the preservation of order in the Frontier Districts, and subsequently sent a force to co-operate with the British Army in the recapture of Lucknow and the final defeat of the rebels. On the conclusion of these operations, the Viceroy and Governor- General in recognition of the eminent services rendered to the British Government by the State of Nipal, declared his intention to restore to the Maharajah the whole of the low lands lying between the River Kali and the District of Gorukpore, which belonged to the State of Nipal in 1815, and were ceded to the British Government in that year by the aforesaid Treaty. These lands have now been identified by Commissioners appointed for the purpose by the British Government, in the presence of Commissioners deputed by the Nipal Darbar; masonry pillars have been erected to mark the future boundary of the two States, and the territory has been formally delivered over to the Nipalese Authorities. In order the more firmly to secure the State of Nipal in the perpetual possession of this territory, and to mark in a solemn way the occasion of its restoration, the following Treaty has been concluded between the two States:

Article 1st

All Treaties and Engagements now in force between the British Government and the Maharajah of Nipal, except in so far as they may be altered by this Treaty, are hereby confirmed.

Article 2nd

The British Government hereby bestows on the Maharajah of Nipal in full sovereignty, the whole of the lowlands between the Rivers Kali and Raptee, and the whole of the lowlands lying between the River Raptee and the District of Gorukpore, which were in the possession of the Nipal State in the year 1815, and were ceded to the British Government by Article III of the Treaty concluded at

Segowlee on the 2nd of December in that year.

Article 3rd

The boundary line surveyed by the British Commissioners appointed for the purpose extending eastward from the River Kali or Sardah to the foot of the hills north of Bagowra Tal, and marked by pillars, shall henceforth be the boundary between the British Province of Oudh and the Territories of the Maharajah of Nipal.

This Treaty, signed by lieutenant-Colonel George Ramsay, on the part of his excellency the Right Honourable Charles John, Earl Canning, G.C.B, Viceroy and Governor-General of India, and by Maharaja Jung Bahadur Rana, G.C.B., on the part of Maharajah Dheraj Soorinder Vikram Sah Bahadoor Shumshere Jung, shall be ratified, and the ratifications shall be exchanged at Kathmandoo within thirty days of the date of signature.

SIGNED and sealed at Kathmandoo, this first day of November, A.D., one thousand eight hundred and sixty corresponding to the third day of Kartik Budee, Sumbut nineteen hundred and seventeen.

G. RAMSAY, LIEUT. COL
Resident at Nipal

CANNING
Viceroy and Governor-General

This Treaty was ratified by His Excellency the Governor-General, at Calcutta, on the 15th of November, 1860.

A.R.YOUNG
Deputy Secretary to the Government of India

MEMORANDUM OF AGREEMENT AMONG THE UNITED KINGDOM, INDIA AND NEPAL RE: GURKHA SOLDIERS, KATHMANDU, NOVEMBER 9, 1947

1.At a meeting held at Kathmandu on Ist May 1947 between representatives of His Majesty's Government in the United Kingdom, the Government of India and Government of Nep al, His Highness the Prime Minister and Supreme Commander-in-Chief of Nepal, stated that he would welcome the proposals to maintain the Gurkha connection with the armies of the United Kingdom and India on the following basis "If the terms and conditions at the final stage do not prove detrimental to the interest or dignity of the Nepalese Government, my Government will be happy to maintain connections with both armies, provided men of the Gurkha regiments are willing so to serve (if they will not be looked upon as distinctly mercenary)".

2. Discussions have taken place in Delhi between the representative of His Majesty's Government in the United Kingdom and of the Government of the Dominion of India and the points of agreement are embodied in the Memorandum dated 7th November 1947 a copy of which forms Annexure I of this document. Necessary financial adjustments between the two Governments are still under consideration.

3. Further discussion between the representatives of the three Governments have taken place at Kathmandu during which the Government of Nepal have put forward certain pertinent observations on the Memorandum of Agreement referred to in the preceding paragraph which are set out in Annexure II. In regard to these points, the representatives of His Majesty's Government in the United Kingdom and of the Government of the Dominion of India have replied as follows:

   (a) *Location of the Recr uiting Depots.* The use of the existing depots at Gorakhpur and Ghum has been sought by His Majesty's Government in the United Kingdom for a temporary period only pending establishment of their own depots in Nepal. The wishes of the Government of Nepal have been noted and arrangements for the establishment in India of the Recruiting Depots required to meet the needs of the Gurkha units of the

British Army will be settled between the United Kingdom and Indian Governments.

(b) Desire of the government of Nepal that the total number of Gurkha units to be employed in the armies of the United Kingdom and of India shall be limited and brought down to the peace time strength of 20 battalions out of which 8 Battalions will be allotted to the British Army.

The representative of His Majesty's Government in the United Kingdom and of the Government of Dominion of India have taken note of the wishes of the Government of Nepal.

The representative of His Majesty's Government in the United Kingdom has explained that the long term planning of British Post-War Army has proceeded on the assumption that the Government of Nepal would be prepared to furnish sufficient men to establish the equivalent of an Infantry Division in South-East Asia and he has received an assurance from the Government of Nepal that a final decision on the question of recruitment of Gurkhas in excess of 8 Battalions at peace-time strength shall be left open until His Majesty's Government in the United Kingdom have had an opportunity of considering the views of the Government of Nepal.

As regards the reduction of the Gurkha units in the Indian Army, the Government of Nepal have informed the representative of the Government of the Dominion of India that the reduction should not be carried out immediately in view of the existing political situation in India.

(c) *Arrangements of the import of the foreign currency belonging tothe Gurkha units of the 8 Battalions serving overseas.*

It is noted that the Government of the Dominion of India has agreed to afford all normal facilities in regard to the import of foreign currency belonging to these men (Annexure I, item 10). A reply to the specific point raised in this connection will be sent to the Government of Nepal in due course.

4. The Government of Nepal being generally satisfied in regard to the terms and conditions of employment of Gurkha troops and taking note of the agreement dated 7th November 1947 reached between His Majesty's Government in the United Kingdom and of the Government of Dominion of

India hereby signify their agreement to the employment of Gurkha troops in the armies of the United Kingdom and of India.

5. In addition to the observations referred to above the Government of Nepal have put forward certain suggestions connected with the employment of Gurkhas in the armies of the United Kingdom and of India. These suggestions are contained in Annexure III of this document and the views of the two Governments therein will be communicated to the Government of Nepal in due course.

6. Note has been taken of the desire of His Majesty's Government in United Kingdom that prompt action be taken to ascertain the wishes of the personnel of the 8 Gurkha Battalions concerned as to whether they desire to be transferred for service under the United Kingdom Government. With this object in view a questionnaire and a Memorandum embodying terms and conditions of service have been prepared by the representative of His Majesty's Government in the United Kingdom. These documents are acceptable to the Governments of India and Nepal. They will be issued to the personnel of the eight units concerned as soon as possible, in accordance with the wishes of the Government of Nepal as well as those of the Government of India. It is agreed that their representative will be present with the eight unit s while the referendum is being taken.

7. The representatives of the three Governments desire to place on record that their deliberations have been conducted in an atmosphere of cordiality and good will and are confident that the friendly relations which have existed in the past will be further cemented as a result of the arrangements which have been agreed for the continued employment of Gurkha soldiers in the armies of the United Kingdom and of India.

8. Signed in triplicate at Kathmandu this 9th day of November 1947.

A.C.B. SYMON
For the Government of United Kingdom.
BEDI
For the Government of the Dominion of India
PADMA SHAMSHERE JUNG BAHADUR RANA
For the Government of Nepal

ANNEXURE I

MEMORANDUM OF AGREEMENT BETWEEN THE GOVERNMENT OF THE DOMINION OF INDIA AND H.M. GOVERNMENT IN THE UNITED KINGDOM

1. That all volunteers from Regular battalions of each of the second, sixth, seventh and tenth Gurkha Rifles, together with personnel of their regimental centres, shall be transferred to H.M. British Army, subject to the negotiation of terms and conditions with the Government of Nepal.

2. That the personal arms and equipment of those units if required by H.M. Government will be issued on payment and removed overseas with the units.

3. That H.M. Government may for the present continue to use the existing recruiting depots at Gorakhpur and Ghum, and that the British and Gurkha military personnel serving in them may wear uniform.

4. That the plans of H.M. Government for recruiting in Nepal up to a possible strength of a Division (say 25,000 men), shall not in any way interfere with recruitment to the Gurkha units in the Indian Army.

5. The Gurkha ofûcers, recruits, soldiers, ex-soldiers and pensioners of Gurkha units serving H.M. Government, and their dependents, shall be permitted to travel freely between Nepal and an Indian port on their lawful occasions, provided mufti is worn in transit through India; the stipulation regarding dress shall not apply to the four Regiments named above during their removal from India.

6. That the normal road and rail transport facilities in India shall be available, at the public rates prevailing from time to time, to all British officers serving with Gurkhas, Gurkha officers and their families, Gurkha other ranks and their families and the necessary maintenance stores and baggage of such personnel in the service of H.M. Government; and that such staging facilities as may be required shall be provided at the expense of H.M. Government.

7. That India's postal, money-order and telegraphic services to and from Nepal shall be available to H.M. Government, and Gurkhas serving H.M. Government, at the normal rates prescribed from time to time.

8. That the Government of India shall make available annually to H.M.Government, for the use of Gurkha soldiers, the following quantities of foodstuffs:

Atta	2,200 tons
Ghee	750 tons
Dhal	1,200 tons
Condiment Powder	150 tons

Provided H.M. Government arrange to supply the Government of India with 2200 tons of wheat in replacement of the atta supplied to them.

9. That the Government of India shall make available to H.M. Government such Indian currency as may be necessary for purposes connected with their employment of Gurkha soldiers, provided that the sterling equivalent thereof shall be credited to the Government of India Sterling Account One.

10. That Gurkha officers, soldiers, ex-soldiers, pensioners and their dependents shall have the right to send or take Indian money back to Nepal subject only to such Indian currency regulations of general application as may be in force from time to time; foreign currency imported into India shall be subject to the general Indian currency regulations obtaining from time to time.

11. That the basic rates of pay admissible to Gurkha officers and soldiers serving H.M. Government shall approximate to those laid down in the present Indian Pay Code, at which rates personnel serving at the recruiting depots in Gorakhpur and Ghum shall be paid: and that a special allowance, to compensate for permanent service overseas and high cost of living, shall in addition be admissible to Gurkha officers and soldiers serving H.M. Government overseas.

12. After the eight battalions have been asked to opt for service under H.M.Government, Government of India will try to make up the deficiency caused by those who do not wish to serve with H.M. Government, by asking other soldiers who have completed their existing engagement and who do not wish to continue to serve in the Indian Army units. If the required number cannot

thus be made good the deficiency will be made up by H.M. Government by direct recruitment.

Sd.

For the Government of
the Dominion of India

Sd.

For His Majesty's Government
in the United Kingdom

Kathmandu
7th November, 1947

ANNEXURE II

NEPALESE REACTION TO POINTS OF AGREEMENT BETWEEN GOVERNMENT OF INDIA AND H.M.G.

1. Para (3)

It appears that the arrangement of having recruiting Depots at Gorakhpur and Ghum for the British Gurkha Regiments has as an after thought been made of a temporary character. Nepal Government feels that it would definitely be more convenient to all three parties, if the recruiting is carried on for both Indian and British Armies at the present depots or any other places in India.

2. Para (4)

In view of our long-standing friendship the Government of Nepal had agreed to raise the strength of the Gurkha Regiments during the period of the last war. But she feels that the continuation of this emer- gency measure will be too much of a drain on the man-power of the country. So she desires that the total be limited and brought down to the peace-time strength of 20 battalions to be divided between the Indian and British Armies, as already arranged.

3. Para (10)

Nepal Government desires that the foreign currency brought by the personnel of the Gurkha Regiments serving abroad be credited to the Nepal Government account in any bank (to be settled afterwards); the Government of Nepal providing Indian currency therefore at the prevailing market rate.

ANNEXURE III

1. In all matters of promotion, welfare and other facilities the Gurkha troops should be treated on the same footing as the other units in the parent army so that the stigma of "mercenary troops" may for all time be wiped out. These troops should be treated as a link between two friendly countries.

2. The Gurkha troops should be given every facility so that it might be officered by their own men and they should be eligible to commissioned ranks with no restrictions whatsoever to the highest level to which qualified offcers may be promoted.

3. The Gurkha troops should not be used against Hindu or any other unarmed mobs.

4. To avoid any clash between the Gurkhas themselves, Gurkha troops should not be used if any contingency of their having to serve in opposite camps arises.

5. To enable us supply better quality men, we request that our following military needs may be met:

   (i) A well equipped arms and ammunition factory producing all modern small arms and ammunitions.

   (ii) A few Army transport planes.

   (iii) Our requirements of army stores and civil supplies could be discussed later on.

6. To establish better liaison between Nepal and the troops, liaison officers would be appointed by the Nepalese Government and would form part of the unit of the Gurkha troops.

7. It is very desirable that the morale of the recruits as well as the armed forces, should remain unimpaired. Therefore all activities prejudicial to the interest and security of one party should be prevented in the territories of the other parties.

POLITICAL

8. The Government of Nepal reserves the right to withdraw all Gurkha troops in case Nepal is involved in any war.

9. All facilities for the training of Nepalese officers in the military academies of India and British should be provided as and when the Nepal Government wants.

10. As Khukri is the religious and national emblem of the Gurkhas forming also a part of the uniform of the Gurkha Army, the carrying of Khukri by Gurkhas of all categories must not be banned in territories where the Gurkhas reside.

11. When Gurkha troops go on active service, intimation might be given to the Government of Nepal.

12. The above mentioned points are to be incorporated in a treaty and or agreement to be signed between the parties in due course.

EXTRACT OF THE TREATY BETWEEN BRITISH INDIA AND BHUTAN SINCHULA 11 NOVEMBER 1865

Article 1 xxxxxxxxxxxx

Article 2

Whereas in consequence of repeated aggressions of the Bhootan Government and of the refusal of that Government to aford satisfaction for those aggressions, and of their insulting treatment of the oficers sent by His Excellency the Governor General in Council for the purpose of procuring an amicable adjustment of differences existing between the two States, the British Government has been compelled to seize by an armed force the whole of the Doars and certain Hill Posts protecting the passes into Bhootan and whereas the Bhootan Government has now expressed its regret for past misconduct and a desire for the establishment of friendly relations with the British Government, it is hereby agreed that the whole of the tract known as the Eighteen Doars, bordering on the Districts of Rungpoor, Cooch Behar and Assam, together with the Talook of Ambaree Fallacottah and the Hill territory on the lef bank of the Teesta up to such points as may be laid down by the British Commissioner appointed for the purpose is ceded by the Bhootan Government to the British Government for ever.

Article 3 xxxxxxxx

Article 4

In consideration of the cession by the Bhootan Government of the territories specified in Article 2 of this Treaty, and of the said Government having expressed its regret for past misconduct, and having hereby engaged for the future to restrain all evil-disposed persons from committing crimes within British territory or the territories of the Rajahs of Sikkim and Cooch Behar and to give prompt and full redress for all such crimes which may be committed in defiance of their commands, the British Government agree to make an annual allowance to the Government of Bhootan of a sum not exceeding fifty thousand rupees (Rupees 50,000) to be paid to officers not below the rank of Jungpen, who shall be deputed by the Government of Bhootan to receive the same. And it is further hereby agreed that the payments shall be made as specified below:

On the fulfillment by the Bhoot an Government of the conditions of this Treaty, twenty-five thousand rupees (Rupees 25,000).

On the 10th January following the first payment, thirty five thousand rupees (Rupees 35,000)

On the 10th January following, forty-five thousand rupees (Rupees 45,000).

On every succeeding 10th January, fifty thousand rupees (Rupees 50,000).

Articles 6-7 xxxxxxxx

Article 8

The Bhootan Government hereby agree to refer to the arbitration of the British Government all disputes with, or causes of complaint against, the Rajahs of Sikkim and Cooch Behar, and to abide by the decision of the British Government; and the British Government hereby engage to enquire into and settle all such disputes and complaints in such manner as justice may require, and to insist on the observance of the decision by the Rajahs of Sikkim and Cooch Behar.

Article 9

There shall be free trade and commerce between the two Governments. No duties shall be levied on Bhootanese goods imported into British territories nor shall the Bhootan Government levy any duties on British goods imported into, or transported through, Bhootan territories .Bhootanese subjects residing in British territories shall have equal justice with British subjects, and British subject s residing in Bhootan shall have equal justice with the subjects of the Bhootan Government.

Article 10

The present Treaty of ten Articles having been concluded at Sinchula on the 11th day of November 1865, corresponding with the Bhootea year Shim Lung 24th day of the 9th month, and signed and sealed by Lieutenant-Colonel Herbert Bruce, C.B., and Samdojey Deb Jimpey and Themseyrensey Denai,the ratifications of the same by His Excellency the Viceroy and Governor-General in Council and by Their Highness the Dhurm and Deb Rajahs shall be mutually delivered within thirty days from this date.

Remarks by the Editor

The Treaty of Sinchula was signed between the Government of Bhutan and British India at Sinchula on November 1 1, 1865. In this treaty , the Bhutan Government agreed to cede the Assam and Bengal Duars to the British Government, mutual extradition of criminals and establishment of free trade between the two countries.

The British Government agreed to pay 25,000 rupees for the fulfillment of the terms of treaty - 35,000 rupees on January 10 as the first payment, 45,000 rupees on January 10 on the following year and 50,000 rupees on January 10 every year following.

As a result of the treaty, 7,122 square km of the land of Bhutan was ceded to British India. Bhutan also lost Ambari Falakata and some of the hill territory on the bank of the Teesta River. In reciprocal basis the Treaty secured the exemption of the levy of duty on goods imported to Bhutan territories. It also subjected the attribution of British Government to all its disputes over Sikkim and Cooch Behar.

The Sinchula Treaty between Bhutan and British India is also the base of the Indo-Bhutan Treaty of 1949.

Treaty Of Punakha
1910

Whereas it is desirable to amend Articles IV and VIII of the Treaty concluded at Sinchula on the 11th day of November 1865, corresponding with the Bhootea year Shing Lang, 24th day of the 9th month, between the British Government and the Government of Bhutan, the undermentioned amendments are agreed to on one part of Mr CA Bell, political Officer in Sikkim, in virtue of the full powers to that effect vested in him by the Right Honourable Sir Gilbert John Elliot-Murray Kynynmound, P.C., G.M.S.I., G.M.I.E.,G.C.M.G., Earl of Minto,Viceroy and Governor-General of India-in-Council and the other part by His Highness Sir Ugyen Wangchuk, K.C.I.E., Maharaja of Bhutan.

The following addition has been made toArticle IV of the Sinchula Treaty of 1865:

> "The British Government has increased the annual allowance to the Government of Bhutan from fifty thousand rupees (Rs.50,000) to one hundred thousand rupees (Rs 1,00,000) with effect from the 10th January, 1910".

Article VIII of the Sinchula Treaty of 1865 has been revised and the revisedArticle runs as follows:

> "The British Government undertaken to exercise no interference in the internal administration of Bhutan. On its part, the Bhutanese Government agrees to be guided by the advice of the British Government in regard to its external relations. In the event of disputes with or causes of complaint against the Maharaja of Sikkim and Cooch Behar, such matters will be referred for arbitration to the British Government which will settle them in such manner as justice may require and insist upon the observance of its decision by the Maharaja named".

Done in quadruplicate at Pinakha, Bhutan, the eighth day of January in the year of our Lord One Thousand Nine Hundred and Ten, corresponding with the Bhutia date, the 27th day of the 11th month of the Earth Bird (Sa-ja) year.

C.A. Bell
Political Officer
in Sikkim
8th January, 1910

Seals of Various
Dignitaries in Sikkim

Seal of Dharama Raja

Seal of Political Officer

Minto
Viceroy and Governor-General of India

The Treaty was ratified by the Viceroy and Governor-General of India-in-Council at Fort William on the twenty fourth day of March, A.D. one thousand nine hundred and ten.

S.H Butler
Secretary to the Government of India
Foreign Department

INDO-BHUTANESE FRIENDSHIP TREATY, 1949

The Government of India on one p art, and His Highness the Druk Gyalpo 's Government on the other part, equally animated by the desire to regulate in a friendly manner and upon a solid and durable basis the state of affairs caused by the termination of the British Government's authority in India, and to promote and foster the relations of friendship and neighbourliness so necessary for the well being of their peoples, have resolved to conclude the following treaty, and for this purpose named their represent atives, that is to say, Sir Harishwar Dayal representing the Government of India, who has full powers to agree to the said treaty on behalf of the Government of India, and Deb Zimpon Sonam Tobgye Dorji, Yang-Lop Sonam, Chho-Zim Thondup, Rin-Zim Taandin and Ha Drung Jigmie Palden Dorji, represent- ing the Government of His Highness the Druk Gyalpo, Maharaja of Bhutan, who have full powers to agree to the same on behalf of the Government of Bhutan.

Article I

There shall be perpetual peace and friendship between the Government of India and the Government of Bhutan.

Article II

The Government of India undertakes to exercise no interference in the internal administration of Bhutan. On its part the Government of Bhutan agrees to be guided by the advice of the Government of India in regard to its external relations.

Article III

In place of the compensation granted to the Government of Bhutan under Article 4 of the Treaty of Sinchula and enhanced by the Treaty of the eighth day of January 1910 and the temporary subsidy of Rupees one lakh per annum granted in 1942, the Government of India agrees to make an annual payment of Rupees five lakhs to the Government of Bhutan. And it is further hereby agreed that the said annual payment shall be made on the tenth day of January every year, the first payment being made on the tenth day of January 1950. This payment shall continue so long as this Treaty remains in force and its terms are duly observed.

Article IV

Further to mark the friendship existing and continuing between the said Governments, the Government of India shall, within one year from the date of signature of this treaty, return to the Government of Bhutan about thirty two square miles of territory in the area known as Dewangiri. The Government of India shall appoint a competent officer or officers to mark out the area so returned to the government of Bhutan.

Article V

There shall, as heretofore, be free trade and commerce between the territories of the Government of India and the Government of Bhutan; and the Government of India agrees to grant the Government of Bhutan every facility for the carriage, by land and water, of its produce through out the territory of the Government of India, including the right to use such forest roads as may be specified by mutual agreement from time to time.

Article VI

The Government of India agrees that the Government of Bhutan shall be free to import with the assistance and approval of the Government of India, from or through India into Bhutan, whatever arms, ammunition, machinery, warlike material or stores may be required or desired for the strength and welfare of Bhutan, and that this arrangement shall hold good for all time as long as the Government of India is satisfied that the intentions of the Government of Bhutan are friendly and that there is no danger to India from such importations. The Government of Bhutan, on the other hand, agrees that there shall be no export of such arms, ammunition, etc., across the fron- tier of Bhutan either by the Government of Bhutan or by private individuals.

Article VII

The Government of India and the Government of Bhutan agree that Bhutanese subjects residing in Indian territories shall have equal justice with Indian subjects, and that Indian subjects residing in Bhutan shall have equal justice with the subjects of the Government of Bhutan.

Article VIII

1. The Government of India shall, on demand being duly made in writing by the Government of Bhutan, take proceedings in accordance with the provisions of the Indian Extradition Act, 1903 (of which a copy shall be furnished to the Government of Bhutan), for the surrender of all Bhutanese subjects accused of any of the crimes specified in the first schedule of the said Act who take refuge in Indian territory.

2. The Government of Bhutan shall, on requisition being duly made by the Government of India, or by any officer authorized by the Government of India in this behalf, surrender any Indian subjects, or subjects of a foreign power, whose extradition may be required in pursuance of any agreement or arrangements made by the Government of India with the said power, accused of any of the crimes, specified in the first schedule of Act XV of 1903, who may take refuge in the territory under the jurisdiction of the Government of Bhutan, and also any Bhutanese subjects who, after committing any of the crimes referred to in Indian territory, shall flee into Bhutan, on such evidence of their guilt being produced as shall satisfy the local court of the district in which the offence may have been committed.

Article IX

Any differences and disputes arising in the application or interpretation of this treaty shall in the first instance be settled by negotiation. If within three months of the start of negotiations no settlement is arrived at, then the matter shall be referred to the arbitrations of three arbitrators, who shall be nationals of either India or Bhutan, chosen in the following manner:

(1) One person nominated by the Government of India;

(2) One person nominated by the Government of Bhutan;

(3) A judge of the Federal court, or of High Court in India, to be chosen by the Government of Bhutan, who shall be the chairman.

The judgment of this tribunal shall be final and executed without delay by either party.

Article X

The treaty shall continue in force in perpetuity unless terminated or modified by mutual consent.

Done in duplicate at Darjeeling this eighth day of August, one thousand nine hundred and forty nine, corresponding with the Bhutanese date the fifteenth day of the sixth month of the Earth-Bull year.

Harishwar Dayal Political Officer in Sikkim	Deb Zimpon Sonam Tobgye Dorji Yang-Lop Sonam Chho-Zim Thondup Rin-Zim Taandin Ha Drung Jigmie Palden Dorji

REMARK BY THE EDITOR

To understand the relationship between India and Bhutan, the study of the following treaties in the recent history is recommended:

(a) Treaty of Peace between East India Company and Bhutan—1774.

(b) Treaty of Peace and Friendship between British India and Bhutan—1865.

(c) Treaty between British India and Bhutan—1910.

The above treaties are a precursor to the Treaty of 1949 between independent India and Bhutan.

INDIA-BHUTAN FRIENDSHIP TREATY 2007

The Government of the Republic of India and the Government of the Kingdom of Bhutan:

Reaffirming their respect for each other's independence, sovereignty and territorial integrity;

Recalling the historical relations that have existed between our two countries;

Recognizing with deep satisfaction the manner in which these relations have evolved and matured over the years into a model of good neighbourly relations;

Being fully committed to further strengthening this enduring and mutually beneficial relationship based on genuine goodwill and friendship, shared interests, and close understanding and cooperation;

Desiring to clearly reflect this exemplary relationship as it stands today;

And having decided, through mutual consent, to update the 1949 Treaty relating to the promotion of, and fostering the relations of friendship and neighbourliness between India and Bhutan;

Have agreed as follows:

Article 1

There shall be perpetual peace and friendship between India and Bhutan.

Article 2

In keeping with the abiding ties of close friendship and cooperation between Bhutan and India, the Government of the Kingdom of Bhutan and the Government of the Republic of India shall cooperate closely with each other on issues relating to their national interests. Neither Government shall allow the use of its territory for activities harmful to the national security and interest of the other.

Article 3

There shall, as heretofore, be free trade and commerce between the territories of the Government of Bhutan and the Government of India. Both the Governments shall provide full cooperation and assistance to each other in the matter of trade and commerce.

Article 4

The Government of India agrees that the Government of Bhutan shall be free to import, from or through India into Bhutan, whatever arms, ammunition, machinery, warlike material or stores as may be required or desired for the strength and welfare of Bhutan, and that this arrangement shall hold good for all time as long as the Government of India is satisfied that the intentions of the Government of Bhutan are friendly and that there is no danger to India from such importations. The Government of Bhutan agrees that there shall be no export of such arms, ammunition and materials outside Bhutan either by the Government of Bhutan or by private individuals.

Article 5

The Government of Bhutan and the Government of India agree that Bhutanese subjects residing in Indian territories shall have equal justice with Indian subjects, and that Indian subjects residing in Bhutan shall have equal justice with the subjects of the Government of Bhutan.

Article 6

The extradition of persons wanted by either state for crimes and for unlawful activities affecting their security shall be in keeping with the extradition agreements between the two countries.

Article 7

The Government of Bhutan and the Government of India agree to promote cultural exchanges and cooperation between the two countries. These shall be extended to such areas as education, health, sports, science and technology.

Article 8

The Government of Bhut an and the Government of India agree to continue to consolidate and expand their economic cooperation for mutual and long term benefit.

Article 9

Any differences and disputes arising in the interpret ation and application of this Treaty shall be settled bilaterally by negotiations in a spirit of trust and understanding in consonance with the historically close ties of friendship and mutually beneficial cooperation that form the bedrock of Bhutan-India relations.

Article 10

This Treaty shall come into force upon the exchange of Instruments of Ratification by the two Governments which shall take place in Thimphu with in one month of the signing of this Treaty.

The Treaty shall continue in force in perpetuity unless terminated or modified by mutual consent.

In witness whereof, the undersigned being duly authorized thereto by their respective Governments, have signed this Treaty.

Done at New Delhi on the Eighth Day of February Two Thousand and Seven, in two originals each in Hindi, Dzongkha and English languages, each text being equally authentic. However, in case of difference, the English text shall prevail.

For the Government of
the Republic of India

Sd/-
(Pranab Mukherjee)
Minister of External Affairs

For the Government of
the Kingdom of Bhutan

Sd/-
(H.R.H.Trongsa Penlop
Jigme Khesar Namgyel
Wangchuck)
The Crown Prince of Bhutan

INDO–NEPAL TREATY OF PEACE AND FRIENDSHIP JULY 31, 1950

The Government of India and the Government of Nepal recognizing the ancient ties which have happily existed between the two countries for centuries;

Desiring still further to strengthen and develop these ties and to perpetuate peace between the two countries,

Have resolved therefore to enter into a Treaty of Peace and Friendship with each other, and have, for this purpose, appointed as their plenipotentiaries the following persons, namely,

The Government of India; His Excellency Shri Chandreshwar Prasad Narain Singh, Ambassador of India in Nepal;

The Government of Nepal, Mohun Shamsher Jang Bahadur Rana, Maharaja, Prime Minister and Supreme Commander-in-Chief of Nepal,

who having examined each other's credentials and found them good and in due form have agreed as follows:

Article 1

There shall be everlasting peace and friendship between the Government of India and the Government of Nepal. The two Governments agree mutually to acknowledge and respect the complete sovereignty, territorial integrity and independence of each other.

Article II

The two Governments hereby undertake to inform each other of any serious friction or misunderstanding with any neighbouring state likely to cause any breach in the friendly relations subsisting between the two Governments.

Article III

In order to establish and maintain the relations referred to in Article 1, the two Governments agree to continue diplomatic relations with each other by means of representatives with such staff as is necessary for the due performance of their functions.

The representatives and such of their staff as may be agreed upon shall enjoy such diplomatic privileges and immunities as are customarily granted by international law on a reciprocal basis, provided that in no case shall these be less than those granted to persons of a similar status of any other state having diplomatic relations with either Government.

Article IV

The two Governments agree to appoint Consuls-Generals, Consuls, Vice Consuls and other consular agents, who shall reside in towns, ports and other places in each other's territory as may be agreed to.

Consuls-Generals, Consuls, Vice Consuls and consular agents shall be provided with exequaturs or other valid authorization of their appointment. Such exequatur or authorization is liable to be withdrawn by the country which issued it, if considered necessary. The reasons for the withdrawal shall be indicated wherever possible.

The persons mentioned above shall enjoy on a reciprocal basis all the rights, privileges, exemptions and immunities that are accorded to persons of corresponding status of any other state.

Article V

The Government of Nepal shall be free to import, from or through the territory of India, arms, ammunition or warlike material and equipment necessary for the security of Nepal. The procedure for giving effect to this arrangement shall be worked out by the two Governments acting in consultation.

Article VI

Each Government undertakes, in token of the neighbourly friendship between India and Nepal, to give to the national of other, in its territory, national treatment with regard to participation in industrial and economic development of such territory and to the grant of concessions and contracts relating to such development.

Article VII

The Governments of India and Nepal agree to grant, on a reciprocal basis, to the nationals of one country in the territories of the other the same privileges in the matter of residence, ownership of property, participation in trade and commerce, movement and privileges of a similar nature.

Article VIII

So far as the matter dealt with herein are concerned, this treaty cancels all other treaties, agreements, and engagements entered into on behalf of India between the British Government and the Government of Nepal.

Article IX

The treaty shall come into force from the date of the signature by both Governments.

Article X

The treaty shall remain in force until it is terminated by either party by giving one years notice.

Done in duplicate at Kathmandu this 31st day of July, 1950.

Chandreshwar Prasad
Narain Singh
For the Government of India

Mohun Shamsher Jang
Bahadur Rana
For the Government of Nepal

Letter Exchanged with this Treaty:

Kathmandu

31st July 1950

Excellency,

In course of our discussion of the Treaties of Peace and Friendship and of Trade and Commerce which have been happily concluded between the Government of India and the Government of Nepal, we agreed that certain matters of details be regulated by an exchange of letters. In pursuance of this understanding, it is hereby agreed between the two Governments:

1. Neither Government shall tolerate any threat to the security of the other by a foreign aggressor. To deal with any such threat, the two Governments shall consult with each other and devise effective counter-measures.
2. Any arms, ammunition or warlike material and equipment necessary for security of Nepal that the Government of Nepal may import through the territory of India shall be so imported with the assistance and agreement of the Government

of India. The Government of India will take steps for the smooth and expeditious transport of such arms and ammunition through India.

3. In regard to Article 6 of the Treaty of Peace and Friendship which provides for national treatment, the Government of India recognize that it may be necessary for some time to come to afford the Nepalese nationals in Nepal protection from unrestricted competition. The nature and extent of this protection will be determined as and when required by mutual agreement between the two Governments.

4. If the Government of Nepal should decide to seek foreign assistance in regard to the development of the natural resources of, or of any industrial project in Nepal, the Government of Nepal shall give first preference to the Government or the nationals of India, as the case may be, provided that the terms offered by the Government of India or Indian nationals, as the case may be, are not less favourable to Nepal than the terms offered by any other Foreign Government or any other foreign nationals.

   Nothing in the foregoing provision shall apply to assistance that the Government of Nepal may seek from the United Nations Organisation or any of its specialized agencies.

5. Both countries agree not to employ any foreigners whose activity may be prejudicial to the security of the other. Either Government may make representations to the other in this behalf, as and when occasion requires.

Please accept Excellency, the assurance of my highest consideration.

Mohun Shamsher Jang Bahadur Rana
Maharaja, Prime Minister and
Supreme commander-in-Chief of Nepal

To
His Excellency
Shri Chandreshwar Prasad Narain Singh,
Ambassador Extraordinary and
Plenipotentiary of India at the court of Nepal,
Indian Embassy, Kathmandu.

INDO–NEPAL TREATY OF TRANSIT

The Government of India and His Majesty's Government of Nepal (hereinafter also referred to as the Contracting Parties).

Animated by the desire to maintain, develop and strengthen the existing friendly relations and co-operation between the two countries.

Recognising that Nepal is a land-locked country needs access to and from sea to promote its international trade.

And recognising the need to facilitate the *traffic in transit* through their territories,

Have resolved to conclude a Treaty of Transit, and

Have for the purpose appointed as their Plenipotentiaries the following persons, namely;

For the Government of India
Shri P Chidambaram
Minister of State for Commerce

For His Majesty's Government of Nepal
Shri Gopal Man Shrestha
Minister of Commerce

Who, having exchanged their full powers, and found them in good and in due form, have agreed as follows:

Article I

The Contracting Parties shall accord to *'traffic in transit'* freedom of transit across their respective territories through routes mutually agreed upon. No distinction shall be made which is based on flag of vessels, the places of origin, departure, entry, exit, destination, ownership of goods or vessels.

Article II

(a) Each Contracting Party shall have the right to take all indispensable measures to ensure that such freedom, accorded by it on its territory does not in any way infringe its legitimate interests of any kind.

(b) Nothing in this Treaty shall prevent either Contracting Party from taking any measures which may be necessary for the protection of its essential security interests.

Article III

The term *'traffic in transit'* means the passage of goods including unaccompanied baggage across the territory of the Contracting Party when the passage is a portion of a complete journey which begins or terminates within the territory of the other Contracting Party. The transhipment, warehousing, breaking bulk and change in the mode of transport of such goods as well as the assembly, dis-assembly or re-assembly of machinery and bulky goods shall not render the passage of goods outside the definition of *'traffic in transit'* provided any such operation is undertaken solely for the convenience of transportation. Nothing in this Article shall be construed as imposing an obligation on either Contracting Party to establish or permit the establishment of permanent facilities on its territory for such assembly, dis-assembly, or re-assembly.

Article IV

Traffic in transit shall be exempt from customs duties and from all transit duties or other charges except reasonable charges for transportation and such other charges as are commensurate with the costs of services rendered in respect of such transit.

Article V

For the convenience of *traffic in transit* the Contracting Parties agree to provide at point or points of entry or exit, on such terms as may be mutually agreed upon and subject to their relevant laws and regulations prevailing in either country, warehouses or sheds, for the storage of *traffic in transit* awaiting customs clearance

---

* The protocol is not being annexed due to reasons of space.

before onward transmission.

Article VI

Traffic in transit shall be subject to the procedure laid down in the Protocol* hereto annexed and as modified by mutual agreement. Except in cases of failure to comply with the procedure prescribed, such *traffic in transit* shall not be subject to avoidable delays or restrictions.

Article VII

In order to enjoy the freedom of the high seas, merchant ships sailing under the flag of Nepal shall be accorded, subject to Indian laws and regulations, treatment no less favourable than that accorded to ships of any other foreign country in respect of matters relating to navigation, entry into and departure from the ports, use of ports and harbour facilities, as well as loading and unloading dues, taxes and other levies, except that the provisions of this Article shall not extend to coastal trade.

Article VIII

Notwithstanding the foregoing provisions, either Contracting Party may maintain or introduce such measures or restrictions as are necessary for the purpose of:

(i) protecting public morals;

(ii) protecting human, animal and plant life;

(iii) safeguarding national treasures;

(iv) safeguarding the implementation of laws relating to the import and export of gold and silver bullion; and

(v) safeguarding such other interests as may be mutually agreed upon.

Article IX

Nothing in this treaty shall prevent either Contracting Party from taking any measures which may be necessary in pursuance of general international conventions, whether already in existence or concluded hereafter, to which it is a party relating to transit, export or import of particular kinds of articles such as narcotics and psychotropic substances or in pursuance of general conventions intended to prevent infringement of industrial, literary or artistic property or relating to false marks, false indications of origin or other methods of unfair competition.

Article X

In order to facilitate effective and harmonious implementation of this Treaty, the Contracting Parties shall consult each other regularly.

Article XI

The Treaty shall enter into force on the 6th December, 1991 and shall remain in force for a period of seven years. It may be renewed for further period of seven years by mutual consent, subject to such modifications as may be agreed upon.

Done in duplicate in Hindi, Nepali and English languages, all the texts being equally authentic, at New Delhi on the 6th December, 1991. In case of doubt, the English text will prevail.

Shri P Chidambram
Minister of State for Commerce
For Government of India

Shri Gopal Man Shrestha
Minister of Commerce
For His Majesty's Government of Nepal

TREATY OF FRIENDSHIP BETWEEN INDIA AND THE UNION OF BURMA, 7 JULY, 1951

The President of India and the President of the Union of Burma being desirous of strengthening and developing the many ties that have bound the two countries for centuries and being urged by mutual recognition of the need for maintaining the peace and friendship that have always existed between the two States, have resolved to conclude this Treaty for the common benefit of their peoples and in furtherance of the objectives of their respective countries, and have, to this end, appointed as their Plenipotentiaries the following persons, namely,

The President of India:
His Excellency Dr MA RAUF,
Ambassador Extraordinary and Plenipotentiary.

The President of the Union of Burma:
The Hon'ble SAO HKUN HKIO, KSM,
Minister of Foreign Affairs.

Who, having examined each other's credentials and found them good and in due form, have agreed to and signed the following articles:

Article I

The two States recognise and respect the independence and rights of each other.

Article II

There shall be everlasting peace and unalterable friendship between the two States who shall ever strive to strengthen and develop further cordial relations existing between the peoples of the two countries.

Article III

The two States agree to continue diplomatic and consular relations with each other by means of representatives of either Party in the territory of the other and agree that such representatives and their agreed staff shall have, on a reciprocal basis, such privileges and immunities as are customarily granted by recognised international principles.

Article IV

The two States agree that their representatives shall meet from time to time and as often as occasion requires to exchange views on matters of common interests and to consider ways and means for mutual co-operation in such matters.

Article V

The two States agree to start negotiations for the conclusion of agreements, on a reciprocal basis, relating to trade, customs, cultural relations, communications, extradition of criminals, immigration or repatriation of nationals of each country resident in the other, or of dual nationals of the two countries, and all other matters of common interest to the two countries.

Article VI

Any difference or dispute arising out of the interpretation or application of this treaty or one or more of its articles shall be settled by negotiations through the ordinary diplomatic channels and if no settlement is reached by that method within a reasonable time, the matter shall be referred to arbitration in such manner as may be mutually determined by a general or special arrangement between the two parties.

Article VII

The Treaty shall be subject to ratification and shall come into force from the date of exchange of the Instruments of Ratification, which shall take place as soon as possible at Rangoon.

Article VIII

The Treaty shall continue in force for five years from the date of its coming into force and thereafter remain in force.

Provided that after the termination of the said period of five years either party may give to the other party a notice of not less than six months intimating its intention to terminate the Treaty and on the expiry of the period of such notice the Treaty shall cease to be in force.

IN FAITH WHEREOF, the said plenipotentiaries have signed the present treaty in the Hindi, Burmese and English languages (the English text shall prevail in case of conflict between the three texts) and have affixed thereto their seals.

Done in duplicate in Rangoon on the seventh day of July ,1951.

For the President of the Union of Burma
SH HKIO
In the presence of
TUN SHEIN

For the President of India
MA RAUF
In the presence of
KM KANNAMPILLY

BRIEF ON INDO–BURMESE BOUNDARY SETTLEMENT, 1967

Indo–Burmese border issue was related to the resolution of the Pakistan–Burma and Sino–Burma border issues, primarily for reasons of determination of the Tri-junctions with India. The negotiations for settlement of Pakistan–Burma border commenced in 1953 and were concluded in 1964. As regards China, after protracted negotiations between Burma and China, and interjections/protestations by India, Sino–Burmese Boundary Treaty and Treaty of Friendship was signed on January 28, 1960. While there were claims and counter claims between Burma and China, India was concerned with the Tri-junction in the north due to its claim on the McMahon line as being the boundary between India and China. Sino–Burmese western terminus on the boundary was terminated at Diphuk Pass (south of McMahon line), not to the liking of India, but Burma declared that as far as India was concerned, this point was negotiable contingent on the resolution of the Sino–Indian border dispute.

Indo–Burma border was never formalised by the British as both India and Burma were under them, and the requirement was not considered pressing. This border was a traditional one based on natural features and historical use even though there were large tracts on either side which were un-administered and also had ethnic contiguity. In a spirit of accommodation, the Agreement between India and Burma was signed on March 10,

1967 and the Instruments of Ratification were exchanged on May 30, 1967. The Tri-junction was kept provisional as described above.

The text of the agreement is not given here as the border is settled with no disputes.

INDO–BANGLADESH TREATY OF CO-OPERATION, FRIENDSHIP AND PEACE, 19 MARCH, 1972

Inspired by common ideals of peace, secularism, democracy, socialism and nationalism;

Having struggled together for the realisation of these ideals and cemented ties of friendship through blood and sacrifices which led to the triumphant emergence of a free, sovereign and independent Bangladesh; Determined to maintain fraternal and good neighbourly relations and

transform their border into a border of eternal peace and friendship; Adhering firmly to the basic tenets of non-alignment, peaceful co-existence, mutual co-operation, non-interference in the internal affairs and respect for territorial integrity and sovereignty;

Determined to safeguard peace, stability and security and to promote progress of their respective countries through all possible avenues of mutual co-operation;

Determined further to expand and strengthen the existing relations of friendship between them;

Convinced that further development of friendship and co-operation meets the national interests of both states as well as the interests of lasting peace in Asia and the world;

Resolved to contribute to strengthening world peace and security and to make efforts to bring about relaxation of international tension and final elimination of vestiges of colonialism, racialism and imperialism;

Convinced that in the present day world international problems can be solved only through co-operation and not through conflict or confrontation; Reaffirming their determination to follow the aims and principles of the United Nations charter;

The People's Republic of Bangladesh, on the one hand, and the Republic of India, on the other, have decided to conclude the present treaty.

Article 1

The high contracting parties, inspired by the ideals of which their respective peoples struggled and made sacrifices together, solemnly declare that there shall be lasting peace and friendship between their two countries and their peoples. Each side shall respect the independence, sovereignty and territorial integrity of the other and refrain from interfering in the internal affairs of the other side.

The high contracting parties shall further develop and strengthen the relations of friendship, good neighbourliness and all-around co-operation existing between them, on the basis of the above-mentioned principles as well as the principles of equality and mutual benefit.

Article 2

Being guided by their devotion to the principle of equality of all peoples and states, irrespective of race or creed, the high contracting parties condemn colonialism and racialism in all their forms and manifestations and reaffirm their determination to strive for their final and complete elimination.

The high contracting parties shall co-operate with other states in achieving these aims and support the just aspirations of peoples in their struggle against colonialism and racial discrimination and for their national liberation.

Article 3

The high contracting parties reaffirm their faith in the policies of non-alignment and peaceful co-existence, as important factors for easing tension in the world, maintaining international peace and security and strengthening national sovereignty and independence.

Article 4

The high contracting parties shall maintain regular contacts with each other on major international problems affecting the interests of both states, through meetings and exchanges of views at all levels.

Article 5

The high contracting parties shall continue to strengthen and widen their mutually advantageous and all-around co-operation in the economic, scientific and technical fields. The two countries shall develop mutual co-operation in the fields of trade, transport and communication between them on the basis of principles of equality, mutual benefit and most favoured nation principle.

Article 6

The high contracting parties further agree to make joint studies and take joint action in the field of flood control, river basin development and the development of hydroelectric power and irrigation.

Article 7

The high contracting parties shall promote relations in the field of art, literature, education, culture, sports and health.

Article 8

In accordance with the ties of friendship existing between the two countries, each of the high contracting parties solemnly declares that it shall not enter into or participate in any military alliance directed against the other party.

Article 9

Each of the high contracting parties shall refrain from any aggression against the other party and shall not allow the use of its territory for committing any act that may cause military damage or to constitute a threat to the security of the other high contracting party.

Article 10

Each of the high contracting parties shall refrain from giving any assistance to any third party taking part in an armed conflict against the other party.

In a case either party is attacked or threatened with attack, the high contracting parties shall immediately enter into mutual consultations in order to take appropriate effective measures to eliminate the threat and thus peace and security of their countries.

Each of the high contracting parties solemnly declares that it shall not undertake any commitment, secret or open, towards one or more states which may be incompatible with the present treaty.

Article 11

The present treaty is signed for a term of 25 years and shall be subject to renewal by mutual agreement of the high contracting parties. The treaty shall come into force with immediate effect from the date of its signature.

Article 12

Any difference in interpreting an article or articles of the present treaty that may arise between the high contracting parties shall be settled on a bilateral basis by peaceful means in a spirit of mutual respect and understanding.

INDO–BANGLADESH AGREEMENT CONCERNING THE DEMARCATION OF LAND BOUNDARY, NEW DELHI, 16 MAY 1974

The Government of the Republic of India the Government of the Peoples Republic of Bangladesh,

BEARING IN MIND the friendly relations existing between the two countries,

DESIRING TO define more accurately at certain points and to complete the demarcation of the land boundary between India and Bangladesh,

HAVE AGREED as follows:

Article 1

The land boundary between India and Bangladesh in the areas mentiond below shall be demarcated in the following manner:

1. Mizoram-Bangladesh Sector

   Demarcation should be completed on the basis of the latest pre- partition notification and records.

2. Tripura-Sylhet Sector

   Demarcation which is already in progress in this area on the agreed basis should be completed as early as possible.

3. Bhagalpur Railway Line

   The boundary should be demarcated at a distance of 75 feet parallel to the toe of the railway embankment towards the east.

4. Sibpur-Gaurangala Sector

   The boundary should be demarcate in continuation of the process started in 1951–52 on the basis of the district settlement maps of 1915–18.

5. Muhuri River (Belonia) Sector

   The boundary in this area should be demarcated along the mid stream of the course of Muhury River at the time of demarcation. This boundary will be a fixed boundary. The two Governments should raise embankments on their respective sides with a view to stabilising the river in its present course.

6. Remaining Portion of the Tripura-Naukhali/Commilla Sector

The demarcation in this sector should be completed on the basis of Chakla-Roshanabad Estate Maps of 1892–1894 and the District settlement Maps of 1915–1918 for areas not covered by the Chakla-Roshanabad Estate Maps.

7. Fenny River

The boundary should be demarcated along the mid-stream of the course at the time of the demarcation of that branch of the Fenny River indicated as the Fenny River on Survey of India Map Sheet no 79 M/15,

1st Edition 1935, till it joins the stream shown as Asalong C on the said map. From that point on, downstream, the boundary should be demarcated along the mid-stream of the course of fenny river at the time of demarcation of the boundary. The boundary in this sector will be fixed boundary.

8. Rest of Tripura-Chittagong Hill Tract Sector

The boundary will follow the mid-stream of that branch of the Fenny River, referred to in para 7 above, up to grid reference 009779 (map sheet as in para 7 above) from where the boundary will follow the mid-stream of the eastern most tributary. From the source of this tributary, the boundary will run along the shortest distance to mid-stream of the stream marked Bayan Asalong, on map referred to above, and thence will run generally northwards along the mid-stream of this river till it reaches its source on the ridge (indicated by grid reference 046681 on the map referred to above). From there it will run along the crest of this ridge upto Bhogoban Trig Station. From Bhogoban Trig Station upto the tri-junction of the Bangladesh–Assam–Tripura boundary (Khan Talang Trig Station), the boundary will run along the watershed of the river system of the two countries. In case of any difference between the map and the ground, the ground shall prevail. The boundary will be a fixed boundary in this sector.

9. Benibazar-Karimganj Sector

The un-demarcated portion of the boundary west of Umapati village should be demarcated in accordance with the agreed basis of demarcation, leaving Umapati in India.

10. Hakar Khal Sector

The boundary should be demarcated in accordance with the Nehru-Noon Agreement of September 1958, treating Hakar Khal as a geographical feature distinct from the Icohamati River. The boundary will be a fixed boundary.

11. Baikari Khal

In the Baikari Khal, the boundary should be demarcated on the agreed basis and principles, namely, that the ground shall prevail, i.e., as per agreement reached between the Directors of Land Records and Surveys of West Bengal and earstwhile East Pakistan in 1949. The boundary will be a fixed boundary.

12. Enclaves

The Indian enclaves in Bangladesh and Bangladesh enclaves in India should be exchanged expeditiousl y, excepting the enclaves mentioned in paragraph 14 without claim to compensation for the additional area going to Bangladesh.

13. Hilli

The area should be demarcated in accordance with Radcliffe Award and the line drawn by him on the map.

14.* Berubari

India will retain the southern half of South Berubari Union No. 12 and the adjacent enclaves, measuring an area of 2.64 square miles approximately, and in exchange Bangladesh will retain the Dahagram and Angarpota enclaves. India will lease in perpetuity to Bangladesh an area of 178 metres X 85 metres near 'Tin Bigha' to connect Dahagram with Panbari Mouza (PS Patgram) of

Bangladesh.

15. Lathitilla-Dumabari

From point Y (the last demarcated boundary pillar position), the boundary shall run southwards along the Patharia Hill RF boundary up to the point where it meets the western boundary of Dumabari Mouza. Thence along the same Mouza boundary up to the tri-junction of Mouzas Dumabari, Lathitilla and Bara Putnigaon through the junction of the two Mouzas Dumabari and Lathitilla. From this point it shall run along the shortest distance to meet the mid-stream of Putni Chara. Thence it shall run generally southwards along the mid-stream of the course of Putni Chara at the time of demarcation, till it meets the boundary between Sylhet (Bangladesh) and Tripura (India).

Article 2

The Government of India and Bangladesh agree that territories in adverse possession in areas already demarcated in respect of which boundary strip maps are already prepared, shall be exchanged within six months of the signing of the boundary strip maps by the plenipotentiaries. They may sign the relevant maps as early as possible and in any case not later than 31 December 1974. Early measures may be taken to print maps in respect of other areas where demarcation has already taken place. These should be printed by 31 May 1975 and signed by the plenipotentiaries thereafter in order that the exchange of adversely held possessions in these areas may take place by 31 December 1975. In sectors still to be demarcated, transfer of territorial jurisdiction may take place within six months of the signature by the plenipotentiaries on the concerned boundary strip maps.

Article 3

The Government of India and Bangladesh agree that when areas are transferred, the people in these areas shall be given the right of staying on where they are, as nationals of the State to which the areas are transferred. Pending demarcation of the boundary and exchange of territory by mutual agreement, there should be no disturbance of the status quo and peaceful conditions shall be maintained in the border regions. Necessary instructions in this regard shall be issued to the local authorities on the border by the two countries.

Article 4

The Government of India and Bangladesh agree that any dispute concerning the interpretation or implementation of this Agreement shall be settled peacefully through mutual consultation.

Article 5

The Agreement shall be subject to ratification by the Government of India and Bangladesh and Instruments of Ratification shall be exchanged as early as possible. The Agreement shall take effect from the date of the exchange of the Instrument of Ratification.

Signed in New Delhi on 16 May 1974, in two originals each of which is equally authentic.

Sd.

REMARKS BY THE EDITOR

A stretch of 6.1 kilometres is a problem area between India and Bangladesh. There are 111 Indian enclaves in Bangladesh comprising approximately 70,000 acres, and 51 Bangladeshi enclaves in India covering an area of approximately 7000 acres.

*Terms of Lease in perpetuity of the Tin Bigha Area have been settled in a separate Agreement dated 7 October 1982 through exchange of letters between the Foreign Ministers of the two countries.

MERGER OF SIKKIM WITH INDIA

The British interests in Sikkim were linked to their trade and political interests in Tibet. Both Bhutan and Sikkim were the gateways to Tibet, Sikkim being the weaker of the two. On 10 February 1817, Sikkim signed a treaty with the East India Company surrendering all her rights to deal with any foreign power and conceded unhindered right of free access to the British to Tibet. Sikkim became a de facto protectorate in 1861 when this treaty was revised. The Anglo Chinese Convention of 1890 put a seal on this status.

With the transfer of power to India in 1947, the Government of India and Sikkim Darbar signed a Stand Still Agreement in 1948, according to which all agreements and administrative arrangements concluded with the British Government were to continue. Negotiations continued and a new treaty was signed in 1950 by which Sikkim was to continue to be protectorate of India, which was responsible for its External Relations, Defence and Communications.

Meanwhile political awakening had swept over Sikkim where two political parties—the Sikkim State Congress and Praja Sammelan, were advocating political rights. There was yet another party, Sikkim National Party which stood for "status quo ante" and was allegedly royalist. The Sikkim State Congress resorted to Satyagraha and demanded a responsible government like in India. The elections were held regularly from 1952 onwards.

Maharaja Tashi Namgyal died in December 1962 and was succeeded by his son Palden Thondut. The Maharaja's request for a change in his title to Chogyal and Maharani to Gyalmo was granted by the Government of India.

The fifth general elections in 1973 led to emergence of Janta Congress. There were allegations of rigging followed by general breakdown of law and order. Chogyal's efforts to suppress this uprising failed. On his request the Government of India took over the administration of the State in April 1973.

The Government of India appointed a constitutional legal adviser to draw up a Constitution for Sikkim. The draft Constitution was presented to the Assembly and passed in June 1974 with eight amendments. One of the amendments gave right to the Assembly to participate in political institutions in India, which, however, were not defined. This became the Government of Sikkim Act of 1974., according to which elections were held. Kazi Lhendup Dorji Khangsarpa's party won 31 out of 32 seats.

After intense and protracted politico-diplomatic activity, the Sikkim assembly met and passed a resolution on 10 April 1975 for removal of the Chogyal and merger with India to protect the interests of the people of Sikkim who chose a democratic system which could only be protected by meeting these demands. A referendum was also organized on 14 April 1975 to seek public opinion on the issue of merger with India. The result was overwhelmingly in favour of merger with India. Accepting this verdict, the 36th Amendment Bill to the Constitution of India was passed and Sikkim became the 22nd state of the Union of India.

AGREEMENT ON FUTURE OF PERSONS OF INDIAN ORIGIN IN CEYLON

An agreement between the Governments of India and Ceylon was signed in New Delhi on October 30, 1964, on the status and future of persons of Indian origin in Ceylon. The agreement was signed in the form of letters exchanged between the two Prime Ministers.

The following is the text of Prime Minister Lal Bahadur Shastri's letter in reply to the letter from the Prime Minister of Ceylon.

No 446/PMO/64

New Delhi
30 October, 1964

Your Excellency,

I have the honour to acknowledge receipt of your letter No. CIT/ICP/62 of date, which reads as follows:-

"I have the honour to refer to the discussions which we have had from the 24th to the 30th October 1964 regarding the status and future of persons of Indian origin in Ceylon and to refer to the main heads of agreement between us which are as follows:-

(1) The declared objective of this agreement is that all persons of Indian origin in Ceylon who have not been recognized either as citizens of Ceylon or as citizens of India should become citizens either of Ceylon or of India.

(2) The number of such persons is approximately 975,000 as of date. This figure does not include illicit immigrants and Indian passport holders.

(3) 300,000 of these persons together with natural increase in their number will be granted Ceylon citizenship by the Government of Ceylon; the Government of India will accept repatriation to India of 525,000 of these persons together with the natural increase in that number. The Government of India will confer citizenship on these persons.

(4) The status and future of the remaining 150,000 of these persons will be the subject matter of a separate agreement between the two Governments.

(5) The Government of India will accept repatriation of the persons to be repatriated within a period of 15 years from the date of this agreement according to a programme as evenly phased as possible.

(6) The grant of Ceylon citizenship under paragraph 3 and the process of repatriation under paragraph 5 shall both be phased over the period of 15 years and shall, as far as possible, keep pace with each other in proportion to the relative numbers to be granted citizenship and to be repatriated respectively.

(7) The Government of Ceylon will grant to the persons to be repatriated to India during the period of their residence in Ceylon the same facilities as are enjoyed by the citizens of their States (except facilities for remittances) and normal facilities for their continued residence, including free visas. The Government of Ceylon agrees that such of these persons as are gainfully employed on the date of this agreement shall continue in their employment until the date of their repatriation in accordance with the requirements of the phased programme or until they attain the age of 55 years, whichever is earlier.

(8) Subject to the Exchange Control Regulations for the time being in force which will not be discriminatory against the persons to be repatriated to India, the Government of Ceylon agrees to permit these persons to repatriate, at the time of their nal departure for India, all their assets including their Provident Fund and gratuity amounts. The Government of Ceylon agrees that the maximum amount of assets which any family shall be permitted to repatriate shall not be reduced to less that Rs. 4,000.

(9) Two registers will be prepared as early as possible, one containing the names of persons who will be granted Ceylon citizenship, the other containing the names of persons to be repatriated to India. The completion of these registers, however, is not a condition precedent to the commencement of the grant of Ceylon citizenship and the process of repatriation.

(10) This Agreement shall come into force with effect from the date hereof and the two Governments shall proceed with all despatch to implement this Agreement and to that end, the officials of the two Governments shall meet as soon as possible to establish joint machinery and to formulate the appropriate procedures for the implementation of this agreement.

I have the honour to propose that the above sets out correctly the Agreement reached between us. My letter and your reply thereto shall constitute an Agreement between the Government of India and the Government of Ceylon.

Accept your Excellency, the assurances of my highest consideration."

I have the honour to confirm that the above correctly sets out the Agreement reached between us. Your letter and my reply thereto shall constitute an Agreement between the Government of India and the Government of Ceylon.

Accept your Excellency, the assurances of my highest consideration.

Yours Sincerely
Sd/-
Lal Bahadur
Prime Minister of India
New Delhi

Her Excellency
Sirimavo RD Bandaranaike
Prime Minister of Ceylon

INDO–SRI LANKA AGREEMENT TO ESTABLISH PEACE AND NORMALCY IN SRI LANKA 1987

The Prime Minister of the Republic of India, His Excellency Mr. Rajiv Gandhi and the President of the Democratic Socialist Republic of Sri Lanka, His Excellency Mr. J.R. Jayewardene having met at Colombo on July 29, 1987.

Attaching utmost importance to nurturing, intensifying and strengthening the traditional friendship of India and Sri Lanka and acknowledging the imperative need of resolving the ethnic problem of Sri Lanka, and the consequent violence, and for the safety, well being and prosperity of people belonging to all communities in Sri Lanka.

1. Have this day entered into the following Agreement to full this objective. In this context:

1.1 desiring to preserve the unity, sovereignty and territorial integrity of Sri Lanka;

1.2 acknowledging that Sri Lanka is a multi-ethnic and multi-lingual plural society consisting inter alia, of Sinhalese, Tamils, Muslims (Moors), and Burghers;

1.3 recognising that each ethnic group has a distinct cultural and linguistic identity which has to be carefully nurtured;

1.4 also recognizing that the Northern and the Eastern Provinces have been areas of historical habitation of Sri Lankan Tamil speaking peoples, who have at all times hitherto lived together in this territory with other ethnic groups;

1.5 conscious of the necessity of strengthening the forces contributing to the unity, sovereignty and territorial integrity of Sri Lanka, and preserving its character as a multi-lingual and multi-religious plural society, in which all citizens can live in equality, safety and harmony, and prosper and full their aspirations;

2. Resolved that:

2.1 Since the Government of Sri Lanka proposes to permit adjoining Provinces to join to form one administrative unit and also by a Referendum to separate as may be permitted to the Northern and Eastern Provinces as outlined below:

2.2 During the period, which shall be considered an interim period (i.e.) from the date of the elections to the Provincial Council, as specied in para 2.8 to the date of the Referendum as specied in para 2.3, the Northern and Eastern Provinces as now constituted, will form one administrative unit, having one elected Provincial Council. Such a unit will have one Governor, one Chief Minister and one Board of Ministers.

2.3 There will be a Referendum on or before 31st December, 1988 to enable the people of the Eastern Province to decide whether:

A. The Eastern province should remain linked with the Northern province as one administrative unit, and continue to be governed together with the Northern Province as specied in para 2.2, or

B. The Eastern province should constitute a separate administrative unit having its own distinct Provincial Council with a separate Governor, Chief Minister and Board of Ministers.

The President may, at his discretion decide to postpone such a Referendum.

2.4 All persons who have been displaced due to ethnic violence, or other reasons, will have right to vote in such a Referendum. Necessary conditions to enable them to return to areas from where they were displaced will be created.

2.5 The Referendum, when held, will be monitored by a committee headed by the Chief Justice, a member appointed by the President, nominated by the Government of Sri Lanka, and a member appointed by the President, nominated by the representatives of the Tamil speaking people of the Eastern Province.

2.6 A simple majority will be sufficient to determine the result of the Referendum.

2.7 Meetings and other forms of propaganda, permissible within the laws of the country, will be allowed before the Referendum.

2.8 Elections to Provincial Councils will be held within the next three months, in any event before December 31, 1987. Indian observers will be invited for elections to the Provincial Council of the North and East.

2.9 The emergency will be lifted in the Eastern and Northern provinces, by August 15, 1987. A cessation of hostilities will come into effect all over the island within 48 hours of the signing of this agreement. All arms presently held by militant groups will be surrendered in accordance with an agreed procedure to authorities to be designated by the Government of Sri Lanka. Consequent to the cessation of hostilities and the surrender of arms by militant groups, the army and other security personnel will be conned to barracks in camps as on May 25, 1987. The process of surrendering of arms and the conning the security personnel moving back to barracks shall be completed within 72 hours of the cessation of hostilities coming into effect.

2.10 The Government of Sri Lanka will utilise for the purpose of law enforcement and maintenance of security in the Northern and Eastern provinces the same organizations and mechanisms of Government as are used in the rest of the country.

2.11 The President of Sri Lanka will grant a general amnesty to political and other prisoners now held in custody under the Prevention of Terrorism Act and other emergency laws, and to combatants, as well as to those persons accused, charged and/or convicted under these laws. The Government of Sri Lanka will make special efforts to rehabilit ate militant youth with a view to bringing them back to the mainstream of national life. India will cooperate in the process.

2.12 The Government of Sri Lanka will accept and abide by the above provisions and expect all others to do likewise.

2.13 If the framework for the resolutions is accepted, the Government of Sri Lanka will implement the relevant proposals forthwith.

2.14 The Government of India will underwrite and guarantee the resolutions, and co-operate in the implementation of these proposals.

2.15 These proposals are conditional to an acceptance of proposals negotiated from 4.5.1986 to 19.12.1986. Residual matters not finalised during the above negotiations shall be resolved between India and Sri Lanka within a period of six weeks of signing this agreement. These proposals are also conditional to the Government of India co-operating directly with Government of Sri Lanka in their implementation.

2.16 These proposals are also conditional to the Government of India taking the following actions if any militant group operating in Sri Lanka do not accept this framework of proposals for a settlement, namely:

A. India will take all necessary steps to ensure that Indian territory is not used for activities prejudicial to the unity, integrity, and security of Sri Lanka.

B. The Indian Navy Coast Guard will co-operate with the Sri Lanka Navy in preventing Tamil militant activities from affecting Sri Lanka.

C. In the event that Government of Sri Lanka requests the Government of India to afford military assistance to implement these proposals the Government of India will co-operate by giving to the Government of Sri Lanka such military assistance as and when requested.

D. The Government of India will expedite repatriation from Sri Lanka of Indian citizens to India who are resident there concurrently with the repatriation of Sri Lanka refugees from Tamil Nadu.

E. The Governments of India and Sri Lanka, will co-operate in ensuring the physical security and safety of all communities inhabiting the Northern and Eastern provinces.

2.17 The Government of Sri Lanka shall ensure free, full and fair participation of voters from all communities in the Northern and Eastern provinces in electoral processes envisaged in this agreement. The Government of India will extend full co-operation to the Government of Sri Lanka in this regard.

2.18 The official language of Sri Lanka shall be Sinhala. Tamil and English will also be official languages.

3. This agreement and the Annexure thereto shall come into force upon signature.

In witness whereof we have set our hands and seals hereunto.

Done in Colombo, Sri Lanka, on this the twenty ninth day of July of the year one thousand nine hundred and eighty seven, in duplicate, both texts being equally authentic.

Rajiv Gandhi
Prime Minister of the Republic of India

Junius Richard Jayewardene
President of the Democratic Socialistic Republic of Sri Lanka

ANNEXURE TO THE AGREEMENT

1. His Excellency the Prime Minister of India and His Excellency, the President of Sri Lanka agree that the Referendum mentioned in paragraph 2 and its sub paragraphs of the agreement will be observed by a representative of the Election Commission of India to be invited by His Excellency the President of Sri Lanka.

2. Similarly, both Heads of Government agree that the elections to the Provincial Council mentioned in paragraph 2.8 of the Agreement will be observed by a representative of the Government of India to be invited by the President of Sri Lanka.

3. His Excellency the President of Sri Lanka agrees that the Home Guards would be disbanded and all paramilitary personnel will be withdrawn from the Eastern and Northern Provinces with a view to creating conditions conductive to fair elections to the Council. The President, in his discretion, shall absorb such para-military forces, which came into being due to ethnic violence into the regular security forces of Sri Lanka.

4. The Prime Minister of India and the President of Sri Lanka, agree that the Tamil militants shall surrender their arms to authorities agreed upon to be designated by the President of Sri Lanka. The surrender shall take place in the presence of one senior representative each of the Sri Lanka Red Cross and the Indian Red Cross.

5. The Prime Minister of India and the President of Sri Lanka agree that a joint Indo-Sri Lankan observer group consisting of qualified representatives of the Government of India and the Government of Sri lanka would monitor the cessation of hostilities from 31 July 1987.

6. The Prime Minister of India and the Prime Minister of Sri Lanka also agree that in terms of paragraph 2.14 and paragraph 2.16 C of the agreement, an Indian Peace Keeping contingent may be invited by the President of Sri Lanka to guarantee and enforce the cessation of hostilities, if so required.

EXCHANGE OF LETTERS BETWEEN THE PRIME MINISTER OF INDIA AND THE PRESIDENT OF SRI LANKA

New Delhi
July 29, 1987

Excellency,

Conscious of the friendship between our two countries stretching over two millenia and more, and recognising the importance of nurturing this traditional friendship, it is imperative that both Sri Lanka and India reaffirm the decision not to allow our respective territories to be used for activities prejudicial to each other's unity, territorial integrity and security.

In this spirit, you had, during the course of our discussions agreed to meet some of India's concerns as follows:

(i) Your excellency and myself will reach an early understanding about the relevance and employment of foreign military and intelligence personnel with a view to ensuring that such presence will not prejudice Indo–Sri Lankan relations.

(ii) Trincomalee or any other ports in Sri Lanka will not be made available for military use by any country in a manner prejudicial to India's interests.

(iii) The work of restoring and operating the 'Trincomalee oil tank farm' will be undertaken as a joint venture between India and Sri Lanka.

(iv) Sri Lanka's agreement with foreign broadcasting organisations will be reviewed to ensure that any facilities set up by them in Sri Lanka are used solely as public broadcasting facilities and not for any military or intelligence purposes.

In the same spirit, India will:

(i) Deport all Sri Lankan citizens who are found to be engaging in terrorist activities or advocating separatism or secessionism.

(ii) Provide training facilities and military supplies for Sri Lankan security forces.

India and Sri Lanka have agreed to set up a joint consultative mechanism to continuously review matters of common concern in the light of objectives stated in para 1 and specifically to monitor the implementation of other matters contained in this letter.

Kindly confirm, Excellency, that above correctly sets out the agreement reached between us.

Please accept, Excellency, the assurances of my highest consideration.

Yours Sincerely
(Rajiv Gandhi)

His Excellency
Mr JR Jayewardene, President of the Democratic
Socialist Republic of Sri Lanka, Colombo.

His Excellency Mr. JR Jayewardene, President of the Democratic Socialist Republic of Sri Lanka confirmed that the contents of the above letter correctly set out the agreement reached between the two heads of the state.

MALDIVES

Maldives is an archipelago comprising approximately 1200 coral islands and islets of which approximately 200 are inhabited, is situated approximately 130 kms south of Minicoy islands (India) and some 600 kms south west of Sri Lanka. None of the islands are more than a couple of kms across or more than a few metres above the sea level. The land area is only 300 sq kms in the total area of approximately 30,000 sq kms which includes lagoons. Its population is approximately 300,000. Once a Buddhist State, all of them converted to Sunni Islam in the twelveth century. Islam is the State religion. Although traditionally a Sultanate, some form of parliamentary democracy existed in Maldives. Male is the capital.

Maldives was an independent State throughout except for a short period under the Portuguese rule in 16th century. It became a British protectorate in 1887 and was granted independence in 1965. As a result of a referendum in 1968, a Republic was established and Sultanate was abolished.

Maldives is not endowed with adequate natural wealth and depends largely on foreign aid. The economy mainly depends upon fish, coconut, millets, fruit and is dominantly linked with Sri Lanka. Tourism is another source of income.

Located strategically on east-west route to/from Malacca Straits, Gan (2.5 X 1.1 kms), one of the islands of Maldives was a British Staging Post till 1976. British military facilities comprised of sophisticate radio communications including an earth station on Hittadu island, an air base at Gan Island, advance navigational aids, satellite meteorological data reception station and a natural harbour. The entire project was a strategic communication and staging facility for the British/NATO with West Asia, South Asia, Pacic region and Australia. On strategic withdrawal of all British forces from east of Suez, the military facility has been wound up, but all the permanent fixtures have been left behind. Also a 5000 feet long civil airstrip exists at Hulule Island (Male), which is under modernisation. Air Maldives operates between Male and Colombo. Maldives has a shipping fleet of 80 freighters with a total tonnage of approximately 150,000 tons. Despite the Maldives desire never to lease its territory again for military purposes, the archipelago nation wields immense strategic importance in the Indian Ocean in close proximity to India and Sri Lanka.

Maldives maintains excellent relations with India as also with other countries in the region. Maldives is a member of the UN and the Non-Aligned Movement. It maintains diplomatic relations with almost all big powers. At one time Maldives also maintained diplomatic relations with Taiwan, but with passage of time it now maintains diplomatic relations with PRC and considers Taiwan as an inalienable part of China. Maldives policy of international relations is one of maintaining equidistance and peace.

THE ANTARCTIC TREATY

Signed at Washington December 1, 1959
U.S. ratication deposited August 18, 1960
Entered into force June 23, 1961

The Government of Argentina, Australia, Belgium, Chile, the French Republic, Japan, New Zealand, Norway, the Union of South Africa, the Union of Soviet Socialist Republics, the United Kingdom of Great Britain and Northern Ireland, and the United States of America,

Recognizing that it is in the interest of all mankind that Antarctica shall continue forever to be used exclusively for peaceful purposes and shall not become the scene or object of international discord;

Acknowledging the substantial contributions to scientic knowledge resulting from international cooperation in scientic investigation in Antarctica;

Convinced that the establishment of a firm foundation for the continuation and development of such cooperation on the basis of freedom of scientific investigation of Antarctica as applied during the International Geo-physical Year accords with the interests of science and progress of all mankind;

Convinced also that a treaty ensuring the use of Antarctica for peaceful purposes only and the continuance of international harmony in Antarctica will further the purposes and principles embodied in the Charter of the United Nations;

Have agreed as follows:

Article I

1. Antarctica shall be used for peaceful purposes only. There shall be prohibited, *inter alia,* any measures of a military nature, such as the establishment of military bases and fortifications, the carrying out of military maneuvers, as well as the testing of any type of weapons.

2. The present Treaty shall not prevent the use of military personnel or equipment for scientific research or for any other purpose.

Article II

Freedom of scientic investigation in Antarctica and cooperation toward that end, as applied during the International Geo-physical Year, shall continue, subject to the provisions of the present Treaty.

Article III

1. In order to promote international cooperation in scientific investigation in Antarctica, as provided for in Article II of the present Treaty, the Contracting Parties Agree that, to the greatest extent feasible and practicable:

   (a) information regarding plans for scientic programs in Antarctica shall be exchanged to permit maximum economy and efficiency of operations;

   (b) scientific personnel shall be exchanged in Antarctica between expeditions and stations;

   (c) scientific observations and results from Antarctica shall be exchanged and made freely available.

2. In implementing this Article, every encouragement shall be given to the establishment of cooperative working relations with those Specialised Agencies of the United Nations and other international organisations having a scientific or technical interest in Antartica.

Article IV

1. Nothing contained in the present Treaty shall be interpreted as:

   (a) a renunciation by any Contracting Party of previously asserted rights of or claims to territorial sovereignty in Antarctica;

   (b) a renunciation or diminution by any Contracting Party of any basis of claim to territorial sovereignty in Antarctica which it may have whether as a result of its activities or those of its nationals in Antarctica, or otherwise;

(c) prejudicing the position of any Contracting Party as regards its recognition or non-recognition of any other State's right of or claim or basis of claim to territorial sovereignty in Antarctica.

2. No acts or activities taking place while the present Treaty is in force shall constitute a basis for asserting, supporting or denying a claim to territorial sovereignty in Antarctica or create any rights of sovereignty in Antarctica. No new claim, or enlargement of an existing claim, to territorial sovereignty in Antarctica shall be asserted while the present Treaty is in force.

Article V

1. Any nuclear explosions in Antarctica and the disposal there of radioactive waste material shall be prohibited.

2. In the event of the conclusion of international agreements concerning the use of nuclear energy, including nuclear explosions and the disposal there of radio active waste material, to which all of the Contracting Parties whose representatives are entitled to participate in the meetings provided for under Article IX are parties, the rules established under such agreements shall apply in Antarctica.

Article VI

The provisions of the present Treaty shall apply to the area south of 60 degree South Latitude, including all ice shelves, but nothing in the present Treaty shall prejudice or in any way affect the rights, or the exercise of the rights, of any State under international law with regard to the high seas within that area.

Article VII

1. In order to promote the objectives and ensure the observance of the pro- visions of the present Treaty, each Contracting Party whose representatives are entitled to participate in the meetings referred to in article IX of theTreaty shall have the right to designate observers to carry out any inspection provided for by the present Article. Observers shall be nationals of the Contracting Parties which designate them. The names of observers shall be communicated to every other Contracting Party having the right to designate observers, and the like notice shall be given to the termination of their appointment.

2. Each observer designated in accordance with the provisions of paragraph1 of this Article shall have complete freedom of access at any time to any or all areas of Antarctica.

3. All areas of Antarctica, including all stations, installations and equipment within those areas, and all ships and aircraft at point of discharging or embarking cargoes of personnel in Antarctica, shall be open at all times to inspection by any observers designated in accordance with paragraph 1 of this Article.

4. Aerial observation may be carried out at any time over any o r all areas of Antarctica by any of the Contracting Parties having the right to designate observers.

5. Each Contracting Party shall, at the time when the present Treaty enters into force for it, inform the other Contracting Parties, and thereafter shall give them notice in advance, of

   (a) all expeditions to and within Antarctica, on the part of its ships or nationals, and all expeditions to Antarctica organised in o r proceeding from its territory.

   (b) all stations in Antarctica occupied by its nationals; and

   (c) any military personnel o r equipment intended to be introduced by it into Antarctica subject to conditions prescribed in paragraph 2 of Article 1 of the present Treaty.

Article VIII

1. In order to facilitate the exercise of their functions under the present Treaty and without prejudice to the respective positions of the Contracting Parties relating to jurisdiction over all other persons in Antarctica, observers designated under paragraph 1 of Article VII and scientific personnel exchanged under subparagraph 1(b) of Article III of the Treaty, and members of the staffs accompanying any such persons, shall be subject only to the jurisdiction of the Contracting Party of which they are nationals in respect of all acts o r omissions occurring while they are in Antarctica for the purpose of exercising their functions.

2. Without prejudice to the provisions of paragraph 1 of this Article, and pending the option of measures in pursuance of sub paragraph 1(e) of Article IX, the Contracting Parties concerned in any case of dispute with regard to the exercise of jurisdiction in Antarctica shall immediately consult together with a view to reaching a mutually acceptable solution.

Article IX

1. Representatives of the Contracting Parties named in the preamble to the present Treaty shall meet at the City of Canberra within two months after the date of entry into force of the Treaty, and thereafter at suitable intervals and places, for the purpose of exchanging information, consulting together on matters of common interest pertaining to Antarctica, and formulating and considering, and recommending to their Governments, measures in furtherance of the principles and objectives of the Treaty, including measures regarding:

   (a) use of Antarctica for peaceful purposes only;

   (b) facilitation of scientific research in Antarctica;

   (c) facilitation of international scientific cooperation in Antarctica;

   (d) facilitation of the exercise of the rights of inspection provided for in Article VII of the Treaty;

   (e) questions relating to the exercise of jurisdiction in Antarctica;

   (f) preservation and conservation of living resources in Antarctica;

2. Each Contracting Party which has become a party to the present Treaty by accession under Article XIII shall be entitled to appoint representatives to participate in the meetings referred to in paragraph 1 of the present Article, during such time as that Contracting Party demonstrates its interest in Antarctica by conducting substantial scientific research activity there, such as the establishment of a scientific station or the dispatch of a scientific expedition.

3. Reports from the observers referred to in Article VII of the present Treaty shall be transmitted to the representatives of the Contracting Parties participating in the meetings referred to in paragraph 1 of the present Article.

4. The measures referred to in paragraph 1 of this Article shall become effective when approved by all the Contracting Parties whose representatives were entitled to participate in the meetings held to consider those measures.

5. Any or all of the rights established in the present Treaty may be exercised as from the date of entry into force of the Treaty whether or not any measures facilitating the exercise of such rights have been proposed, considered or approved as provided in this Article.

Article X

Each of the Contracting Parties undertakes to exert appropriate efforts, consistent with the Charter of the United Nations, to the end that no one engages in any activity in Antarctica contrary to the principles or purposes of the present Treaty.

Article XI

1. If any dispute arises between two or more of the Contracting Parties concerning the interpretation or application of the present Treaty, those Contracting Parties shall consult among themselves with a view to having the dispute resolved by negotiation, inquiry, mediation, conciliation, arbitration, judicial settlement or other peaceful means of their own choice.

2. Any dispute of this character not so resolved shall, with the consent, in each case, of all parties to the dispute, be referred to the International Court of Justice for settlement; but failure to reach agreement on reference to the International Court shall not absolve parties to the dispute from the responsibility of continuing to seek to resolve it by any of the various peaceful means referred to in paragraph 1 of this Article.

Article XII

1. (a) The present Treaty may be modified or amended at any time by unanimous agreement of the Contracting Parties whose representatives are entitled to participate in the meetings provided for under Article IX. Any such modification or amendment shall enter into force when the Depositary Government has received notice from all such Contracting Parties that they have ratified it.

(b) Such modification or amendment shall thereafter enter into forces as to any other Contracting Party when notice of ratication by it has been received by the Depositary Government. Any such Contracting Party from which no notice of ratication is received within a period of two years from the date of entry into force of the modification or amendment in accordance with the provisions of sub paragraph 1(a) of this Article shall be deemed to have withdrawn from the present Treaty on the date of the expiration of such period.

2. (a) If after the expiration of thirty years from the date of entry into force of the present Treaty, any of the Contracting Parties whose representatives are entitled to participate in the meetings provided for under Article IX so requests by a communication addressed to the Depositary Government, a Conference of all the Contracting Parties shall be held as soon as practicable to review the operation of the Treaty.

(b) Any modification or amendment to the present Treaty which is approved at such a Conference by a majority of the Contracting Parties there represented, including a majority of those whose representatives are entitled to participate in the meetings provided for under Article IX, shall be communicated by the Depositary Government to all the Contracting Parties immediately after the termination of the Conference and shall enter into force in accordance with the provisions of paragraph 1 of the present Article.

(c) If any such modification or amendment has not entered into force in accordance with the provisions of sub paragraph 1(a) of this Article within a period of two years after the date of its communication to all the Contracting Parties, any Contracting Party may at any time after the expiration of that period give notice to the Depositary Government of its withdrawal from the present Treaty, and such withdrawal shall take effect two years after the receipt of the notice by the Depositary Government.

Article XIII

1. The present Treaty shall be subject to ratification by the signatory States. It shall be open for accession by any State which is a Member of the United Nations, or by any other State which may be invited to accede to the Treaty with the consent of all the Contracting Parties whose representatives are entitles

to participate in the meetings provided for under Article IX of the Treaty.

2. Ratification or accession to the present Treaty shall be effected by each State in accordance with its constitutional processes.

3. Instrument s of ratification and instruments of accession shall be deposited with the Government of the United States of America, hereby designated as the Depositary Government.

4. The Depositary Government shall inform all signatory and acceding States of the date of each deposit of an instrument of ratification or accession, and the date of entry into force of the Treaty and of any modification or amendment thereto.

5. Upon the deposit of instruments of ratification by all the signatory States, the present Treaty shall enter into force for those States and for States which have deposited instruments of accession. Thereafter the Treaty shall enter into force for any acceding State upon the deposit of its instrument of accession.

6. The present treaty shall be registered by the Depositary Government pursuant to the Article 102 of the Charter of the United Nations.

Article XIV

The present Treaty, done in the English, French, Russian and Spanish languages each version being equally authentic, shall be deposited in the archives of the Government of the United States of America, which shall transmit duly certified copies thereof to the Government of the signatory and acceding States.

In the WITNESS WHEREOF the undersigned Plenipotentiaries, duly authorised, have signed the present Treaty.

DONE at Washington this first day of December, one thousand nine hundred and fifty-nine.

IV

RIVER WATER TREATIES/ AGREEMENT

BRIEF ON INDUS WATER TREATY

The Indus and its tributaries comprise one of the most important river systems in the world. The basin was converted into an extensively cultivated area by the British, with millions of acres irrigated by large canals. At the time of p artition of the subcontinent in 1947, the layout of the Indus Basin was ignored.

The total area of the Indus Basin (the area draining the Himalayan water into the Arabian Sea) is about 934,000 sq.km. Pakist an covers the major p art of the Indus Basin. The Indus River system consist s mainly of the Indus River and it s major eastern tributaries, ie Jehlum, Chenab, Ravi, Beas and Sutlej rivers.A number of relatively small rivers join the Indus on its west side. The largest being the Kabul River.

In 1960, after years of negotiations, the World Bank brokered the Indus Water Treaty, which regulated the use of the Indus Basin rivers. The Treaty was signed on September 19, 1960 by Pakistan's President Mohammad Ayub Khan, Indian Prime Minister Jawahar Lal Nehru and Mr. W.A.B Iliff from the World Bank. The text of the treaty runs into approximately 113 pages, as such only a brief of the Treaty is given. For convenience of describing use of waters, the systems have been described as eastern rivers to mean Ravi, Beas and Sutlej rivers and their tributaries, and western rivers to mean Indus, Jehlum and Chenab rivers and their tributaries.

The document consist s of three part s: the preamble, twelve articles and annexure A to H. The principal subjects covered in the Treaty's annexure are - the exchange of notes between the Government s of India and Pakist an, India's agricultural use of certain tributaries of the Ravi river, India's agricultural use of the upper reaches of the western rivers, India's generation of hydroelectric power and the storage of water from the western rivers, a procedure to solve disputes and differences through a Commission, a neutral court of arbitration, and allocation to Pakistan of some waters from the eastern rivers during the period of transition.

Under the Treaty, the waters of western rivers have been provisioned for unrestricted use by Pakistan except waters utilized by India for domestic, non-consumptive and agricultural use, limited to:-

(a) Ranbir Canal - 1000 cusecs from 15April to 14 October and 350 cusecs from 15 October to 14 April.

(b) Pratap Canal - 400 cusecs from 15April to 14 October and 100 cusecs from 15 October to 14 April.

(c) Irrigation from western rivers may continue by India in those areas which were so irrigated as on the ef fective date. In addition, the waters of the western rivers can be used for generation of hydro electric power limited as follows:

(i) No restrictions on the operation of existing plant s at Pahalgam, Bandipura, Dachhigam, Ranbir Canal, Udhampur and Poonch.

(ii) No restriction on completion of plants at Mahora, Gunderbal, Kupwara, Bhaderwah, Kishtwar, Rajouri, Chinani and Nichalani Banihal to the laid down design capacity.

(iii) Design of any Run-of-River plant shall conform to certain laid down criteria.

(iv) No restriction on any hydro-electric power plant s on irrigation channels.

Waters of eastern River shall be available for unrestricted use of India except where otherwise specified. Except for domestic use and non-consumptive use, Pakistan shall be under an obligations to let flow the waters of eastern rivers at specified places without any interference.

Both Pakistan and India shall create posts of commissioners for exchange of data and for implementing content s of this Treaty. The two commissioners shall together form permanent Indus Water Commission.

The Indus Water Treaty has survived hostilities between India and Pakist an over the years but patience may be running out and the recent developments may threaten to undermine it. The Treaty provides India a strategic leverage during a military confrontation and could well be utilized as an answer to the export of terror by Pakistan.

Lately, Pakistan has been raising the water issues with India, possibly to divert the attention of its masses from the internal unstable situation. The blowback is not appreciated. It will be naïve to presume that India will not have contingencies like Swal Kot and Basrar dams on River Chenab, if the weapon of terror continues to operate.

TREATY BETWEEN NEPAL AND INDIA CONCERNING THE INTEGRATED DEVELOPMENT OF THE MAHAKALI RIVER INCLUDING SARADA BARRAGE, TANAKPUR BARRAGE AND PANCHESHWAR PROJECT

His Majesty's Government of Nepal and the Government of India (here- inafter referred to as the "Parties"),

Reaffirming the determination to promote and strengthen their relations of friendship and close neighbourliness for the co-operation in the development of water resources;

Recognising that the Mahakali River is a boundary river on major stretches between the two countries;

Realising the desirability to enter into a treaty on the basis of equal partnership to define their obligations and corresponding rights and duties thereto in regard to the waters of Mahakali River and its utilization;

Noting the Exchange of Letters of 1920 through which both the Parties had entered into an arrangement for the construction of the Sarada Barrage in the Mahakali River, whereby Nepal is to receive some waters from the said Barrage;

Recalling the decision taken in the Joint Commission dated 4–5 December, 1991 and the Joint Communiqué issued during the visit of the Prime Minister of India to Nepal on 21st October, 1992 regarding the Tanakpur Barrage which India has constructed in a course of the Mahakali River with a part of the eastern afflux bund at Jimuwa and the adjoining pondage area of the said Barrage lying in the Nepalese territory;

Noting that both the parties are jointly preparing a Detailed Project Report of the Pancheshwar Multipurpose Project to be implemented in the Mahakali River;

Now, therefore, the Parties hereto hereby have agreed as follows:

Article I

1. Nepal shall have the right to a supply of 28.35 m^3/s (1000 cusecs) of water from the Sarada Barrage in the wet season (i.e. from 15th May to 15th October) and 4.25 m^3/s (150 cusecs) in the dry season (i.e. from 16th October to 14th May).

2. India shall maintain a flow of not less than 10 m^3/s (350 cusecs) down-stream of the Sarada Barrage in the Mahakali River to maintain and preserve the river ecosystem.

3. In case the Sarada Barrage becomes non-functional due to any cause:

   (a) Nepal shall have the right to a supply of water as mentioned in Paragraph 1 of Article 1, by using the head regulator(s) mentioned in paragraph 2 of Article 2 herein. Such a supply of water shall be in addition to the water to be supplied to Nepal pursuant to Paragraph 2 of Article 2.

   (b) India shall maintain the river flow pursuant to Paragraph 2 of this Article from the tailgate of the Tanakpur Power Station downstream of the Sarada Barrage.

Article 2

In continuation of the decision taken in the Joint Commission dated 4–5 December, 1991 and the Joint Communiqué issued during the visit of the Prime Minister of India to Nepal on 21st October 1992, both the Parties agree as follows:

1. For the construction of the eastern afflux bund of the Tanakpur Barrage, at Jimuwa and tying it up to the high ground in the Nepalese territory at EL 250 M, Nepal gives it s consent to use a piece of land of about 577 meters in length (an area of about 2.9 hectares) of the Nepalese territory at the Jimuwa village in Mahendranagar Municipal area and a certain portion of the No-Man's land on either side of the border. The Nepalese land consented to be so used and the land lying on the west of the said land (about 9 hectares) up to Nepal–India border which forms a part of the pondage area, including the natural resources endowment lying within that area, remains under the continued sovereignty and control of Nepal and Nepal is free to exercise all attendant rights thereto.

2. In lieu of the eastern afflux bund of the Tanakpur barrage, at Jimuwa thus constructed, Nepal shall have the right to:

   (a) a supply of 28.35 m^3/s (1000 cusecs) of water in the wet season (i.e. from 15th May to 15th October) and 8.50 m^3/s (300 cusecs) in the dry season (i.e. from 16th October to 14th May) from the date of entry into force of this Treaty. For this purpose and for the purposes of Article 1 herein, India shall construct the head regulator(s) near the left under-sluice of the Tanakpur Barrage and also the waterways of the required capacity up to the Nepal–India border. Such head regulator(s) and waterways shall be operated jointly.

   (b) a supply of 70 million kilowatt-hour (unit) of energy on a continuous basis annually, free of cost, from the date of entry into force of this Treaty. For this purpose, India shall construct a 132 KV transmission line up to the Nepal–India border from the Tanakpur Power Station

   (which has, at present, an installed capacity of 120,000 kilowatt generating 448.4 millions kilowatt-hour of energy annually on 90 per cent dependable year flow).

3. Following arrangements shall be made at the Tanakpur Barrage at the time of development of any storage project(s) including Pacheshwar Multipurpose Project upstream of the Tanakpur Barrage:

   (a) Additional head regulator and the necessary waterways, as required, up to the Nepal–India borders shall be constructed to supply additional water to Nepal. Such head regulator and waterways shall be operated jointly.

   (b) Nepal shall have additional energy equal to half of the incremental energy generated from the Tanakpur Power Station, on a continuous basis from the date of augmentation of the flow of the Mahakali River and shall bear half of the additional operation cost and, if required, half of the additional capital cost at the Tanakpur Power Station for the generation of such incremental energy.

Article 3

Pancheshwar Multipurpose Project (hereinafter referred to as the "Project") is to be constructed on a stretch of the Mahakali River where it forms the boundary between the two countries and hence both the parties agree that they have equal entitlement in the utilization of the waters of the Mahakali River without prejudice to their respective existing consumptive uses of the waters of the Mahakali River in accordance with the Detailed Project Report (DPR) being jointly prepared by them. The project shall be designed and implemented on the basis of the following principles:

1. The Project shall, as would be agreed between the Parties, be designed to produce the maximum total net benefit. All benefits accruing to both the Parties with the development of the Project in the forms of power, irrigation, flood control etc, shall be assessed.

2. The Project shall be implemented or cause to be implemented as an integrated Project including power stations of equal capacity on each side of the Mahakali River. The two power stations shall be operated in an integrated manner and the total energy shall be shared equally between the Parties.

3. The cost of the Project shall be borne by the Parties in proportion to the benefits accruing to them. Both the Parties shall jointly endeavour to mobilize the finance required for the implementation of the Project.

4. A portion of Nepal's share of energy shall be sold to India. The quantum of such energy and its price shall be mutually agreed upon between the Parties.

Article 4

India shall supply 10 m^3/s (350 cusecs) of water for the irrigation of Dodhara-Chandani area of Nepalese Territory. The technical and other details will be mutually worked out.

Article 5

1. Water requirement of Nepal shall be given prime consideration in the utilization of the waters of the Mahakali River.

2. Both the Parties shall be entitled to draw their share of waters of the Mahakali River from the Tanakpur Barrage and/or other mutually agreed points as provided for in this Treaty and any subsequent agreement between the Parties.

Article 6

Any project, other than those mentioned herein, to be developed in the Mahakali River, where it is a boundary river, shall be designed and implemented by an agreement between the Parties on the principles established by this Treaty.

Article 7

In order to maintain the flow and level of waters of Mahakali Rive r, each Party undertakes not to use or obstruct or divert the waters of Mahakali River adversely affecting its natural flow and level except by an agreement between the Parties. Provided, however, this shall not preclude the use of the waters of the Mahakali River by the local communities living along both sides of the Mahakali River, not exceeding ve (5) percent of the average annual flow at Pancheshwar.

Article 8

The Treaty shall not preclude planning, survey, development and operation of any work on the tributaries of the Mahakali River, to be carried out independently by each Party in its own territory without adversely affecting the provision of Article 7 of this Treaty.

Article 9

1. There shall be a Mahakali River Commission (hereinafter referred to as the "Commission"). The Commission shall be guided by the principle of equality, mutual benefit and no harm to either Party.

2. The Commission shall be composed of equal number of representatives from both the Parties.

3. The function of the Commission shall, inter alia, include the following:

   (a) To seek information on and, if necessary, inspect all structures included in the Treaty and make recommendations to both the Parties to take steps which shall be necessary to implement the provisions of this Treaty.

   (b) To make recommendations to both the Parties for the conservation and utilization of the Mahakali River as envisaged and provided for in this Treaty.

   (c) To provide expert evaluation of the projects and recommendations thereto.

(d) To co-ordinate and monitor plans of actions arising out of the implementation of this Treaty, and

(e) To examine any differences arising between the Parties concerning the interpretation and application of this Treaty.

4. The expenses of the Commission shall be borne equally by both the Parties.

5. As soon as the Commission has been constituted pursuant to paragraphs 1 and 2 of this Article, it shall draft its rules of procedure which shall be submitted to both the Parties for their concurrence.

6. Both the Parties shall reserve their rights to deal directly with each other on matters which may be in competence of the Commission.

Article 10

Both the Parties may form project specic joint entity/ies for the development, execution and operation of new projects including Pancheshwar Multipurpose Project in the Mahakali River for their mutual benet.

Article 11

1. If the Commission fails under Article 9 of this Treaty to recommend its opinion after examining the differences of the Parties within three (3) months of such reference to the Commission or either Party disagrees with the recommendations of the Commission, then a dispute shall be deemed to have been arisen which shall then be submitted to arbitration for decision. In so doing either Party shall give three (3) months prior notice to the other Party.

2. Arbitration shall be conducted by a tribunal composed of three arbitrators. One arbitrator shall be nominated by Nepal, one by India, with neither country to nominate its own national and the third arbitrator shall be appointed jointly, who, as a member of the tribunal, shall preside over such tribunal. In the event that the Parties are unable to agree upon the third arbitrator within ninety (90) days after receipt of a proposal, either Party may request the Secretary-General of the Permanent Court of Arbitration at The Hague to appoint such arbitrator who shall not be a national of either country.

3. The procedures of the arbitration shall be determined by the arbitration tribunal and the decision of a majority of the arbitrators shall be the decision of the tribunal. The proceedings of the tribunal shall be conducted in

English and the decision of such a tribunal shall be in writing. Both the Parties shall accept the decision as nal, denitive and binding.

4. Provision for the venue of arbitration, the administrative support of the arbitration tribunal and the remuneration and expenses of its arbitrators shall be as agreed in an exchange of notes between the Parties. Both the Parties may also agree by such exchange of notes on alternative procedures for settling differences arising under this Treaty.

Article 12

1. Following the conclusion of this Treaty, the earlier understanding reached between the Parties concerning the utilization of the waters of the Mahakali River from the Sarada Barrage and the T anakpur Barrage, which have been incorporated herein, shall be deemed to have been replaced by this Treaty.

2. This Treaty shall be subject to ratification and shall enter into force on the date of exchange of Instruments of Ratification. It shall remain valid for a period of seventy-five (75) years from the date of its entry into force.

3. This Treaty shall be reviewed by both the Parties at ten (10) years interval or earlier as required by either Party and make amendments thereto, if necessary.

4. Agreements, as required, shall be entered into by the Parties to give effect to the provisions of this Treaty.

IN WITNESS WHEREOF the undersigned being duly authorised thereto by their respective governments have hereto signed this treaty and affixed thereto their seals in two originals each in Hindi, Nepali and English languages, all texts being equally authentic. In case of doubt, the English text shall prevail.

Done at New Delhi, India, on the twelfth day of February of the year one thousand nine hundred ninety six.

(PV NARASIMHA RAO)	(SHER BAHADUR DEUBA)
Prime Minister of India	Prime Minister
	His Majesty's Government of Nepal

Letter Exchanged with the Treaty

Kathmandu
Nepal
12 February 1996

Excellency,

I have the honour to refer to the Treaty concluded between us concerning the Integrated Development of the Mahakali River including Sarada Barrage, the Tanakpur Barrage and Pancheshwar Project (Treaty). At this juncture, may I recall for Your Excellency the decisions taken in the Joint Commission dated 4–5 December, 1991 and the Joint Communiqué issued during visit to Nepal on 21st October, 1992.

In order to give effect to the desires expressed by our respective Governments, I have the honour to make the following proposals on the basis of the provisions of the said understandings and the said Treaty.

1. The all weather link road connecting the Tanakpur Barrage to East–West Highway at the Mahendranagar in Nepal shall be completed by India within one (1) year from the date of entry into force of the Treaty.
2. The supply of 20 million kilowatt-hour (unit) of energy annually, free of cost, to Nepal from the Tanakpur Power Station as indicated in the said Joint Communiqué from the date of commissioning of the Tanakpur power Station in July 7, 1992 till the start of the supply of 70 million kilowatt-hour (unit) of energy annually, free of cost, for Nepal as provided in the Treaty, shall be reconciled with the energy procured or to be procured by Nepal from India under the existing power exchange arrangement.
3. Regarding Pancheshwar Multipurpose Project (Project) the following principles shall be adopted and arrangements made for finalisation of the Detailed Project Report (DPR), completion of negotiation and implementation of the project:
   (a) The DPR shall be finalised by both the countries within six (6) months of date of entry into force of the Treaty. For this purpose, necessary data and reports shall be exchanged expeditiously. While assessing the benefits from the project during the preparation of the DPR, net power benefit shall be assessed on the basis of, inter alia, saving in cost to the beneficiaries as compared to the relevant alternatives available. Irrigation benefit shall be assessed on the basis of incremental and additional benefits due

to augmentation of river flow and flood control benefit shall be assessed on the basis of the value of works saved and damages avoided.

(b) It is understood that paragraph 3 of Article 3 of the Treaty precludes the claim, in any form, by either party on the unutilised portion of the share of the waters of the Mahakali River of that party without affecting the provision of the withdrawal of the respective shares ofthe waters of the Mahakali River by each party under this Treaty.

(c) Agreement of the financing and implementation of the Project, including the proposal for the establishment of the Pancheshwar Development Authority shall be negotiated and finalised by both the countries within one (1) year from the finalisation of the DPR.

(d) In order to expedite the implementation of the Project, field investigation and detailed design including tender document preparation shall start immediately after the finalisation of the DPR and run parallel to the negotiation on agreement for implementation of the Project. For this purpose, a separate financing arrangement for such activities shall be agreed upon by both the countries.

(e) The Project shall be aimed to be completed within eight (8) years from the date of the agreement for its implementation, subject to the provision of the DPR.

I shall be grateful if Your Excellency will kindly confirm that the above correctly sets out the understanding reached between our two Governments. This letter and Your Excellency's reply confirming the understanding will constitute an agreement between our two Governments which also shall come into force on the date of exchange of Instruments of Ratification between the Parties as set forth in paragraph 2 of Article 12 of the Treaty.

Please accept Your Excellency, the assurances of my highest considerations.

Sher Bahadur Deuba
Prime Minister his Majesty's Government of Nepal

HE Mr Narsimha Rao Prime Minister,
Government of India

The contents of the above letter were conrmed as correct vide Indian Prime minister letter dated 12 February 1996.

TREATY ON SHARING OF GANGA/GANGES WATERS AT FARAKKA BETWEEN INDIA AND BANGLADESH, 1996

The Government of the Republic of India and the Government of the Republic of Bangladesh,

DETERMINED to promote and strengthen their relations of friendship and good neighbourliness,

INSPIRED by the common desire of promoting the well being of their peoples,

BEING desirous of sharing by mutual agreement the waters of the inter national rivers flowing through the territories of the two countries and of making the optimum utilisation of the water resources of their region in the fields of flood management, irrigation, river basin development and generation of hydropower for the mutual benet of the peoples of the two countries,

RECOGNISING that the need for making an arrangement for sharing of the Ganga/Ganges waters at Farakka in a spirit of mutual accommodation and need for a solution to the long-term problem of augmenting the flows of the Ganga/Ganges are in mutual interests of the peoples of the two countries,

BEING desirous of finding a fair and just solution without affecting the rights and entitlements of either country other than those covered by this Treaty, or establishing any general principles of law or precedent,

HAVE AGREED AS FOLLOWS:

Article I

The quantum of waters agreed to be released by India to Bangladesh will be at Farakka.

Article II

(i) The sharing between India and Bangladesh of the Ganga/Ganges waters at Farakka by ten day periods from 1st January to 31 May every year will be with reference to the formula at Annexure I and an indicative schedule giving the implications of the sharing arrangement under Annexure I is at Annexure II.

(ii) The indicative schedule at Annexure II, as referred to in sub para (i) above, is based on 40 years (1949–1988) 10-day period average availability of water at Farakka. Every effort would be made by the upper riparian to protect flow of water at Farakka as in the 40 year average availability as mentioned above.

(iii) In the event flow at Farakka falls below 50,000 cusecs in any 10-day period, the two Governments will enter into immediate consultations to make adjustments on an emergency basis, in accordance with the principles of equity, fair play and no harm to either party.

Article III

The waters released to Bangladesh at Farakka under Article I shall not be reduced below Farakka except for reasonable uses of waters, not exceeding 200 cusecs, by India between Farakka and the point on the Ganga/Ganges where both its banks are in Bangladesh.

Article IV

A Committee consisting of representatives nominated by the two Governments in equal numbers (hereinafter called the Joint Committee) shall be constituted following the signing of this Treaty. The Joint Committee shall set up suitable teams at Farakka and Hardinge Bridge to observe and record at Farakka the daily flows below Farakka Barrage, in the Feeder Canal, and at the Navigation lock, as well as at the Hardinge Bridge.

Article V

The Joint Committee shall decide its own procedure and method of functioning.

Article VI

The Joint Committee shall submit to the two governments all data collected by it and shall also submit a yearly report to both the Governments. Following submission of the reports the two Governments will meet at appropriate levels to decide upon such further actions as may be needed.

Article VII

The Joint Committee shall be responsible for implementing the arrangements contained in this Treaty and examining any difficulty arising out of the implementation of the above arrangements and of the operation of Farakka Barrage. Any difference or dispute arising in this regard, if not resolved by the Joint Committee, shall be referred to the Indo–Bangladesh Joint Rivers Commission. If the difference or dispute still remains unresolved, it shall be referred to the two Governments which shall meet urgently at the appropriate level to resolve it by mutual discussion.

Article VIII

The two Governments recognise the need to cooperate with each other in finding a solution to the long-term problem of augmenting the flows of the Ganga/Ganges during the dry season.

Article IX

Guided by the principle of equity, fairness and no harm to either party, both the Governments agree to conclude water sharing Treaties/Agreements with regard to other common rivers.

Article X

The sharing arrangement under this Treaty shall be reviewed by the two Governments at five years interval or earlier, as required by either party and needed adjustments, based on principle of equity, fairness and no harm to either party made thereto, if necessary. It would be open to either party to seek first review after two years to assess the impact and working of the sharing arrangement as contained in this Treaty.

Article XI

For the period of this Treaty, in the absence of mutual agreement on adjustments following reviews as mentioned in Article X, India shall release downstream of Farakka Barrage, water at a rate not less than 90 (ninety) percent of

Bangladesh's share according to the formula referred to in Article II, until such time as mutually agreed ows are decided upon.

Article XII

This treaty shall enter into force upon signature and shall remain in force for a period of thirty years and it shall be renewable on the basis of mutual consent.

IN WITNESS WHEREOF the undersigned, being duly authorised thereto by the respective governments, have signed this Treaty.

DONE at New Delhi 12th December 1996 in Hindi, Bangla and English languages. In the event of any conflict between the text s, the English text shall prevail.

HD DEVA GOWDA
Prime Minister
Republic of India

SHEIKH HASINA
Prime Minister
People's, Republic of Bangladesh

Annexure I

Availability at Farakka	**Share of India**	**Share of Bangladesh**
70,000 cusecs or less	50%	50%
70,000–75,000 cusecs	Balance of Flow	35,000 cusecs
75,000 cusecs or more	40,000 cusecs	Balance of Flow

Subject to condition that India and Bangladesh each shall receive guaranteed 35,000 cusecs of water in alternate three 10 days periods during the period March 1 to May 10.

Annexure II

SCHEDULE

(Sharing of waters at Farakka between January 01 and May 31 every year)

If actual availability corresponds to average flows of the period 1949 to1988, the implication of the formula in Annexure I for the share of each side is:

Period	Average of total flow	India's share	Bangladesh's share
Jan			
1–10	107,516	40,000	67,516
11–20	97,673	40,000	57,673
21–31	90,154	40,000	50,154
Feb			
1–10	86,323	40,000	46,323
11–20	82,859	40,000	42,859
21–28	79,106	40,000	39,106
March			
1–10	74,419	39,419	35,000
11–20	68,931	33,931	35,000
21–31	64,688	35,000	29,688
April			
1–10	63,180	28,180	35,000
11–20	62,633	35,000	27,633
21–30	60,992	25,992	35,000
May			
1–10	67,351	35,000	32,351
11–20	73,590	38,590	35,000
21–31	81,854	40,000	41,854

V

BRIEF DESCRIPTION OF THE UN CONVENTION OF THE LAW OF THE SEA AND INDIA'S MARITIME BOUNDARIES

BRIEF DESCRIPTION OF THE UN CONVENTION OF THE LAW OF THE SEA (UNCLOS), AND INDIA'S MARITIME BOUNDARIES

UNCLOS

The first United Nations Conference on the Law of the Sea (UNCLOS I) was held in Geneva in 1958. Four key conventions emerged from the deliberations:

- The Convention on the Territorial Sea and Contiguous Zone.
- The Convention on the Continental Shelf.
- The Convention on the High Seas.
- The Convention on Fishing and Conservation of the Living Resources of the High Seas.

The 1958 Convention could not arrive at an agreement on the maximum width of the territorial sea. In 1960, 88 nations met for UNCLOS II, almost succeeded in establishing a 6 n mile territorial sea and 6 n mile shing zone beyond the territorial sea, but two-third majority fell short by just one vote.

The Third United Nations Conference on the Law of the Sea (UNCLOSIII) finalised after nine years of deliberations, comprises 320 articles and nine annexes governing virtually all aspects of ocean space like boundary delimitation, environmental control, scientic research, economic and commercial activity, transfer of technology and the settlement of disputes relating to ocean matters. The new Law of the Sea came into force with effect from 16 November 1994. As of February 2000, 158 states had signed and 132 had ratified the **United Nations Convention on the Law of the Sea.** The important features of the Convention are given in the succeeding paragraphs.

Baseline

The baseline represents the outer limit of a state's internal waters. It is the low water mark along the coast. The Baseline could be 'Normal' as has been described, or in case of an indented or deeply cut into coastline or if there is an island on the fringes or in case of a delta resulting into an unstable coastline, the baseline could be 'Straight' drawn along selected parts as allowed by Article 7 of the **UNCLOS.** However, the provision could give rise to various queries as the precise definitions of some of the terms used have not been provided.

Inter-Tidal Foreshore

The coastal state maintains sovereignty over the area that lies between the high and low tidemarks.

Internal Waters

Waters on the landward side of the baseline of the territorial sea are Internal Waters.

Territorial Waters

The sovereignty of a coastal state runs beyond its land territory and the internal waters up to 12 n miles over the adjacent belt of sea. This sovereignty extends to airspace as well. The regime envisages ships of other states to be given right of innocent passage. Submarines and underwater craft are required to navigate on the surface of the sea and exhibit the flag of their nationality while in the territorial waters.

Contiguous Zone

Contiguous Zone extends to 24 nm including the territorial waters. This zone provides for preventive jurisdiction in respect of customs, immigration, fiscal and sanitary measures to be exercised by the coastal state.

Exclusive Economic Zone (EEZ)

Provides for sovereign rights and jurisdiction over all living and non-living resources superjacent to the sea-bed and of the sea-bed and subsoil up to 200 nm from the baseline. However, grants freedom of navigation, communication, overights and laying of submarine cables and pipelines to other states.

Continental Shelf

The Continental Shelf of a coastal state comprises the sea-bed and subsoil of the submarine areas that extend beyond its territorial sea throughout its natural prolongation of its land territory to the outer edge of the continental margin, or to a distance of 200 n miles from the baseline where the outer edge of the continental margin does not extend to that distance. In case the continental margin extends beyond 200 n miles from the baseline, the upper limit of the continental shelf will be 350 n miles, although where the line 100 nm beyond the 2500 meters isobath lies beyond the 350 n miles line, that may be used instead. The states claiming continental shelf beyond 200 n miles must have their claims approved by the UN Commission on the Limits of the Continental Shelf.

Beyond the limits of the Continental Shelf jurisdiction, the sea is the common heritage of the mankind and is to be managed by the International Seabed Authority.

Deep Sea Mining Regime Controversy

This was a controversial aspect of the Convention of the Law of the Sea. After protracted negotiations the Convention was modiûed as follows:

(a) Transfer of Technology—Countries wishing to obtain transfer of technology on seabed mining shall do so on fair and reasonable terms and conditions of open market. The obligation of transfer of technology was deleted.

(b) Production Policy—The production policy and technical formula envisaged in the original Convention was deleted.

(c) Financial Terms—The financial terms of contracts have been attenuated. A Finance Committee would be established as part of the International Authority to decide on the financial matters.

(d) Review Conferences—Certain changes have been made with regard to the Review Conferences and Economic Assistance to developing countries. The concept of "Pioneer Investor" however remains unchanged. This status has already been conferred on India because of its leading role in steering the world-view on important matters concerning India and other developing countries.

INDIA'S MARITIME BOUNDARIES

The length of the Indian coastline, including the island territories is 7516.5 kilometres. In view of the prospective changes in the international law of the sea,

Indian Parliament extended Constitutional recognition to the new concept of the EEZ in May 1976. Article 297 of Chapter III, Part XII of the Constitution of India reads as follows:

> "All lands, minerals and other things of value underlying the ocean within the territorial waters, or the continental shelf, o r the exclusive economic zone of India, shall vest in the Union and be held for the purposes of the Union."

In August 1976, the "Territorial Waters, Continental Shelf, Exclusive Economic Zone and Other Maritime Zones Act" entered into force. Section 5 on Contiguous Zone and section 7 on EEZ entered into force in January 1977. In December 1982, India signed **UNCLOS** and ratified it along with the implementation of Part XI (dealing with the International Seabed Area) on 29 June 1995.

With **UNCLOS** coming in to force the India 's responsibility increased from 83200 square kilometres to 2.2 million square kilometres of sea.

India's maritime boundaries necessitate delimitation with seven neighbouring and opposite coasts, viz Pakistan, Maldives, Sri Lanka, Indonesia, Thailand, Myanmar and Bangladesh. The details of agreements* concluded between India and her neighbours are given below:

Country	**Signature/entry into Force**	**Type of Agreement**
Indonesia	8-8-74/17-12-74	Delimitation of Continental Shelf Boundary.
Indonesia	14-1-77/15-8-77	Extension of the above boundary in Andaman Sea and in Indian Ocean.
Maldives	28-12-76/8-6-78	Maritime Boundary and related matters.
Myanmar	23-12-86/14-9-87	Delimitation of maritime boundary in Andaman Sea, in Coco Channel and in Bay of Bengal.

*Rahul Roy Chaudhury, India's Maritime Security

Sri Lanka	26/28-6-74/8-7-74	On boundary in historic waters and related matters.
	23-3-76/10-5-76	Maritime Boundary and related matters.
	22-11-76/5-2-77	Supplementary Agreement on the extension of the maritime boundary in the Gulf of Mannar from position 13 m to the Tri-Junction between India,Sri Lanka and Maldives (Point T).
Thailand	22-6-78/15-12-78	Delimitation of seabed boundary in Andaman Sea.
	27-10-78/17-1-96	Maritime Boundary in Andaman Sea from Point 7 to Tri-Junction Point (Point T) between India, Thailand and Myanmar.
Sri Lanka, Maldives and India	24-7-76/31-7-76	Determining the Tri-Junction between the three countries.
Indonesia, Thailand and India	22-6-78/2-3-79	Determining the Tri-Junction and delimitation of the related boundaries between the three countries.
Myanmar, Thailand and India	27-10-93/24-5-95	Determining the Tri-Junction in Andaman Sea.

Thus India has settled her maritime boundaries with all her neighbours except Pakistan and Bangladesh. The delay with these countries are related to the resolution of the Sir Creek dispute with Pakistan and differing principles being advocated by India and Bangladesh to demarcate the maritime boundary between them as also the dispute over a three kilometres island lying in an estuary in the Bay of Bengal.

India–Pakistan Maritime Boundaries Settlement, Sir Creek Dispute

The details of the dispute have already been explained in this book. Once the Sir Creek Dispute is resolved, the resolution of the maritime boundary will follow.

India–Bangladesh Maritime Boundary Settlement

As per **UNCLOS** all maritime international disputes including the resolution of the maritime boundaries will be carried out by peaceful means, and are not confined to any particular method to resolve such disputes even though some methods of dispute resolution have been listed. States can adopt their own methods. One of the popular methods is to follow the method of equidistance from the respective baselines. India and Bangladesh maritime dispute primarily emerges out of difference of opinion by which the boundary should be delimited between the two countries and also the disputed sovereignty over a three kilometres island lying in the estuary of Haribhanga and Raimongal rivers in the Bay of Bengal, known as New Moore or Purbhasha in India and South Talpatty in Bangladesh.

Because of the concave nature of the coastline of Bangladesh and the zigzagging of the coastline, the delimitation of this maritime boundary is full of complications with economic ramifications for both nations.

VI

ARMS CONTROL AND DENIAL REGIMES

ARMS CONTROL AND DENIAL REGIMES

History of arms control dates back to the dropping of atomic bombs on Hiroshima and Nagasaki which demonstrated the enormous destructive power of the nuclear devices. Arms control aims at war prevention, reduction of lethality of war and reduction of defence budgets besides maintenance of preeminence of the United States of America and other Nuclear-Weapon States.

Denial regimes aim to restrict the horizontal proliferation of weapons of mass destruction by restricting the knowledge, technology and materials which go to manufacture such weapons. Third world countries at present are mainly concerned with the denial regimes. Keeping the scope of this book in view only Geneva Protocol of 1925; Biological Weapons Convention of 1972; Treaty Banning Nuclear-Weapon Tests in the Atmosphere, in Outer Space and Under Water; NPT and India's Nuclear Doctrine in full texts and brief description of CTBT, FMCT, MTCR and CWC have been included.

PROTOCOL FOR PROHIBITION OF THE USE IN WAR OF ASPHYXIATING, POISONOUS OR OTHER GASES, AND OF BACTERIOLOGICAL METHODS OF WARFARE

Signed at Geneva: 17 June 1925

Entered in to Force: For each signatory as from the date of deposit of Ratification etc.

Depositary Government: France

The undersigned Plenipotentiaries, in the name of their respective Governments:

Whereas the use in war of asphyxiating, poisonous or other gases, and of all analogous liquids, materials or devices, has been justly condemned by general opinion of the civilized world; and

Whereas the prohibition of such use has been declared in Treaties to which the majority of powers of the world are Parties; and

To the end that this prohibition shall be universally accepted as a part of International Law, binding alike the conscience and practice of nations;

Declare:

That the High Contracting Parties, so far as they are not already Parties to the Treaties prohibiting such use, accept this prohibition, agree to extend this prohibition to the use of bacteriological methods of warfare and agree to be bound as between themselves according to the terms of this declaration.

The High Contracting Parties will exert every effort to induce other States to accede to the present Protocol. Such accession will be notified to the Government of French Republic, and by the latter to all signatory and acceding Powers, and will take effect on the date of the notication by the Government of the French Republic.

The present Protocol, of which the French and English texts are both authentic, shall be ratified as soon as possible. It shall bear today's date.

The Ratification of the present Protocol shall be addressed to the Government of the French Republic, which will at once notify the deposit of such Ratification to each of the signatory and acceding Powers.

The Instrument of Ratification and accession to the present Protocol will remain deposited in the archives of the Government of French Republic.

The present Protocol will come into force for each signatory Power as from the date of its Ratification, and from the moment, each Power will be bound as regards other Powers which have already deposited their Ratifications.

In witness whereof the Plenipotentiaries have signed the present Protocol.

Done at Geneva in a single copy, the seventeenth day of June, one thousand nine hundred and twenty five.

CONVENTION ON THE PROHIBITION OF THE DEVELOPMENT, PRODUCTION AND STOCKPILING OF BACTERIOLOGICAL (BIOLOGICAL) AND TOXIN WEAPONS AND ON THEIR DESTRUCTION, 1972

The States Parties to the Convention,

Determined to act with a view to achieving effective progress towards general and complete disarmament, including the prohibition and elimination of all types of weapons of mass destruction, and convinced that the prohibition of the development, production and stockpiling of chemical and bacteriological (biological) weapons and their elimination, through effective measures, will facilitate the achievement of general and complete disarmament under strict and ef fective international control,

Recognizing the important signicance of the Protocol for the prohibition of the Use in War of Asphyxiating, Poisonous or other Gases, and of Bacteriological Methods of Warfare, signed at Geneva on 17 June 1925, and conscious also of the contribution which the said Protocol has already made, and continues to make, to mitigating the horrors of war,

Reaffirming their adherence to the principles and objectives of that Protocol and calling upon all States to comply strictly with them,

Recalling that the General Assembly of the United Nations has repeatedly condemned all actions contrary to the Principles and Objectives of the Geneva Protocol of 17 June 1925,

Desiring to contribute to the strengthening of confidence between peoples and general improvement of the international atmosphere,

Desiring also to contribute to the realization of the purposes and principles of the Charter of the United Nations,

Convinced of the importance and urgency of eliminating from the arsenals of the States, through effective measures, such dangerous weapons of mass destruction as those using chemical or bacteriological (biological) agents,

Recognizing that an agreement on the prohibition of bacteriological (biological) and toxin weapons represents a first possible step towards the achievement of agreement on effective measures also for the prohibition of development, production and stockpiling of chemical weapons, and determined to continue negotiations to that end,

Determined for the sake of all mankind, to exclude completely the possibility of bacteriological (biological) agents and toxins being used as weapons,

Convinced that such use would be repugnant to the conscious of mankind and that no effort should be spared to minimize this risk,

Have agreed as follows:

Article I

Each State Party to this Convention undertakes never in any circumstances to develop, produce, stockpile or otherwise acquire or retain:

(1) Microbial or other biological agents, or toxins whatever their origin or method of production, of types and in quantities that have no justification for prophylactic, protective or other peaceful purposes;

(2) Weapons, equipment or means of delivery designed to such agents or toxins for hostile purposes or in armed conflict.

Article II

Each State Party to this Convention undertakes to destroy, or to divert to peaceful purposes, as soon as possible but not later than nine months after the entry into force of the Convention, all agents, toxins, weapons, equipment and means of delivery specied in Article I ofthe Convention, which are in its possession or under its jurisdiction or control. In implementing the provisions of this article all necessary safety precautions shall be observed to protect populations and the environment.

Article III

Each State Party to this Convention undertakes not to transfer to any recipient whatsoever, directly or indirectly, and not in any way to assist, encourage or induce any State, group of States or international organisations to manufacture or otherwise acquire any of the agents, toxins, weapons, equipment or means of delivery specied in Article I of the Convention.

Article IV

Each State Party to this Convention shall, in accordance with its constitutional processes, take any necessary measures to prohibit and prevent the development, production, stockpiling, acquisition or retention of the agents, toxins, weapons, equipment or means of delivery specied in Article I of the Convention, within the territory of such State, under its jurisdiction or under its control anywhere.

Article V

The States Parties to this Convention undertake to consult one another and to co-operate in solving any problems which may arise in relation to the objective of, or in application of the provisions of the Convention. Consultation and cooperation pursuant to this article may also be undertaken through appropriate international procedures within the framework of the United Nations and in accordance with its Charter.

Article VI

1. Any State Party to this Convention which finds that any other State Party is acting in breach of obligations deriving from the provisions of the Convention may lodge a complaint with the Security Council of the United Nations. Such a complaint should include all possible evidence confirming its validity, as well as its request for its consideration by the Security Council.

2. Each state Party to this Convention undertakes to co-operate in carrying out any investigation which the Security Council may initiate, in accordance with the provisions of the Charter of the United Nations, on the basis of the complaint received by the Council. The Security Council shall inform the States Parties to the Convention of the result of the investigation.

Article VII

Each State Party to this Convention undertakes to provide or support assistance, in accordance with the United Nations Charter, to any Party to the Convention which so requests, if the Security Council decides that such party has been exposed to danger as a result of violation of the Convention.

Article VIII

Nothing in this Convention shall be interpreted as in any way limiting or detracting from the obligations assumed by any State under the protocol for the Prohibition of the Use in War of Asphyxiating, Poisonous or Other gases, and of Bacteriological Methods of Warfare, signed at Geneva on 17 June 1925.

Article IX

Each State Party to the Convention affirms the recognized objective of effective prohibition of chemical weapons and, to this end, undertakes to continue negotiations in good faith with a view to reaching early agreement on effective measures for the prohibition of their development, production and stockpiling and for their destruction, and on appropriate measures concerning equipment and means of delivery specifically designed for the production or use of chemical agents for weapons purposes.

Article X

1. The States Parties to this Convention undertake to facilitate, and have the right to participate in the fullest possible exchange of equipment, materials and scientific and technological information for the use of bacteriological (biological) agents and toxins for peaceful purposes. Parties to the Convention in a position to do so shall also co-operate contributing individually or together with other States or international organisations to the further development and application of scientific discoveries in the field of bacteriology (biology) for the prevention of disease, or for other peaceful purposes.

2. This Convention shall be implemented in a manner designed to avoid hampering the economic or technological development of States Parties to the Convention or international co-operation in the field of peaceful bacteriological (biological) activities, including the international exchange of bacteriological (biological) agents and toxins and equipment for processing, use or production of bacteriological (biological) agents and toxins for peaceful purposes in accordance with the provisions of the Convention.

Article XI

Any State Party may propose amendments to this Convention. Amendments shall enter into force for each State Party accepting the amendments upon their acceptance by a majority of the States Parties to the Convention and thereafter for each remaining State Party on the date of acceptance by it.

Article XII

Five years after the entry into force of this Convention, or earlier if it is requested by a majority of Parties to the Convention by submitting a proposal to this effect to the Depositary Governments, a conference of States Parties to the Convention shall be held at Geneva, Switzerland, to review the operation of the Convention, with a view to assuring that the purposes of Preamble and the provisions of the Convention, including the provisions concerning negotiations on chemical weapons, are being realized. Such review shall take into account any new scientific and technological developments relevant to the Convention.

Article XIII

1. This Convention shall be of unlimited duration.

2. Each State Party to this Convention shall in exercising its national sovereignty have the right to withdraw from the Convention if it decides that extraordinary events, related to the subject matter of the Convention, have jeopardized the supreme interests of its country. It shall give notice of such withdrawal to all other States Parties to the Convention and to United Nations Security Council three months in advance. Such notice shall include a statement of the extraordinary events it regards as having jeopardized its supreme interests.

Article XIV

1. This Convention shall be open to all States for signature. Any State which does not sign the Convention before its entry into force in accordance with paragraph 3 of this Article, may accede to it at any time.

2. This Convention shall be subject to ratification and instrument of accession shall be deposited with the Government of the Union of Soviet Socialist Republics, the United Kingdom of Great Britain and Northern Ireland and the United States of America, which are hereby designated the Depositary Gov-

ernments.

3. This Convention shall enter into force after the deposit of Instruments of Ratification by twenty-two Governments, including the Government s designated as Depositaries of the Convention.

4. For States whose Instruments of Ratification or accession are deposited subsequent to the entry into force of this Convention, it shall enter into force on the date of the deposit of their Instruments of Ratification or accession.

5. The Depositary Governments shall promptly inform all signatory and acceding states of the date of each signature, the date of deposit of each Instrument of Ratification or of accession and the date of the entry into force of this Convention, and of the receipt of other notices.

6. This Convention shall be registered by the Depositary Governments pursuant to Article 102 of the Charter of the United Nations.

Article XV

This Convention, the Chinese, English, French, Russian and Spanish texts of which are equally authentic, shall be deposited in the archives of the Depositary Governments. Duly certied copies of the Convention shall be transmitted by the Depositary Governments to the Governments of the signatory and acceding States

IN WITNESS WHEREOF the undersigned, duly authorized, have signed this Convention.

DONE in triplicate, at ...., this............day of............, ...

REMARKS BY THE EDITOR

While the Geneva Protocol prohibits the use of Biological or Toxin weapons, the BW Convention of 1972 prohibits their production, possession etc. The states adhering to the BW Convention are not necessarily parties to the Geneva Protocol. Some parties to the Geneva Protocol also have reserved the right to use such weapons against those not parties to the Protocol and use in response to use by the engaging states.

India is a signatory of both Geneva Protocol 1925 and BW Convention 1972.

TREATY BANNING NUCLEAR-WEAPON TESTS IN THE ATMOSPHERE, IN OUTER SPACE AND UNDER WATER

Done at Moscow August 5, 1963

US Ratification deposited October 10, 1963

Entered into force October 10, 1963

The Governments of United States of America, the United Kingdom of Great Britain and Northern Ireland, and the Union of Soviet Socialist Republics, hereinafter referred to as the "Original Parties",

Proclaiming as their principal aim the speediest possible achievement of an agreement on general and complete disarmament under strict international control in accordance with the objectives of the United Nations which would put an end to the armaments race and eliminate the incentive to the production and testing of all kinds of weapons, including nuclear weapons,

Seeking to achieve the discontinuance of all test explosions of nuclear weapons for all time, determined to continue negotiations to this end, and desiring to put an end to the contamination of man's environment by radioactive substances,

Have agreed as follows:

Article I

1. Each of the Parties to this Treaty undertakes to prohibit, to prevent, and not to carry out any nuclear-weapon test explosion, at any place under its jurisdiction or control:

   (a) In the atmosphere; beyond its limits, including outer space; or under water, including territorial waters or high seas; or

   (b) In any other environment if such explosion causes radioactive debris to be present outside the territorial limits of the State under whose jurisdiction or control such explosion is conducted. It is understood in this connection that the provisions of this paragraph are without prejudice to the conclusion of a treaty resulting in the permanent banning of all nuclear test explosions, including all such explosions underground, the conclusion of which, as the Parties have stated in the Preamble to this Treaty, they seek to achieve.

2. Each of the Parties to this Treaty undertakes furthermore to refrain from causing, encouraging, or in any way participating in, the carrying out of any nuclear weapon test explosion, or any other nuclear explosion, anywhere which would take place in any of the environments described, or have the effect referred to, in paragraph 1 of this Article.

Article II

1. Any Party may propose amendments to this Treaty. The text of any proposed amendment shall be submitted to the Depositary Governments which shall circulate it to all Parties to this Treaty. Thereafter, if requested to do so by one-third or more of the Parties, the Depositary Governments shall convene a conference, to which they shall invite all of the Parties, to consider such amendment.

2. Any amendments to this Treaty must be approved by a majority of the votes of all Parties to this Treaty, including the votes of all of the Original Parties. The amendment shall enter into force for all Parties upon the deposit of instrument of ratification of all of the Original Parties.

Article III

1. This Treaty shall be open to all states for signature. Any State which does not sign this Treaty before its entry into force in accordance with paragraph 3 of this Article may accede to it at any time.

2. This Treaty shall be subject to ratification by signatory States. Instruments of ratification and instruments of accession shall be deposited with the Governments of the Original Parties—the United States of America, the United Kingdom of Great Britain and Northern Ireland, and the Union of Soviet Socialist Republics—which are hereby designated the Depositary Governments.

3. This Treaty shall enter into force after its ratification by all the Original Parties and the deposit of their instruments of ratification or accession.

4. For States whose instruments of ratification or accession are deposited sub-

sequent to the entry into force of this Treaty, it shall enter into force on the date of the deposit of their instruments of ratification or accession.

5. The Depositary Governments shall promptly inform all signatory and acceding States of the date of each signature, the date of its entry into force, and the date of receipt of any requests for conferences or other notices.

6. This Treaty shall be registered by the Depositary Governments pursuant to Article 102 of the Charter of the United Nations.

Article IV

This Treaty shall be of unlimited duration.

Each Party shall in exercising its national sovereignty have the right to withdraw from the Treaty if it decides that extraordinary events, related to the subject matter of this Treaty, have jeopardized the supreme interests of its country. It shall give notice of such withdrawal to all other Parties to the Treaty three months in advance.

Article V

This Treaty, of which the English and Russian texts are equally authentic, shall be deposited in the archives of the Depositary Governments. Duly certified copies of this Treaty shall be transmitted by the Depositary Governments to the Governments of the signatory and acceding States.

IN WITNESS WHEREOF the undersigned, duly authorised, have signed this Treaty.

Done in triplicate at the city of Moscow the fth day of August, one thousand nine hundred and sixty-three.

For the Government of the United States of America	For the Government of the United Kingdom of Great Britain and Northern Ireland	For the Government of the Union of Soviet Socialist Republics
Sd.	Sd.	Sd.

TREATY ON THE NON-PROLIFERATION OF THE NUCLEAR WEAPONS (NPT) SIGNED AT LONDON, MOSCOW, AND WASHINGTON JULY 1, 1968

(Entered into force March 5, 1970)

The States concluding this treaty, hereinafter referred to as the "Parties to the Treaty"

Considering the devastation that would be visited upon all mankind by a nuclear war and the consequent need to make every effort to avert the danger of such a war and measures to safeguard the security of the peoples, Believing that the proliferation of nuclear-weapons would seriously enhance the danger of nuclear war,

In conformity with resolution of the United Nations General Assembly calling for the conclusion of an agreement on the prevention of wider dissemination of nuclear weapons,

Undertaking to cooperate in facilitating the application of International Atomic Energy Agency safeguards on peaceful nuclear activities,

Expressing their support for research, development and other efforts to further the application of, within the frame work of the International Atomic Energy Agency safeguards system, the principle of safeguarding effectively the flow of source and special fissionable materials by use of instruments and other techniques at certain strategic points,

Affirming the principle that the benefit of peaceful applications of nuclear technology, including any technological by-products which may be derived by nuclear-weapons states from the development of nuclear explosive devices, should be available for peaceful purposes to all parties to the treaty, whether nuclear-weapons or non-nuclear-weapons states,

Convinced that, in furtherance of this principle, all Parties to the treaty are entitled to participation in the fullest possible exchange of scientic information for, and to contribute alone or in co-operation with other states to, the further development of the applications of atomic energy for peaceful purposes.

Declaring their intention to achieve at the earliest possible date the cessation of nuclear arms race and to undertake effective measures in the direction of nuclear disarmament,

Urging the co-operation of all states in the attainment of this objective, Recalling the determination expressed by the Parties to the 1963 Treaty banning nuclear weapon tests in the atmosphere, in the outer space and under water in its Preamble to seek to achieve the discontinuance of all test explosions of nuclear weapons for all times and to continue negotiations to this end,

Desiring to further the erasing of the international tension and the strengthening of trust between States in order to facilitate the cessation of the manufacture of nuclear weapons, the liquidation of all their existing nuclear stockpiles, and the elimination from national arsenal of nuclear weapons and the means of their delivery pursuant to a treaty on general and complete disarmament under strict and effective international control,

Recalling that, in accordance with the Charter of the United Nations, States must refrain in their international relations from the threat or use of force against the territorial integrity or political independence of any States, or in any other manner inconsistent with the Purpose of the United Nations, and that the establishment and international peace and security are to be promoted with the least diversion for armaments of the world's human and economic resources,

Have agreed as follows:

Article I

Each nuclear-weapon State Party to the Treaty undertakes not to transfer to any recipient whatsoever nuclear weapons or other nuclear explosive devices or control over such weapons or explosive devices directly or indirectly; and not in any way to assist, encourage, or induce any non-nuclear-weapon State to manufacture or otherwise acquire nuclear weapons or nuclear explosive devices, or control over such weapons or explosive devices.

Article II

Each non-nuclear-weapon State Party to the Treaty undertakes not to receive the transfer from any transferor whatsoever of nuclear weapons or other nuclear explosive devices or of control over such weapons or explosive devices directly, or indirectly; nor to manufacture or otherwise acquire nuclear-weapons or other nuclear explosive devices; and not to seek or receive any assistance in the manufacture of nuclear weapons or other nuclear explosive devices.

Article III

1. Each non-nuclear-weapon State Party to the Treaty undertakes to accept safeguards, as set forth in an agreement to be negotiated and concluded with the International Atomic Energy Agency in accordance with the statute of the International Atomic Energy Agency and the Agency's safeguard system for the exclusive purpose of verification of the fullment of its obligations assumed under this Treaty with a view to preventing diversion of nuclear explosive devices. Procedures for the safeguards required by this article shall be followed with respect to source or special fissionable material whether it is being produced, processed or used in any principal nuclear facility or is outside any such facility. The safeguards required by this article shall be applied on all sources or special fissionable material in all peaceful nuclear activities within the territory of such state, under its jurisdiction, or carried out under its control anywhere.

2. Each state party to the Treaty undertakes not to provide:

   (a) Source or special fissionable material, or

   (b) Equipment or material especially designed or prepared for the processing, use or production of special fissionable material, to any non-nuclear-weapon State for peaceful purposes, unless the source or special fissionable material shall be subject to the safeguards required by this article.

3. The safeguards required by this article shall be implemented in a manner designed to comply with article IV of this Treaty, and to avoid hampering the economic or Technological development of the Parties or international co-operation in the field of peaceful nuclear activities, international exchange of nuclear activities, including the international exchange of nuclear material and

equipment for the processing, use or production of nuclear material for peaceful purposes in accordance with the provisions of this article and the principle of safeguarding set forth in the Preamble of the Treaty.

4. Non-nuclear weapon States Party to the Treaty shall conclude agreements with the International Atomic Energy Agency to meet the requirements of this article either individually or together with other States in accordance with the statute of International Atomic Energy Agency. Negotiations of such agreements shall commence within 180 days from the original entry into force of this Treaty. For states depositing their Instruments of Ratication or accession after the 180 days period, negotiation of such agreements shall commence not later than the date of such deposit. Such agreements shall enter into force not later than eighteen months after the date of initiation of negotiations.

Article IV

1. Nothing in this Treaty Shall be interpreted as affecting the inalienable right of all Parties to the T reaty to develop research, production and use of nuclear energy for peaceful purposes without discrimination and in conformity with Articles I and II of this Treaty.

2. All the Parties to the treaty undertake to facilitate, and have the right to participate in, the fullest possible exchange of equipment, materials and scientific and technological information for the peaceful uses of nuclear energy. Parties to the Treaty in a position to do so shall also cooperate in contributing alone or together with other States or international organizations to the further development of applications of nuclear energy for peaceful purposes, specially in the territories of non-nuclear-weapon States Party to the Treaty, with due consideration for the needs of the developing areas of the world.

Article V

Each Party to the Treaty undertakes to take appropriate measures to ensure that, in accordance with this Treaty, under appropriate international observation and through appropriate international procedures, potential benefits from any peaceful application of nuclear explosions will be made available to non-nuclear-weapon States Party to the Treaty on a non-discriminatory basis and that the charge to such Parties for the explosive devices used will be as low as possible and exclude any charges for research and development. Non-nuclear-weapon States Party to the Treaty shall be able to obtain such benefits, pursuant to special international agreement or agreements, through an appropriate international body with adequate representation of non-nuclear-weapon States. Negotiations on this subject shall commence as soon as possible after the Treaty enters into force. Non-nuclear weapon States Party to the Treaty so desiring may also obtain such benefits pursuant to bilateral agreements.

Article VI

Each of the Parties to the Treaty undertakes to pursue negotiations in good faith on effective measures relating to cessation of nuclear arms race at an early date and to nuclear disarmament, and on a treaty on general and complete disarmament, under strict effective international control.

Article VII

Nothing in this Treaty affects the right of any group of states to conclude regional treaties in order to assure the total absence of nuclear weapons in their respective territories.

Article VIII

1. Any Party to the Treaty may propose amendments to this Treaty. The text of any proposed amendment shall be submitted to the Depositary Governments which shall circulate it to all Parties to the Treaty. There- upon if requested to do so by one-third or more of the Parties to the Treaty, the Depositary Governments shall convene a conference, to which they shall invite all the Parties to the Treaty, to consider such an amendment.

2. Any amendments to this Treaty must be approved by a majority of the votes of all Parties to the Treaty, including the votes of all nuclear weapon States Party to the Treaty and all other Parties which, on the date the amendment is circulated, are members of the Board of Governors of the International Atomic Energy Agency. The amendment shall enter into force for each Party that deposits its Instrument ofRatification of the amendment. Upon the deposit of such Instrument of Ratification by a majority of all the Parties, including the Instrument of Ratification of all nuclear weapon States Party to the Treaty and

all other Parties which, on the date the amendment is circulated, are members of the board of Governors of the International Atomic Energy Agency. Therefore, it shall enter into force for any other Party upon the deposit of the Instrument of Ratification of the amendment.

3. Five years after the entry into force of this Treaty, a conference of Parties to the Treaty shall be held in Geneva, Switzerland, in order to review the operation of this Treaty with a view to assuring that the purpose of the Preamble and the provisions of the Treaty are being realised. An interval of five years thereafter, a majority of the Parties to the Treaty may obtain, by submitting a proposal to this effect to the Deposit ary Governments the convening of further conferences with the same objective of reviewing the operation of the Treaty.

Article IX

1. This Treaty shall be open to all States for signature. Any State which does not sign the Treaty before its entry into force in accordance with paragraph 3 of this Article may accede to it at any time.

2. This Treaty shall be subject to ratification by signatory States. Instruments of Ratification and Instruments of accession shall be deposited with the Governments of the United Kingdom of Great Britain and Northern Ireland, the Union of Soviet Socialist Republics and the United States of America, which are hereby designated the Depositary Governments.

3. This Treaty shall enter into force after its ratification by the states, the Governments of which are designated Depositaries of the Treaty, and forty other states signatory to this Treaty and the Deposit of their Instruments of Ratification. For the purpose of this Treaty, a nuclear weapon state is one which has manufactured and exploded a nuclear weapon or other nuclear explosive device prior to January 1, 1967.

4. For the States whose Instruments of Ratification or accession are deposited subsequent to the entry into force of this Treaty, it shall enter into force on the date of the deposit of their Instruments of Ratification or accession.

5. The Depositary Governments shall promptly inform all signatory and acceding States of the date of each signature, the date of deposit of each signature, the date of deposit of each Instrument of Ratification or of accession, the

date of entry into force of this Treaty, and the date of receiptof any requests for convening a conference or other notices.

6. This Treaty shall be registered by the Depositary Governments pursuant to Article 102 of the Charter of the United Nations.

Article X

1. Each Party shall in exercising its national sovereignty have the right to withdraw from the T reaty if it decides that extraordinary events related to the subject matter of this Treaty, have jeopardized the supreme interests of its country. It shall give notice of such withdrawal to all other Parties to the Treaty and to United Nations Security Council three months in advance. Such notice shall include a statement of the extraordinary events it regards as having jeopardized its supreme interests.

2. Twenty five years after the entry into force of this Treaty, a conference shall be convened to decide whether the Treaty shall continue in force indefinitely, or shall be extended for an additional fixed period or periods. This decision shall be taken by a majority of the Parties to the Treaty.

Article XI

This Treaty, the English, Russian, French, Spanish and Chinese texts of which are equally authentic, shall be deposited in the archives of the Depositary Governments. Duly certified copies of this Treaty shall be transmitted by the Depositary Governments to the Governments of the signatory and acceding States.

IN WITNESS WHEREOF the undersigned, duly authorized, have signed this Treaty.

Done in triplicate, at the cities of London, Moscow and Washington, the first day of July, one thousand nine hundred and sixty eight.

Sd.

REMARK BY THE EDITOR

The Treaty is reviewed every five years. Among other important decisions, the Treaty has been extended indefinitely during the 1995 Review.

BRIEF DESCRIPTION OF COMPREHENSIVE TEST BAN TREATY (CTBT)

The concept of Comprehensive Test Ban can be traced to the Partial Test Ban Treaty (PTBT) signed in 1963. India is a signatory to PTBT, which allows only underground nuclear testing. The draft CTBT has seventeen articles, two annexes and a protocol with two annexes and aims at complete ban on nuclear explosions of any kind and refrains the States Parties from causing, encouraging or in any way participating in carrying out any type of nuclear explosion. CTBT aims at limiting the horizontal proliferation of nuclear weapons and would ensure the pre-eminence of the nuclear weapons states in future.

All States Parties to the Treaty will be members of the 'organisation'. There shall be:

(a) a Conference of the States Parties represented by each State Party. This shall be the principal organ of the organisation to oversee the compli- ance of the Treaty.

(b) an Executive Council shall be the executive organ of the Conference and shall comprise of:

(i) 10 States Parties from Africa,

(ii) 7 States Parties from Eastern Europe,

(iii) 9 States Parties from Latin America and Carribean countries,

(iv) 7 States Parties from Middle East and South Asia,

(v) 10 States Parties from America and Europe,

(vi) 8 States Parties from SE Asia, the Pacic and the Far East.

(c) a Technical Secretariat under a Director General and technical staff appointed by the Conference.

Article IV lays down the Verification Regime which comprises of an international monitoring system, consultation and clarification, on site inspections, and confidence building measures. Article V lays down redress and compliance including sanctions.

India has not signed the Treaty as it bans only explosive testing and keeps the laboratory testing, sub critical testing and computer simulation out of its preview. India also insisted that such a treaty should be linked to a time bound global nuclear disarmament schedule. The Treaty also ignores the security compulsions of India.

On 10 September 1996, a resolution on a draft similar to the CTBT was passed in the UN General Assembly with an overwhelming majority. India voted against the resolution.

BRIEF DESCRIPTION OF FISSILE MATERIAL CUT-OFF TREATY (FMCT)

In December 1993, the UN General Assembly adopted, by consensus, calling for negotiation for a "non discriminatory, multilateral effectively veriable treaty banning the production of fissile material for nuclear weapons or other nuclear explosive devices." In March 1995, the Geneva-based Conference on Disarmament (CD) agreed to a mandate to begin negotiations on FMCT.

No progress has been made so far due to dispute over the scope and linkage with disarmament, amongst the nuclear weapons states, the non- nuclear-weapons States parties to the NPT and the nuclear capable states. The most basic issues that will have to be negotiated at the CD will relate to:

• The existing stocks of the fissile material and other nuclear explosive devices with the nuclear-weapons States (NWS).

• Extension into the NWS of the international safeguards as for non- nuclear-weapons States in the NPT.

• Separation and stockpiling by some countries of huge quantities of directly weapon-usable plutonium for non-weapon purposes.

The proposed treaty in the present form and intention is another instrument which aims to curtail the proliferation of the nuclear weapons and retain the pre-eminence of the nuclear-weapons States. The Treaty does not address the issue of complete nuclear disarmament.

BRIEF DESCRIPTION OF MISSILE TECHNOLOGY CONTROL REGIME (MTCR)

In April 1987 the United States, Canada, France, West Germany, Italy, Japan and United Kingdom created the MTCR to restrict the proliferation of missiles and missile technology. The MTCR is the only multilateral missile non-proliferation regime. It is a voluntary arrangement and not an agreement or a treaty amongst the countries not wanting missile proliferation. In 1993 the MTCR guidelines were expanded to include missiles and unmanned air vehicles with a range of 300 kilometers and capable of delivering a payload of 500 kilograms or a weapon of mass destruction. The guidelines are sensitive as the ballistic missile and space launch vehicle technology are virtually identical.

EXTRACT OF CHEMICAL WEAPONS CONVENTION, 1997 (CWC)

1. **Important definitions.**

   (a) *Chemical Weapons*. Chemicals, any Precursor and any other equipment in use with the weapon system directly or indirectly.

   (b) *Old Chemical Weapons*. Pre 1925 weapons, and weapons of 1925–46 vintage which are unfit for use.

   (c) *Abandoned Chemical Weapons*. Chemical weapons including old chemical weapons, abandoned by a state after 01 Jun 25 on the territory of another state w/o the consent of the latter.

   (d) *Chemical Weapon Production Facility*. Self-explanatory. Certain dual use chemicals may be produced/stored but would be subject to inspection.

2. CWC entered into force in April 97. Organisation for Prohibition of Chemical Weapons (OPCW) was also put into place simultaneously. Salient features of the Convention are as follows:

   (a) Each State Party is to undertake never to develop, produce, otherwise acquire, stockpile or retain chemical weapons or transfer, directly or indirectly chemical weapons to any other State.

   (b) Never to use chemical weapons.

   (c) Never to engage in any military preparations to use chemical weapons.

   (d) Never to assist/encourage/induce in any way, or to engage in any activity prohibited to a State Party under this Convention.

   (e) Each State Party to destroy all Chemical Weapons and chemical weapon producing facilities under its control within a period of 10 years (2007).

(f) Each state will declare (has declared) the quantity and location of chemical weapons including Old and Abandoned Chemical Weapons.

(g) Each state will also declare the destructions plan and submit progress to OPCW periodically.

(h) Each state will also enact law to prevent production etc of Chemical Weapons.

3. **Organisation.**

(a) *Location*. The Hague

(b) *Components.*

(i) Conference of the States Parties (Principal Organ).

(ii) The Executive Council (41 members on the principle of rotation).

(iii) Technical Secretariat (to assist Conference of States Parties and Executive Council).

Procedure

4. In case of a doubt about non-compliance of the Convention, an inspection may be ordered by the Executive Council after following a laid down procedure as given at Article IX of the Convention. The procedure in brief is as follows:

(a) A State Party has the right to request the Executive Council to assist in clarifying any situation which may be considered ambiguous or which gives rise to a concern about the possible non-compliance of another State Party with this Convention. The Executive Council shall provide appropriate information in its possession relevant to such a concern.

(b) A State Party also has the right to request the Executive Council to obtain clarication from another State Party on any situation which may be considered ambiguous or which gives rise to a concern about its possible non-compliance with this Convention. In such a case, the following procedure shall be adopted:

(i) The Executive Council shall forward the request for clarification to the State Party concerned within 24 hours after its receipt.

(ii) The requested State Party shall provide the clarification to the Executive Council within 10 days after the receipt of the request.

(iii) The Executive Council shall take note of the clarification and forward it to the requesting State Party within 24 hours after its receipt.

(iv) If the requesting State Party deems the clarification to be inadequate, it shall have the right to request the Executive Council to obtain from the requested State Party further clarication.

(v) For the purpose of obtaining further clarification, the Executive Council may call on the Directo r-General of OPCW to establish a group of experts from the Technical Secretariat who shall submit a factual report to the Executive Council.

(vi) If the requesting State Party considers the clarification obtained to be unsatisfactory, it shall have the right to request a special session of the Executive Council which may recommend any measure it deems appropriate to resolve the situation.

(c) If the doubt o r concern of a State Party about a possible non-compliance has not been resolved within 60 days after the submission of the request for clarification to the Executive Council, or it believes its doubts warrant urgent consideration, notwithstanding its right to request a Challenge Inspection, it may request a Special Session of the Conference of the State Parties.

(d) **Challenge Inspection**.

(i) Each State Party has the right to request an on-site Challenge Inspection of any facility or location in the territory or in any other place under the jurisdiction or control of any other State Party for the sole purpose of clarifying and resolving any questions concerning possible non-compliance with the provisions of this Convention, and to have this inspection conducted anywhere without delay by an inspection team designated by the Director- General and in accordance with the Verification Annexure.

(ii) Each State Party is under the obligation to keep the inspection request within the scope of this Convention and to provide in the inspection request all appropriate information on the basis of which a concern has arisen regarding possible non-compliance with this Convention as specified in the Verification Annexure. Each State Party shall refrain from unfounded inspection requests, care being taken to avoid abuse. The Challenge Inspection shall be carried out for the sole purpose of determining facts relating to the possible non-compliance with this Convention.

(iii) Pursuant to a request for a Challenge Inspection of a facility or location, and in accordance with the procedures provided for in the Verification Annexure, the inspected State Party shall be obliged to make every reasonable effort to demonstrate its compliance with this Convention and, to this end, to enable the inspection team to full its mandate.

(e) The final report shall contain the factual findings as well as an assessment by the inspection team of the degree and nature of access and cooperation granted for the satisfactory implementation of the Challenge Inspection. The Director-General shall promptly transmit the final report of the inspection team to the requesting State Party, to the inspected State Party, to the Executive Council and to all other States Parties.

(f) The Executive Council shall, in accordance with its powers and functions, review the final report of the inspection team as soon as it is presented, and address any concerns as to:

(i) Whether any non-compliance has occurred.

(ii) Whether the request had been within the scope of the Convention; and

(iii) Whether the right to request a Challenge Inspection had been abused.

5. In India, Cabinet Secretary is the co-ordinating authority. Chairman National Authority for Chemical Weapons Convention functions under him.

6. Only USA, Russia, South Korea and India have accepted existence of Chemical Weapons on their soil.

AMENDED PROTOCOL ON PROHIBITIONS OR RESTRICTIONS ON THE USE OF MINES, BOOBY-TRAPS AND OTHER DEVICES (AMENDED PROTOCOL II) ANNEXED TO THE CONVENTION ON PROHIBITIONS OR RESTRICTIONS ON THE USE OF CERTAIN CONVENTIONAL WEAPONS WHICH MAY BE DEEMED TO BE EXCESSIVELY INJURIOUS OR TO HAVE INDISCRIMINATE EFFECTS

Article 1—Scope of Application

1. This Protocol relates to the use on land of the mines, booby-traps and other devices, defined herein, including mines laid to interdict beaches, waterway crossings or river crossings, but does not apply to the use of anti-ship mines at sea or in inland waterways.

2. This Protocol shall apply, in addition to situations referred to in Article 1 of this Convention, to situations referred to in Article 3 common to the Geneva Conventions of 12 Augusts 1949. This Protocol shall not apply to situations of internal disturbances and tensions such as riots, isolated and sporadic acts of violence and other acts of a similar nature, as not being armed conflicts.

3. In case of armed conflicts not of an international character in the territory of one of the High Contracting Parties, each party to the conflict shall be bound to apply the prohibitions and restrictions of this Protocol.

4. Nothing in this Protocol shall be involved for the purpose of affecting the sovereignty of a State or the responsibility of the Government, by all legitimate means, to maintain or re establish law and order in the State or to defend the national unity and territorial integrity of the State.

5. Nothing in this Protocol shall be invoked as a justification for intervening, directly or indirectly, for any reason whatever, in the armed conflict or in the internal or external affairs of the High Contracting Party in the territory of which that conflict occurs.

6. The application of the provisions of this Protocol to parties to a conflict, which are not high Contracting Parties that have accepted this Protocol, shall not change their legal status or the legal status of a disputed territory, either explicitly or implicitly.

Article 2—Definitions

For the purpose of this Protocol:

1. **"Mine"** means a munition placed under, on or near the ground or other surface area and designed to be exploded by the presence, proximity or contact of a person or vehicle.
2. **"Remotely-delivered mine"** means a mine not directly emplaced but delivered by artillery, missile, rocket, mortar, or similar means, or dropped from an aircraft. Mines delivered from a land-based system from less than 500 meters are not considered to be "remotely delivered", provided that they are used in accordance with Article 5 and other relevant Articles of this Protocol.
3. **"Anti-personnel mine"** means a mine primarily designed to be exploded by presence, proximity or contact of a person and that will incapacitate, injure or kill one or more persons.
4. **"Booby-trap"** means any device or material which is designed, constructed, or adapted to kill or injure, and which functions unexpectedly when a person disturbs or approaches apparently harmless object or performs an apparently safe act.
5. **"Other devices"** means manually-emplaced munitions and devices including improvised explosive devices designed to kill, injure or damage and which are actuated manually, by remote control or automatically after a lapse of time.
6. **"Military objective"** means, so far as objects are concerned, any object which by its nature, location, purpose or use makes an effective contribution to military action and whose total or partial destruction, capture or neutralization in the circumstances ruling at the time, offers a definite military advantage.
7. **"Civilian objects"** are all objects which are not military objectives as defined

in paragraph 6 of this Article.

8. **"Minefield"** is a defined area in which mines have been emplaced and "mined area" is an area, which is dangerous due to the presence of mines. "Phoney minefield" means an area free of mines that simulates a minefield. The term "minefield" includes phoney minefields.

9. **"Recording"** means a physical, administrative and technical operation designed to obtain, for the purpose of registration in official records, all available information facilitating the location of minefields, mined areas, mines, booby-traps and other devices.

10. **"Self-destruction mechanism"** means an incorporated or externally attached automatically-functioning mechanism which secures the destruction of the munitions into which it is incorporated or to which it is attached.

11. **"Self-neutralization mechanism"** means an incorporated automatically-functioning mechanism which renders inoperable the munitions into which it is incorporated.

12. **"Self-deactivating"** means automatically rendering a munition inoperable by means of the irreversible exhaustion of a component, for example, a battery, that is essential to the operation of the munition.

13. **"Remote control"** means control by commands from distance.

14. **"Anti-handling device"** means a device intended to protect a mine and which is part of, linked to, attached to or placed under the mine and which activates when an attempt is made to tamper with the mine.

15. **"Transfer"** involves, in addition to the physical movement of mines into or from national territory, the transfer of title to and control over the mines, but does not involve the transfer of territory containing emplaced mines.

Article 3—General Restrictions on the Use of Mines, Booby-Traps and Other Devices

1. This article applies to:

   (a) Mines.

(b) Booby-Traps.

(c) Other Devices.

2. Each High Contracting Party or party to a conflict is in accordance with the provisions of this Protocol, responsible for all mines, booby-traps, and other devices employed by it and undertakes to clear, remove, destroy or maintain them as specied in Article 10 of this Protocol.

3. It is prohibited in all circumstances to use any mine, booby-trap or other device which is designed or of a nature to cause superfluous injury or unnecessary suffering.

4. Weapons to which this Article applies shall strictly comply with the standards and limitations specified in the Technical Annex with respect to each particular category.

5. It is prohibited to use mines, booby-traps or other devices which employ a mechanism or device specically designed to detonate the munitions by the presence of commonly available mine detectors as a result of their magnetic or other non-contact influence during normal use in detection operations.

6. It is prohibited to use a self deactivating mine equipped with an anti- handling device that is designed in such a manner that the anti-handling device is capable of functioning after the mines has ceased to be capable of functioning.

7. It is prohibited in all circumstances to direct weapons to which this Article applies, either in offence, defence or by way of reprisals, against the civilian population as such or against individual civilians or civilian objects.

8. The indiscriminate use of weapons to which this Article applies is prohibited. Indiscriminate use is any placement of such weapons:

   (a) Which is not on, or directed against a military objective. In case of doubt as to whether an object which is normally dedicated to civilian purposes, such as a place of worship, a house or other dwelling or a school, is being used to make an effective contribution to military action, it shall be presumed not to be so used; or

   (b) Which employs a method or means of delivery which cannot be directed at a specic military objective; or

(c) Which may be expected to cause incidental loss of civilian life, injury to civilians, damage to civilian objects, or a combination thereof, which would be excessive in relation to the concrete and direct military advantage anticipated.

9. Several clearly separated and distinct military objectives located in a city, town, village or other area containing a similar concentration of civilians or civilian objects are not to be treated as a single military objective.

10. All feasible precautions shall be taken to protect civilians from the effects of weapons to which this Article applies. Feasible precautions are those precautions which are practicable or practically possible taking into account all circumstances ruling at the time, including humanitarian and military considerations. These circumstances include, but are not limited to:

(a) The short and long-term effect of mines upon the local civilian population for the duration of the minefield.

(b) Possible measures to protect civilians (for example, fencing, signs, warning and monitoring).

(c) The availability and feasibility of using alternatives; and

(d) The short and long-term military requirements for a minefield.

11. Effective advance warning shall be given of any emplacement of mines, booby-traps and other devices which may affect the civilian population, unless circumstances do not permit.

Article 4—Restrictions on the use of Anti-Personnel Mines

1. It is prohibited to use anti-personnel mines which are not detectable, specified in paragraph 2 of the Technical Annex.

Article 5—Restrictions on the use of Anti-Personnel Mines Other Than Remotely Delivered Mines

1. This Article applies to anti-personnel mines other than remotely-delivered mines.

2. It is prohibited to use weapons to which this Article applies which are not in compliance with the provisions on self-destruction and self- deactivation in the Technical Annex, unless:

   (a) Such weapons are placed within a perimeter-marked area which is monitored by military personnel and protected by fencing or other means, to ensure the effective exclusion of civilians from the area. The marking must be of a distinct and durable character and must at least be visible to a person who is about to enter the perimeter- marked area; and

   (b) Such weapons are cleared before the area is abandoned, unless the area is turned over to the forces of another state which accepts responsibility for the maintenance of the protections required by this Article and the subsequent clearance of those weapons.

3. A party to a conflict is relieved from further compliance with the provisions of sub-paragraphs 2(a) and 2(b) of this Article only if such compliance is not feasible due to forcible loss of control of the area as a result of enemy action, including situations where direct enemy military action makes it impossible to comply. If that party regains control of the area, it shall resume compliance with the provisions of sub-paragraphs 2 (a) and 2 (b) of this Article.

4. If the forces of a party to a conflict gain control of an area in which weapons to which this Article applies have been laid, such forces shall, to the maximum extent feasible, maintain and, if necessary, establish the protections required by this Articles until such weapons have been cleared.

5. All feasible measures shall be taken to prevent the unauthorized removal, defacement, destruction or concealment of any device, system o r material used to establish the perimeter of a perimeter-marked area.

6. Weapons to which this Article applies which propel fragments in a horizontal arc of less than 90 degrees and which are placed on or above the ground may be used without the measures provided for in sub-paragraph 2 (a) of this Article for a maximum period of 72 hours, if:

   (a) They are located in immediate proximity to the military unit that emplaced them; and

(b) The area is monitored by military personnel to ensure the effective exclusion of civilians.

Article 6—Restrictions on the Use of Remotely Delivered Mines

1. It is prohibited to use remotely-delivered mines unless they are recorded in accordance with sub-paragraph 1(b) of the Technical Annex.

2. It is prohibited to use remotely-delivered anti-personnel mines which are not in compliance with the provisions on self-destruction and self- deactivation in the Technical Annex.

3. It is prohibited to use remotely-delivered mines other than anti- personnel mines, unless, to the extent feasible, they are equipped with an effective self-destruction or self-neutralization mechanism and have a back-up self-deactivation feature, which is designed so that mine will no longer function as mine when the mine no longer serves the military purpose for which it was placed in position.

4. Effective advance warning shall be given of any delivery or dropping of remotely-delivered mines which may affect the civilian population, unless circumstances do not permit.

Article 7—Prohibitions on the Use of Booby-Traps and Other Devices

1. Without prejudice to the rules of international law applicable in armed conflict relating to treachery and perfidy, it is prohibited in all circumstances to use booby-traps and other devices which are in any way attached to or associated with:

   (a) Internationally recognized protective emblems, signs or signals;

   (b) Sick, wounded or dead persons;

   (c) Burial or cremation sites or graves;

   (d) Medical facilities, medical equipment, medical supplies or medical transportation;

   (e) Children's toys or other portable objects or products specially designed for the feeding, health, hygiene, clothing or education of children;

(f) Food or drink;

(g) Kitchen utensils or appliances except in military establishments, military locations or military supply depots;

(h) Objects clearly of a religious nature;

(j) Historic monuments, works of art or places of worship which constitute the cultural or spiritual heritage of people; or

(k) Animals or their carcasses.

2. It is prohibited to use booby-traps or other devices in the form of apparently harmless portable objects which are specifically designed and constructed to contain explosive material.

3. Without prejudice to the provisions of Article 3, it is prohibited to use weapons to which the Article applies in any city, town, village or other area containing a similar concentration of civilians in which combat between ground forces is not taking place or does not appear to be imminent, unless either:

(a) They are placed on or in the close vicinity of a military objective; or

(b) Measures are taken to protect civilians from their effects, for example, the posting of warning sentries, the issuing of warnings or the provision of fences.

Article 8—Transfers

1. In order to promote the purposes of this Protocol, each High Contracting Party:

(a) Undertakes not to transfer any mine the use of which is prohibited by this Protocol;

(b) Undertakes not to transfer any mine to any recipient other than a State or a State agency authorized to receive such transfer;

(c) Undertakes to exercise restraint in the transfer of any mine the use of which is restricted by this Protocol. In particular, each High Contracting Party undertakes not to transfer any anti-personnel mines to States which are not bound by this Protocol, unless the recipient State agrees to apply this protocol; and

(d) Undertakes to ensure that any transfer in accordance with this Article takes in full compliance, by both the transferring and the recipient State, with the relevant provisions of this Protocol and the applicable norms of international humanitarian law.

2. In the event that High Contracting Party declares that it will defer compliance with specic provisions on the use of certain mines, as provided for in the Technical Annex, sub-paragraph 1(a) of this Article shall how ever apply to such mines.

3. All High Contracting Parties, pending the entry into force of this Protocol, will refrain from any actions which would be inconsistent with sub- paragraph 1(a) of this Article.

Article 9—Recording and Use of Information on Minefields, Mined Areas, Mines, Booby-Traps and Other Devices

1. All information concerning minefields, mined areas, mines, booby-traps and other devices shall be recorded in accordance with the provisions of the Technical Annex.

2. All such records shall be retained by the parties to a conflict, who shall, without delay after the cessation of active hostilities, take all necessary and appropriate measures, including the use of such information, to protect civilians from the effects of minefields, mined areas, mines, booby-traps and other devices in areas under their control. At the same time, they shall also make available to the other party or parties to the conflict and to the Secretary-General of the United Nations all such in- formation in their possession concerning minefields, mined areas, mines, booby-traps and other devices laid by them in areas no longer under their control; provided, however, subject to reciprocity, where the forces of a party to a conflict are in the territory of an adverse party, either party may withhold such information from the Secretary- General and the other party, to the extent that security

interests require such withholding, until neither party is in the territory of the other. In the latter case, the information withheld shall be disclosed as soon as those security interests permit. Wherever possible, the parties to the conflict shall seek, by mutual agreement, to provide for the release of such information at the earliest possible time in a manner consistent with the security interests of each party.

3. This Article is without prejudice to the provisions of Articles 10 and 12 of this Protocol.

Article 10—Removal of Minefields, Mined Areas, Mines, Booby-Traps and Other Devices and International Cooperation

1. Without delay after the cessation of active hostilities, all minefields, mined areas, mines, booby-traps and other devices shall be cleared, removed, destroyed or maintained in accordance with Article 3 and paragraph 2 of Article 5 of this Protocol.

2. High Contracting Parties and parties to a conflict bear such responsibility with respect to minefields, mined areas, mines, booby-traps and other devices in areas under their control.

3. With respect to minefields, mined areas, mines, booby-traps and other devices laid by a party in areas over which it no longer exercises control, such party shall provide to the party in control of the area pursuant to paragraph 2 of this Article, to the extent permitted by such party, technical and material assistance necessary to full such responsibility.

4. At all times necessary, the parties shall endeavour to reach agreement, both among themselves and, where appropriate, with other States and with international organizations, on the provision of technical and material assistance, including, in appropriate circumstances, the undertaking of joint operations necessary to full such responsibilities.

Article 11—Technological Cooperation and Assistance

1. Each High Contracting Party undertakes to facilitate and shall have the right to participate in the fullest possible exchange of equipment, material and scientific and technological information concerning the implementation of this Pro-

tocol and means of mine clearance. In particular, High Contracting Parties shall not impose undue restrictions on the provision of mine clearance equipment and related technological information for humanitarian purposes.

2. Each High Contracting Party undertakes to provide information to the database on mine clearance established within the United Nations System, especially information concerning various means and technologies of mine clearance, and list s of experts, expert agencies or national points of contact on mine clearance.

3. Each High Contracting Party in a position to do so shall provide assistance for mine clearance through the United Nations System, other international bodies or on a bilateral basis, or contribute to the United Nations Voluntary Trust Fund for Assistance in Mine Clearance.

4. Requests by High Contracting Parties for assistance, substantiated by relevant information, may be submitted to the United Nations, to other appropriate bodies or to other States. These requests may be submitted to the Secretary-General of the United Nations, who shall transmit them to all High Contracting Parties and to relevant international organizations.

5. In the case of requests to the United Nations, the Secretary-General of the United Nations, within the resources available to the Secretary- General of the United Nations, may take appropriate steps to assess the situation and in cooperation with the requesting High Contracting Party, determine the appropriate provision of assistance in mine clearance or implementation of the Protocol. The Secretary-General may also report to High Contracting Parties on any such assessment as well as on the type and scope of assistance required.

6. Without prejudice to their constitutional and other legal provisions, the High Contracting Parties undertake to cooperate and transfer technology to facilitate the implementation of the relevant prohibitions and restrictions set out in this Protocol.

7. Each High Contracting Party has the right to seek and receive technical assistance, where appropriate, from another High Contracting Party on specific relevant technology, other than weapons technology, as necessary and

feasible, with a view to reducing any period of deferral for which provision is made in the Technical Annex.

Article 12—Protection from the Effects of Minefields, Mined Areas, Mines, Booby-Traps and Other Devices

1. **Application.**

(a) With the exception of the forces and missions referred to in sub paragraph 2 (a) (i) of this Article, this Article applies only to missions which are performing functions in an area with the consent of the High Contracting Party on whose territory the functions are performed.

(b) The application of the provisions of this Article to parties to a conflict which are not High Contracting Parties shall not change their legal status or the legal status of a disputed territory, either explicitly or implicitly.

(c) The provisions of this Article are without prejudice to existing international humanitarian law, or other international instruments as applicable, or decisions by the Security Council of the United Nations which provide for a higher level of protection to personnel functioning in accordance with this Article.

2. **Peace-Keeping and Certain Other Forces and Missions.**

(a) This paragraph applies to:

(i) Any United Nations force or mission performing peace-keeping, observation or similar functions in any area in accordance with the Charter of the United Nations.

(ii) Any mission established pursuant to Chapter VIII of the Charter of the United Nations and performing its functions in the area of a conflict.

(b) Each High Contracting Party or party to a conflict, if so requested by the head of a force or mission to which this paragraph applies, shall:

(i) So far as it is able, take such measures as are necessary to protect the force or mission from the effects of mines, booby-traps and other devices in any area under its control;

(ii) If necessary in order effectively to protect such personnel, remove or render harmless, so far it is able, all mines, booby-traps and other devices in that area; and

(iii) Inform the head of the force or mission of the location of all known minefields, mined areas, mines, booby-traps and other devices in the area in which the force or mission is performing its functions and, so far as is feasible, make available to the head of the force or mission all information in its possession concerning such minefields, mined areas, mines, booby-traps and other devices.

3. **Humanitarian and Fact-Finding Missions of the United Nations System.**

(a) This paragraph applies to any humanitarian fact-finding mission of the United Nations System.

(b) Each High Contracting Party or Party to a conflict, if so requested by the head of a mission to which this paragraph applies, shall:

(i) Provide the personnel of the mission with the protections set out in sub-paragraph 2 (b) (i) of this Article, and

(ii) If access to or through any place under its control is necessary for the performance of the mission and in order to provide the personnel of the mission with safe passage to or through that place:

(aa) Unless on-going hostilities prevent, inform the head of the mission of a safe route to that place if such information is available, or

(ab) If information identifying a safe route is not provided in accordance with sub-paragraph (aa) so far as is necessary and feasible, clear a lane through minefields.

4. **Missions of the International Committee of the Red Cross.**

(a) This paragraph applies to any mission of the International Committee of the Red Cross performing functions with the consent of the host State or States as provided for by the Geneva Conventions of 12 August 1949 and, where applicable, their Additional Protocols.

(b) Each High Contracting Party or Party to a conflict, if so requested by the head of a mission to which this paragraph applies, shall:

(i) Provide the personnel of the mission with the protections set out in sub-paragraph 2 (b) (i) of this Article; and

(ii) Take the measures set out in sub-paragraph 3 (b) (ii) of this Article.

5. **Other Humanitarian Missions and Missions of Enquiry.**

(a) In so far as paragraph 2, 3 and 4 above do not apply to them, this paragraph applies to the following missions when they are performing functions in the area of a conflict or to assist the victims of a conflict:

(i) Any Humanitarian mission of a National Red Cross or Red Crescent Society or of their International Federation;

(ii) Any mission of an impartial humanitarian organization, including any impartial humanitarian demining mission; and

(iii) Any mission of enquiry established pursuant to the provisions of the Geneva Conventions of 12 August 1949 and, where applicable, their Additional Protocols.

(b) Each High Contracting Party or party to a conflict, if so requested by the head of a mission to which this paragraph applied, shall, so far as is feasible:

(i) Provide the personnel of the mission with the protections set out in sub-paragraph 2 (b) (i) of this Article; and

(ii) Take the measures set out in sub-paragraph 3 (b) (ii) of this Article.

6. **Confidentiality.** All information provided in confidence pursuant to this Article shall be treated by the recipient in strict confidence and shall not be released outside the force or mission concerned without the express authorization of the provider of the information.

7. **Respect for Laws and Regulations.** Without prejudice to such privileges and immunities as they may enjoy or to the requirements of their duties, personnel participating in the forces and missions referred to in this Article shall:

(a) Respect the laws and regulations of the host State; and

(b) Refrain from any action or activity incompatible with the impartial and international nature of their duties.

Article 13—Consultations of High Contracting Parties

1. The High Contracting Parties undertake to consult and cooperate with each other on all issues related to the operation of this Protocol. For this purpose, a conference of High Contracting Parties shall be held annually.

2. Participation in the annual conferences shall be determined by their agreed Rules of Procedure.

3. The work of the conference shall include:

(a) Review of the operation and status of this Protocol;

(b) Consideration of matters arising from reports by High Contracting Parties according to paragraph 4 of this Article;

(c) Preparation for review conferences; and

(d) Consideration of the development of technologies to protect civilians against indiscriminate effects of mines.

4. The High Contracting Parties shall provide annual reports to the Depositary, who shall circulate them to all High Contracting Parties in advance of the Conference, on any of the following matters:

(a) Dissemination of information on this Protocol to their armed forces and to the civilian population;

(b) Mine clearance and rehabilitation programmes;

(c) Steps taken to meet technical requirements of this Protocol and any other relevant information pertaining thereto;

(d) Legislation related to this Protocol;

(e) Measures taken on international technical information exchange, on international cooperation on mine clearance, and on technical cooperation and assistance; and

(f) Other relevant matters.

5. The cost of the Conference of High Contracting parties shall be borne by the High Contracting Parties and states not parties participating in the work of the Conference, in accordance with the United Nations scale of assessment adjusted appropriately.

Article 14—Compliance

1. Each High Contracting Party shall take appropriate steps, including legislative and other measures, to prevent and suppress violations of this Protocol by persons on territory under its jurisdiction or control.

2. The measures envisaged in paragraph 1 of this Article include appropriate measures to ensure the imposition of penal sanctions against persons who, in relation to an armed conflict and contrary to the provisions of this Protocol, willfully kill or cause serious injury to civilians and to bring such persons to justice.

3. Each High Contracting Party shall also require that its armed forces issue relevant military instructions and operating procedures and that armed forces personnel receive training commensurate with their duties and responsibilities to comply with the provisions of this Protocol.

4. The High Contracting Parties undertake to consult each other and to cooperate with each other bilaterally, through the Secretary-General of the United Nations or through other appropriate international procedures, to resolve any problems that may arise with regard to the interpretation and application of the provisions of this Protocol.

TECHNICAL ANNEX

1. **Recording.**

(a) Recording of the location of mines other than remotely delivered mines, minefields, mined areas, booby-traps and other devices shall be carried out in accordance with the following provisions:

(i) The location of the mines other than remotely-delivered mines, minefields, mined areas, booby-traps and other devices shall be specied by relation to the coordinates of at least two reference points and the estimated dimensions of the area containing these weapons in relation to those reference points;

(ii) Maps, diagrams or other records shall be made in such a way so as to indicate the location of minefields, mined areas, booby-traps and other devices in relation to reference points, and these records shall also indicate their perimeters and extent;

(iii) For purposes of detection and clearance of mines, booby-traps and other devices, maps, diagrams or other records shall contain complete information on the type, number, emplacing method, type of fuse and life time, date and time of laying, anti-handling devices (if any) and other relevant information on all these weapons laid. Whenever feasible the minefield record shall show the exact location of every mine, except in row minefields where the row location is sufficient. The precise location and operating mechanism of each booby-trap laid shall be individually recorded.

(b) The estimated location and area of remotely-delivered mines shall be specied by coordinates ofreference points (normally corner points) and shall be ascertained and when feasible marked on the ground at the earliest opportunity. The total number and type of mines laid, the date and time of laying and the self-destruction time periods shall also be recorded.

(c) Copies of records shall be held at a level of command sufficient to guarantee their safety as far as possible.

(d) The use of mines produced after the entry into force of this Protocol is prohibited unless they are marked in English or in the respective national language or languages with the following information:

(i) Name of the country of origin;

(ii) Month and year of production; and

(iii) Serial number or lot number.

The marking should be visible, legible, durable and resistant to environmental effects, as far as possible.

2. **Specification on Detectability.**

(a) With respect to anti-personnel mines produced after 1 January 1997, such mines shall incorporate in their construction a material or device that enables the mine to be detected by commonly-available technical mine detection equipment and provides a response signal equivalent to a signal from 8 grams or more of iron in a single coherent mass.

(b) With respect to anti-personnel mines produced before 1 January 1997, such mines shall either incorporate in their construction, or have attached prior to their emplacement, in a manner not easily removable, a material or device that enables the mine to be detected by commonly-available technical mine detection equipment and provides a response signal equivalent to a signal from 8 grams or more of iron in a single coherent mass.

(c) In the event that a High Contracting Party determines that it cannot immediately comply with sub-paragraph (b), it may declare at the time of its notication of consent to be bound by this Protocol that it will defer compliance with sub-paragraph (b) for a period not to exceed 9 years from the entry into force of this Protocol. In the mean time it shall, to the extent feasible, minimize the use of anti-personnel mines that do not so comply.

3. **Specifications on Self-destruction and Self-deactivation.**

(a) All remotely-delivered anti-personnel mines shall be designed and constructed so that no more than 10% of activated mines will fail to self-destruct within 30 days after emplacement, and each mine shall have a back-up self-deactivation feature designed and constructed so that, in combination with the self-destruction mechanism, no more than one in one thousand activated mines will function as a mine 120 days after emplacement.

(b) All non-remotely delivered anti-personnel mines, used outside marked areas, as dened in Article 5 of this Protocol, shall comply with the requirement for self-destruction and self-deactivation stated in subparagraph (a).

(c) In the event that a High Contracting Party determines that it cannot immediately comply with sub-paragraphs (a) and/or (b), it may declare at the time of its notication of consent to be bound by this Protocol, that it will, with respect to mines produced prior to the entry into force of this Protocol defer compliance with sub- paragraphs (a) and/or (b) for period not to exceed 9 years from the entry into force of this Protocol.

(d) During this period of deferral, the High Contracting Party shall:

(i) Undertake to minimize, to the extent feasible, the use of anti- personnel mines that do not so comply, and

(ii) With respect to remotely-delivered anti-personnel mines, comply with either the requirements for self-destruction or the requirements for self-deactivation and, with respect to other anti- personnel mines comply with at least the requirements for self-deactivation.

4. **International Signs for Minefields and Mined Areas.** Signs similar to the example attached and as specied below* shall be utilized in the marking of minefields and mined areas to ensure their visibility and recognition by the civilian population:

(a) **Size and Shape:** a triangle or square not smaller than 28 centimeters (11 inches) by 20 centimeters (7.9 inches) for a triangle, and 15 centimeters (6 inches) per side for a square;

(b) **Colour:** red or orange with a yellow reflecting border;

(c) **Symbol:** the symbol illustrated in the attachment or an alternative readily

---

*Example not attached.

recognizable in the area in which the sign is to be displayed as identifying a dangerous area;

(d) **Language:** the sign should contain the word **"mines"** in one of the six official languages of the Convention (Arabic, Chinese, English, French, Russian and Spanish) and the languages prevalent in that area;

(e) **Spacing:** signs should be placed around the minefield or mined area at a distance sufficient to ensure their visibility at any point by a civilian approaching the area.

REMARKS BY THE EDITOR

India is a signatory to the UN 'Convention On Prohibitions or Restrictions on the use of Certain Conventional Weapons which may be Deemed to be Excessively Injurious or to have Indiscriminate Effects.'

There are four Protocols in the Convention:

(a) **Protocol I -** Non-Detectable fragments.

(b) **Protocol II -** Mines, Booby Traps and Other Devices.

(c) **Protocol III -** Incendiary Weapons.

(d) **Protocol IV -** Blinding Lasers.

Large number of civilian and non-combatant casualties due to indiscriminate use of land mines by warring factions in strife-torn countries caused growing concern and led to the review of Protocol II. The Amended Protocol II came into force in Dec 1998. India has ratified the original Convention in 1984 and Amended Protocol II in July 1999.

EXTRACT OF OTTAWA CONVENTION

The Convention consists of 22 articles and completely prohibits use, stock- piling, production and transfer of APLs and their destruction. The Convention obliges States Parties to destroy stocks of APLs in four years and destroy emplaced mines in their areas within 10 years. With 40 countries ratifying it, the convention has become international law on 17 Sep 98. India, Pak, China, Russia, USA and Finland are some countries who have not ratified the Convention.

INDIA'S NUCLEAR DOCTRINE

Table of Contents

1. PREAMBLE.

1.1 The use of nuclear weapons in particular as well as other weapons of mass destruction constitutes the gravest threat to humanity and to peace and stability in the international system. Unlike the other two categories of weapons of mass destruction, biological and chemical weapons which have been outlawed by international treaties, nuclear weapons remain instruments for national and collective security, the possession of which on a selective basis has been sought to be legitimised through permanent extension of the Nuclear Non-Proliferation Treaty [NPT] in May 1995. Nuclear-weapon states have asserted that they will continue to rely on nuclear weapons with some of them adopting policies to use them even in a non-nuclear context. These developments amount to virtual abandonment of nuclear disarmament. This is a serious setback to the struggle of the international community to abolish weapons of mass destruction.

1.2 India's primary objective is to achieve economic, political, social, scientific and technological development within a peaceful and democratic framework. This requires an environment of durable peace and insurance against potential risks to peace and stability. It will be India's endeavour to proceed towards this overall objective in cooperation with the global democratic trends and to play a constructive role in advancing the international system toward a just, peaceful and equitable order.

1.3 Autonomy of decision making in the development process and strategic matters is an inalienable democratic right of the Indian people. India will strenuously guard this right in a world where nuclear weapons for select few are sought to be legitimised for an indefinite future and where there is growing complexity and frequency in the use of force for political purposes.

1.4 India's security is an integral component of its development process.India continuously aims at promoting an everexpanding area of peace and stability around it so that developmental priorities can be pursued without disruption.

1.5 However, the very existence of offensive doctrines pertaining to the first use of nuclear weapons and insistence of some nuclear-weapon states on the legitimacy of their use even against non-nuclear-weapon countries constitute a threat to peace, stability and sovereignty of States.

1.6 This document outlines the broad principles for the development, deployment and employment of India's nuclear forces. Details of policy and strategy concerning force structures, deployment and employment of nuclear forces will flow from this framework and will be laid down separately and kept under constant review.

2. OBJECTIVES.

2.1 In the absence of global nuclear disarmament, India's strategic interests require effective, credible nuclear deterrence and adequate retaliatory capability should deterrence fail. This is consistent with the UN Charter, which sanctions the right of self-defence.

2.2 The requirements of deterrence should be carefully weighed in the design of Indian nuclear forces and in the strategy to provide for a level of capability consistent with maximum credibility, survivability, effectiveness, safety and security.

2.3 India shall pursue a doctrine of 'credible minimum nuclear deterrence'. In this policy of "retaliation only", the survivability of our arsenal is critical. This is a dynamic concept related to the strategic environment, technological imperatives and the needs of national security. The actual size, components, deployment and employment of nuclear forces will be decided in the light of these factors. India's peace-time posture aimed at convincing any potential aggressor that:

(a) Any threat of use of nuclear weapons against India shall invoke measures to counter the threat, and

(b) Any nuclear attack on India and its forces shall result in punitive retaliation with nuclear weapons to inflict damage unacceptable to the aggressor.

2.4 The fundamental purpose of Indian nuclear weapons is to deter the use and threat of use of nuclear weapons by any State or entity against India and its forces. India will not be the first to initiate a nuclear strike, but will respond with punitive retaliation should deterrence fail.

2.5 India will not resort to the use or threat of use of nuclear weapons against States which do not possess nuclear weapons, or are not aligned with nuclear weapon powers.

2.6 Deterrence requires that India maintain:

(a) Sufficient, survivable and operationally prepared nuclear forces,

(b) A robust command and control system,

(c) Effective intelligence and early warning capabilities, and

(d) Comprehensive planning and training for operations in line with the strategy, and

(e) The will to employ nuclear forces and weapons.

2.7 Highly effective conventional military capabilities shall be maintained to raise the threshold of outbreak both of conventional military conflict as well as that of threat or use of nuclear weapons.

3. NUCLEAR FORCES.

3.1 India's nuclear forces will be effective, enduring, diverse, exible, and responsive to the requirements in accordance with the concept of credible minimum deterrence. These forces will be based on a triad of aircraft, mobile land-based missiles and sea-based assets in keeping with the objectives outlined above. Survivability of the forces will be enhanced by a combination of multiple redundant systems, mobility, dispersion and deception.

3.2 The doctrine envisages assured capability to shift from peace-time deployment to fully employable forces in the shortest possible time, and ability to retaliate effectively even in a case of signicant degradation by hostile strikes.

4. CREDIBILITY AND SURVIVABILITY.

The following principles are central to India's nuclear deterrent:

4.1 Credibility: Any adversary must know that India can and will retaliate with sufficient nuclear weapons to inflict destruction and punishment that the aggressor will find unacceptable if nuclear weapons are used against India and its forces.

4.2 Effectiveness: The efficacy of India's nuclear deterrent be maximised through synergy among all element s involving reliability, timelines, accuracy and weight of the attack.

4.3 Survivability:

(i) India's nuclear forces and their command and control shall be organised for very high survivability against surprise attacks and for rapid punitive response. They shall be designed and deployed to ensure survival against a first strike and to endure repetitive attrition attempts with adequate retaliatory capabilities for a punishing strike, which would be unacceptable to the aggressor.

(ii) Procedures for the continuity of nuclear command and control shall ensure a continuing capability to effectively employ nuclear weapons.

5. COMMAND AND CONTROL.

5.1 Nuclear weapons shall be tightly controlled and released for use at the highest political level. The authority to release nuclear weapons for use resides in person of the Prime Minister of India, or the designated successor(s).

5.2 An effective and survivable command and control system with requisite exibility and responsiveness shall be in place. An integrated operational plan, or a series of sequential plans, predicated on strategic objectives and a targeting policy shall form part of the system.

5.3 For effective employment the unity of command and control of nuclear forces including dual capable delivery systems shall be ensured.

5.4 The survivability of the nuclear arsenal and effective command, control, communications, computing, intelligence and information (C4I2) systems shall be ensured.

5.5 The Indian defence forces shall be in a position to, execute operations in an NBC environment with minimal degradation.

5.6 Space based and other assets shall be created to provide early warning, communications, damage/detonation assessment and as far as possible.

6. SECURITY AND SAFETY.

6.1 Security: Extraordinary precautions shall be taken to ensure that nuclear weapons, their manufacture, transportation and storage are fully guarded against possible theft, loss, sabotage, damage or unauthorized access or use.

6.2 Safety: Safety is an absolute requirement and tamper proof procedures and systems shall be instituted to ensure that unauthorized or inadvertent activation/use of nuclear weapons does not take place and risks of accidents are avoided.

6.3 Disaster Control: India shall develop an appropriate disaster control system capable of handling the unique requirements of potential incidents involving nuclear weapons and material.

7. RESEARCH AND DEVELOPMENT.

7.1 India should step up efforts in research and development to keep up with technological advances in this field.

7.2 While India is committed to maintain the deployment of a deterrent which is both minimum and credible, it will not accept any restraints on building its R&D capability.

8. DISARMAMENT AND ARMS CONTROL.

8.1 Global, veriable and non-discriminatory nuclear disarmament is a national security object. India shall continue its efforts to achieve the goal of a nuclear-weapon free world at an early date.

8.2 Since no first use of nuclear weapons is India's basic commitment, every effort shall be made to persuade other states possessing nuclear weapons to join an international treaty banning first use.

8.3 Having provided unqualied negative security assurances, India shall work for internationally binding negative security assurances by nuclear weapons states to non-nuclear weapon States.

8.4 Nuclear arms control measures shall be sought as part of national security policy to reduce potential threats and to protect our own capability and effectiveness.

8.5 In view of the very high destructive potential of nuclear weapons, appropriate nuclear risk reduction and confidence building measures shall be sought, negotiated and instituted.

AGREEMENT FOR COOPERATION BETWEEN THE GOVERNMENT OF INDIA AND THE GOVERNMENT OF THE UNITED STATES OF AMERICA CONCERNING PEACEFUL USES OF NUCLEAR ENERGY

India - U.S. Joint Statement

Washington, DC

July 18, 2005

Prime Minister Manmohan Singh and President Bush today declare their resolve to transform the relationship between their countries and est ablish a global partnership. As leaders of nations committed to the values of human freedom, democracy and rule of law , the new relationship between India and the United States will promote stability, democracy, prosperity and peace throughout the world. It will enhance our ability to work together to provide global leadership in areas of mutual concern and interest.

Building on their common values and interests, the two leaders resolve:

- To create an international environment conducive to promotion of democratic values, and to strengthen democratic practices in societies which wish to become more open and pluralistic.

- To combat terrorism relentlessly . They applaud the active and vigorous counterterrorism cooperation between the two countries and support more international efforts in this direction.Terrorism is a global scourge and the one we will fight everywhere. The two leaders strongly affirm their commitment to the conclusion by September of a UN comprehensive convention against international terrorism.

The Prime Minister's visit coincides with the completion of the Next Steps in Strategic Partnership (NSSP) initiative, launched in January 2004.The two leaders agree that this provides the basis for expanding bilateral activities and commerce in space, civil nuclear energy and dual-use technology.

Drawing on their mutual vision for the U.S.-India relationship, and our joint objectives as strong long-st anding democracies, the two leaders agree on the following:

FOR THE ECONOMY

• Revitalize the U.S.-India Economic Dialogue and launch a CEO Forum to harness private sector energy and ideas to deepen the bilateral economic relationship.

• Support and accelerate economic growth in both countries through greater trade, investment, and technology collaboration.

• Promote modernization of India's infrastructure as a prerequisite for the continued growth of the Indian economy. As India enhances its investment climate, opportunities for investment will increase.

• Launch a U.S.-India Knowledge Initiative on Agriculture focused on promoting teaching, research, service and commercial linkages.

FOR ENERGY AND THE ENVIRONMENT

• Strengthen energy security and promote the development of stable and efficient energy markets in India with a view to ensuring adequate, affordable energy supplies and conscious of the need for sustainable development. These issues will be addressed through the U.S.-India Energy Dialogue.

• Agree on the need to promote the imperatives of development and safeguarding the environment, commit to developing and deploying cleaner, more efficient, affordable, and diversified energy technologies.

FOR DEMOCRACY AND DEVELOPMENT

• Develop and support, through the new U.S.-India Global Democracy Initiative in countries that seek such assistance, institutions and resources that strengthen the foundations that make democracies credible and effective. India and the U.S. will work together to strengthen democratic practices and capacities and contribute to the new U.N. Democracy Fund.

• Commit to strengthen cooperation and combat HIV/AIDs at a global level through an initiative that mobilizes private sector and government resources, knowledge, and expertise.

FOR NON-PROLIFERATION AND SECURITY

- Express satisfaction at the New Framework for the U.S.-India Defense Relationship as a basis for future cooperation, including in the field of defense technology.

- Commit to play a leading role in international efforts to prevent the proliferation of Weapons of Mass Destruction. The U.S. welcomed the adoption by India of legislation on WMD (Prevention of Unlawful Activities Bill).

- Launch a new U.S.-India Disaster Relief Initiative that builds on the experience of the Tsunami Core Group, to strengthen cooperation to prepare for and conduct disaster relief operations.

FOR HIGH-TECHNOLOGY AND SPACE

- Sign a Science and Technology Framework Agreement, building on the U.S.–India High-Technology Cooperation Group (HTCG), to provide for joint research and training, and the establishment of public-private partnerships.

- Build closer ties in space exploration, satellite navigation and launch, and in the commercial space arena through mechanisms such as the U.S.-India Working Group on Civil Space Cooperation.

- Building on the strengthened nonproliferation commitments undertaken in the NSSP, to remove certain Indian organizations from the Department of Commerce's Entity List.

Recognizing the significance of civilian nuclear energy for meeting growing global energy demands in a cleaner and more efficient manner, the two leaders discussed India's plans to develop its civilian nuclear energy program.

President Bush conveyed his appreciation to the Prime Minister over India's strong commitment to preventing WMD proliferation and stated that as a responsible state with advanced nuclear technology, India should acquire the same benefits and advantages as other such states. The President told the Prime Minister that he will work to achieve full civil nuclear energy cooperation with India as it realizes its goals of promoting nuclear power and achieving energy security. The President would also seek agreement from Congress to adjust U.S. laws and policies, and the United States will work with friends and allies to adjust international regimes to enable full civil nuclear energy cooperation and trade with India, including but not limited to expeditious consideration of fuel supplies for safeguarded nuclear reactors at Tarapur. In the meantime, the United States will encourage its partners to also consider this request expeditiously. India has expressed its interest in ITER and a willingness to contribute. The United States will consult with its partners considering India's participation. The United States will consult with the other participants in the Generation IV International Forum with a view toward India's inclusion.

The Prime Minister conveyed that for his part, India would reciprocally agree that it would be ready to assume the same responsibilities and practices and acquire the same benefits and advantages as other leading countries with advanced nuclear technology, such as the United States. These responsibilities and practices consist of identifying and separating civilian and military nuclear facilities and programs in a phased manner and filing a declaration regarding it s civilians facilities with the International Atomic Energy Agency (IAEA); taking a decision to place voluntarily its civilian nuclear facilities under IAEA safeguards; signing and adhering to an Additional Protocol with respect to civilian nuclear facilities; continuing India's unilateral moratorium on nuclear testing; working with the United States for the conclusion of a multilateral Fissile Material Cut Of Treaty; refraining from transfer of enrichment and reprocessing technologies to states that do not have them and supporting international efforts to limit their spread; and ensuring that the necessary steps have been taken to secure nuclear materials and technology through comprehensive export control legislation and through harmonization and adherence to Missile Technology Control Regime (MTCR) and Nuclear Suppliers Group (NSG) guidelines.

The President welcomed the Prime Minister's assurance. The two leaders agreed to establish a working group to undertake on a phased basis in the months ahead the necessary actions mentioned above to fulfill these commitments. The President and Prime Minister also agreed that they would review this progress when the President visits India in 2006.

The two leaders also reiterated their commitment that their countries would play a leading role in international efforts to prevent the proliferation of weapons of mass destruction, including nuclear, chemical, biological and radiological weapons.

In light of this closer relationship, and the recognition of India's growing role in enhancing regional and global security the Prime Minister and the President agree that international institutions must fully reflect changes in the global scenario that have taken place since 1945. The President reiterated his view that international institutions are going to have to adapt to reflect India's central and growing role. The two leaders state their expectations that India and the United States will strengthen their cooperation in global forums.

Prime Minister Manmohan Singh thanks President Bush for the warmth of his reception and the generosity of his hospitality. He extends an invitation to President Bush to visit India at his convenience and the President accepts that invitation.

AGREEMENT FOR COOPERATION BETWEEN THE GOVERNMENT OF INDIA AND THE GOVERNMENT OF THE UNITED STATES OF AMERICA CONCERNING PEACEFUL USES OF NUCLEAR ENERGY

AGREED TEXT

The Government of India and the Government of the United S tates of America, hereinafter referred to as the Parties,

RECOGNIZING the significance of civilian nuclear energy for meeting growing global energy demands in a cleaner and more efficient manner;

DESIRING to cooperate extensively in the full development and use of nuclear energy for peaceful purposes as a means of achieving energy securityon a stable, reliable and predictable basis;

WISHING to develop such cooperation on the basis of mutual respect for sovereignty, non-interference in each other's internal affairs, equality, mutual benefit, reciprocity and with due respect for each other's nuclear programmes;

DESIRING to establish the necessary legal framework and basis for cooperation concerning peaceful uses of nuclear energy;

AFFIRMING that cooperation under this Agreement is between two S tates possessing advanced nuclear technology, both Parties having the same benefits and advantages, both committed to preventing WMD proliferation;

NOTING the understandings expressed in the India - U.S. Joint S tatement of July 18, 2005 to enable full civil nuclear energy cooperation with India covering aspects of the associated nuclear fuel cycle;

AFFIRMING their support for the objectives of the InternationalAtomic Energy Agency (IAEA) and its safeguards system, as applicable to India and the United States of America, and its importance in ensuring that international cooperation in development and use of nuclear energy for peaceful purposes is carried out under arrangements that will not contribute to the proliferation of nuclear weapons or other nuclear explosive devices;

NOTING their respective commitments to safety and security of peaceful uses of nuclear energy, to adequate physical protection of nuclear material and effective national export controls;

MINDFUL that peaceful nuclear activities must be undertaken with a view to protecting the environment;

MINDFUL of their shared commitment to preventing the proliferation of weapons of mass destruction; and

DESIROUS of strengthening the strategic partnership between them;

Have agreed on the following:

ARTICLE 1 - DEFINITIONS

For the purposes of this Agreement:

(A) "By-product material" means any radioactive material (except special fissionable material) yielded in or made radioactive by exposure to the radiation incident to the process of producing or utilizing special fissionable material. By-product material shall not be subject to safeguards or any other form of verification under this Agreement, unless it has been decided otherwise by prior mutual agreement in writing between the two Parties.

(B) "Component" means a component part of equipment, or other item so designated by agreement of the Parties.

(C) "Conversion" means any of the normal operations in the nuclear fuel cycle, preceding fuel fabrication and excluding enrichment, by which uranium is transformed from one chemical form to another - for example, from uranium hexafluoride (UF6) to uranium dioxide (UO2) or from uranium oxide to metal.

(D) "Decommissioning" means the actions taken at the end of a facility's useful life to retire the facility from service in the manner that provides adequate protection for the health and safety of the decommissioning workers and the general public, and for the environment.These actions can range from closing down the facility and a minimal removal of nuclear material coupled with continuing maintenance and surveillance, to a complete removal of residual radioactivity in excess of levels acceptable for unrestricted use of the facility and its site.

(E) "Dual-Use Item" means a nuclear related item which has a technical use in both nuclear and non-nuclear applications.

(F) "Equipment" means any equipment in nuclear operation including reactor, reactor pressure vessel, reactor fuel charging and discharging equipment, reactor control rods, reactor pressure tubes, reactor primary coolant pumps, zirconium tubing, equipment for fuel fabrication and any other item so designated by the Parties.

(G) "High enriched uranium" means uranium enriched to twenty percent or greater in the isotope 235.

(H) "Information" means any information that is not in the public domain and is transferred in any form pursuant to this Agreement and so designated and documented in hard copy or digital form by mutual agreement by the Parties that it shall be subject to this Agreement, but will cease to be information whenever the Party transferring the information or any third party legitimately releases it into the public domain.

(I) "Low enriched uranium" means uranium enriched to less than twenty percent in the isotope 235.

(J) "Major critical component" means any part or group of parts essential to the operation of a sensitive nuclear facility or heavy water production facility.

(K) "Non-nuclear material" means heavy water, or any other material suitable for use in a reactor to slow down high velocity neutrons and increase the likelihood of further fission, as may be jointly designated by the appropriate authorities of the Parties.

(L) "Nuclear material" means (1) source material and (2) special fissionable material. "Source material" means uranium containing the mixture of isotopes occurring in nature; uranium depleted in the isotope 235; thorium; any of the foregoing in the form of metal, alloy, chemical compound, or concentrate; any other material containing one or more of the foregoing in such concentration as the Board of Governors of the IAEA shall from time to time determine; and such other materials as the Board of Governors of the IAEA may determine or as may be agreed by the appropriate authorities of both Parties. "Special fissionable material" means plutonium, uranium-233, uranium enriched in the isotope 233 or 235, any substance containing one or more of the foregoing, and such other substances as the Board of Governors of the IAEA may determine or as may be agreed by the appropriate authorities of both Parties. "S pecial fissionable material" does not include "source material"Any determination by the Board of Governors of the IAEA under Article XX of that Agency's Statute or otherwise that amends the list of materials considered to be "source material" or "special fissionable material" shall only have ef fect under this Agreement when both Parties to this Agreement have informed each other in writing that they accept such amendment.

(M) "Peaceful purposes" include the use of information, nuclear material, equipment or components in such fields as research, power generation, medicine, agriculture and industry, but do not include use in, research on, or development of any nuclear explosive device or any other military purpose. Provision of power for a military base drawn from any power network, production of radio isotopes to be used for medical purposes in military environment for diagnostics, therapy and sterility assurance, and other similar purposes as may be mutually agreed by the Parties shall not be regarded as military purpose.

(N) "Person" means any individual or any entity subject to the territorial jurisdiction of either Party but does not include the Parties.

(O) "Reactor" means any apparatus, other than a nuclear weapon or other nuclear explosive device, in which a self-sustaining fission chain reaction is maintained by utilizing uranium, plutonium, or thorium or any combination thereof.

(P) "Sensitive nuclear facility" means any facility designed or used primarily for uranium enrichment, reprocessing of nuclear fuel, or fabrication of nuclear fuel containing plutonium.

(Q) "Sensitive nuclear technology" means any information that is not in the public domain and that is important to the design, construction, fabrication, operation, or maintenance of any sensitive nuclear facility, or other such information that may be so designated by agreement of the Parties.

ARTICLE 2 - SCOPE OF COOPERATION

1. The Parties shall cooperate in the use of nuclear energy for peaceful purposes in accordance with the provisions of this Agreement. Each Party shall implement this Agreement in accordance with its respective applicable treaties, national

laws, regulations, and license requirements concerning the use of nuclear energy for peaceful purposes.

2. The purpose of the Agreement being to enable full civil nuclear energy cooperation between the Parties, the Parties may pursue cooperation in all relevant areas to include, but not limited to, the following:

   a. Advanced nuclear energy research and development in such areas as may be agreed between the Parties;

   b. Nuclear safety matters of mutual interest and competence, as set out in Article 3;

   c. Facilitation of exchange of scientists for visits, meetings, symposia and collaborative research;

   d. Full civil nuclear cooperation activities covering nuclear reactors and aspects of the associated nuclear fuel cycle including technology transfer on an industrial or commercial scale between the Parties or authorized persons;

   e. Development of a strategic reserve of nuclear fuel to guard against any disruption of supply over the lifetime of India's reactors;

   f. Advanced research and development in nuclear sciences including but not limited to biological research, medicine, agriculture and industry, environment and climate change;

   g. Supply between the Parties, whether for use by or for the benefit of the Parties or third countries, of nuclear material;

   h. Alteration in form or content of nuclear material as provided for in Article 6;

   i. Supply between the Parties of equipment, whether for use by or for the benefit of the Parties or third countries;

   j. Controlled thermonuclear fusion including in multilateral projects; and

   k. Other areas of mutual interest as may be agreed by the Parties.

3. Transfer of nuclear material, non-nuclear material, equipment, components and information under this Agreement may be undertaken directly between the Parties or through authorized persons. Such transfers shall be subject to this

Agreement and to such additional terms and conditions as may be agreed by the Parties. Nuclear material, non-nuclear material, equipment, component s and information transferred from the territory of one Party to the territory of the other Party, whether directly or through a third countrywill be regarded as having been transferred pursuant to this Agreement only upon confirmation, by the appropriate authority of the recipient Party to the appropriate authority of the supplier Party that such items both will be subject to the Agreement and have been received by the recipient Party.

4. The Parties affirm that the purpose of this Agreement is to provide for peaceful nuclear cooperation and not to af fect the unsafeguarded nuclear activities of either Party. Accordingly, nothing in this Agreement shall be interpreted as affecting the rights of the Parties to use for their own purposes nuclear material, non-nuclear material, equipment, component s, information or technology produced, acquired or developed by them independent of any nuclear material, non-nuclear material, equipment, component s, information or technology transferred to them pursuant to this Agreement. This Agreement shall be implemented in a manner so as not to hinder or otherwise interfere with any other activities involving the use of nuclear material, non-nuclear material, equipment, components, information or technology and military nuclear facilities produced, acquired or developed by them independent of this Agreement for their own purposes.

ARTICLE 3 - TRANSFER OF INFORMATION

1. Information concerning the use of nuclear energy for peaceful purposes may be transferred between the Parties.Transfers of information may be accomplished through reports, data banks and computer programs and any other means mutually agreed to by the Parties. Fields that may be covered include, but shall not be limited to, the following:

   a. Research, development, design, construction, operation, maintenance and use of reactors, reactor experiments, and decommissioning;

   b. The use of nuclear material in physical, chemical, radiological and biological research, medicine, agriculture and industry;

c. Fuel cycle activities to meet future world-wide civil nuclear energy needs, including multilateral approaches to which they are p arties for ensuring nuclear fuel supply and appropriate techniques for management of nuclear wastes;

d. Advanced research and development in nuclear science and technology;

e. Health, safety, and environmental considerations related to the foregoing;

f. Assessments of the role nuclear power may play in national energy plans;

g. Codes, regulations and standards for the nuclear industry;

h. Research on controlled thermonuclear fusion including bilateral activities and contributions toward multilateral project s such as the International Thermonuclear Experimental Reactor (ITER); and

i. Any other field mutually agreed to by the Parties.

2. Cooperation pursuant to this Article may include, but is not limited to, training, exchange of personnel, meetings, exchange of samples, materials and instruments for experiment al purposes and a balanced p articipation in joint studies and projects.

3. This Agreement does not require the transfer of any information regarding matters outside the scope of this Agreement, or information that the Parties are not permitted under their respective treaties, national laws, or regulations to transfer

4. Restricted Data, as defined by each Party , shall not be transferred under this Agreement.

ARTICLE 4 - NUCLEAR TRADE

1. The Parties shall facilit ate nuclear trade between themselves in the mutual interests of their respective industry, utilities and consumers and also, where appropriate, trade between third countries and either Party of items obligated to the other Party. The Parties recognize that reliability of supplies is essential to ensure smooth and uninterrupted operation of nuclear facilities and that industry in both the Parties needs continuing reassurance that deliveries can be made on time in order to plan for the efficient operation of nuclear installations.

2. Authorizations, including export and import licenses as well as authorizations or consents to third parties, relating to trade, industrial operations or nuclear material movement should be consistent with the sound and efficient administration of this Agreement and should not be used to restrict trade. It is further agreed that if the relevant authority of the concerned Party considers that an application cannot be processed within a two month period it shall immediately upon request, provide reasoned information to the submitting Party. In the event of a refusal to authorize an application or a delay exceeding four months from the date of the first application the Party of the submitting persons or undertakings may call for urgent consultations under Article 13 of this Agreement, which shall take place at the earliest opportunity and in any case not later than 30 days after such a request.

ARTICLE 5 - TRANSFER OF NUCLEAR MATERIAL, NON-NUCLEAR MATERIAL, EQUIPMENT, COMPONENTS AND RELATED TECHNOLOGY

1. Nuclear material, non-nuclear material, equipment and components may be transferred for applications consistent with this Agreement. Any special fissionable material transferred under this Agreement shall be low enriched uranium, except as provided in paragraph 5.

2. Sensitive nuclear technology, heavy water production technology, sensitive nuclear facilities, heavy water production facilities and major critical components of such facilities may be transferred under this Agreement pursuant to an amendment to this Agreement. Transfers of dual-use items that could be used in enrichment, reprocessing or heavy water production facilities will be subject to the Parties' respective applicable laws, regulations and license policies.

3. Natural or low enriched uranium may be transferred for use as fuel in reactor experiments and in reactors, for conversion or fabrication, or for such other purposes as may be agreed to by the Parties.

4. The quantity of nuclear material transferred under this Agreement shall be consistent with any of the following purposes: use in reactor experiments or the loading of reactors, the efficient and continuous conduct of such reactor experiments or operation of reactors for their lifetime, use as samples, standards, detectors, and targets, and the accomplishment of other purposes as may be agreed by the Parties.

5. Small quantities of special fissionable material may be transferred for use as samples, standards, detectors, and targets, and for such other purposes as the Parties may agree.

6. (a) The United States has conveyed its commitment to the reliable supply of fuel to India. Consistent with the July 18, 2005, Joint Statement, the United States has also reaffirmed its assurance to create the necessary conditions for India to have assured and full access to fuel for its reactors. As part of its implementation of the July 18, 2005, Joint Statement the United States is committed to seeking agreement from the U.S. Congress to amend its domestic laws and to work with friends and allies to adjust the practices of the Nuclear Suppliers Group to create the necessary conditions for India to obtain full access to the international fuel market, including reliable, uninterrupted and continual access to fuel supplies from firms in several nations.

(b) To further guard against any disruption of fuel supplies, the United States is prepared to take the following additional steps:

(i) The United States is willing to incorporate assurances regarding fuel supply in the bilateral U.S.-India agreement on peaceful uses of nuclear energy under Section 123 of the U.S. Atomic Energy Act, which would be submitted to the U.S. Congress.

(ii) The United States will join India in seeking to negotiate with the IAEA an India-specific fuel supply agreement.

(iii) The United States will support an Indian effort to develop a strategic reserve of nuclear fuel to guard against any disruption of supply over the lifetime of India's reactors.

(iv) If despite these arrangements, a disruption of fuel supplies to India occurs, the United States and India would jointly convene a group of friendly supplier countries to include countries such as Russia, France and the United Kingdom to pursue such measures as would restore fuel supply to India.

(c) In light of the above understandings with the United States, an India-specific safeguards agreement will be negotiated between India and the IAEA providing for safeguards to guard against withdrawal of safeguarded nuclear material from civilian use at any time as well as providing for corrective measures that India may take to ensure uninterrupted operation of its civilian nuclear reactors in the event of disruption of foreign fuel supplies. Taking this into account, India will place it s civilian nuclear facilities under India-specific safeguards in perpetuity and negotiate an appropriate safeguards agreement to this end with the IAEA.

ARTICLE 6 - NUCLEAR FUEL CYCLE ACTIVITIES

In keeping with their commitment to full civil nuclear cooperation, both Parties, as they do with other st ates with advanced nuclear technology , may carry out the following nuclear fuel cycle activities:

(i) Within the territorial jurisdiction of either Party, enrichment up to twenty percent in the isotope 235 of uranium transferred pursuant to this Agreement, as well as of uranium used in or produced through the use of equipment so transferred, may be carried out.

(ii) Irradiation within the territorial jurisdiction of either Party of plutonium, uranium-233, high enriched uranium and irradiated nuclear material transferred pursuant to this Agreement or used in or produced through the use of non-nuclear material, nuclear material or equipment so transferred may be carried out.

(iii) With a view to implementing full civil nuclear cooperation as envisioned in the Joint Statement of the Parties of July 18, 2005, the Parties grant each other consent to reprocess or otherwise alter in form or content nuclear material transferred pursuant to this Agreement and nuclear material and by-product material used in or produced through the use of nuclear material, non-nuclear material, or equipment so transferred. To bring these right s into ef fect, India will est ablish a new national reprocessing facility dedicated to reprocessing safeguarded nuclear material under IAEA safeguards and the Parties will agree on arrangements and procedures under which such reprocessing or other alteration in form or content will take place in this new facility Consultations on arrangements and procedures will begin within six months of a request by either Party and will be concluded within one year The Parties agree on the application of IAEA safeguards to all facilities concerned with the above activities. These arrangements and procedures shall include provisions with respect to physical protection standards set out in Article 8, storage standards set out in Article 7, and environmental protections set forth in Article 11 of this Agreement, and such other provisions as may be agreed by the Parties. Any special fissionable material that may be separated may only be utilized in national facilities under IAEA safeguards.

iv) Post-irradiation examination involving chemical dissolution or separation of irradiated nuclear material transferred pursuant to this Agreement or irradiated nuclear material used in or produced through the use of non-nuclear material, nuclear material or equipment so transferred may be carried out.

ARTICLE 7 - STORAGE AND RETRANSFERS

1. Plutonium and uranium 233 (except as either may be contained in irradiated fuel elements), and high enriched uranium, transferred pursuant to this Agreement or used in or produced through the use of material or equipment so transferred, may be stored in facilities that are at all times subject, as a minimum, to the levels of physical protection that are set out in IAEA document INFCIRC 225/ REV 4 as it may be revised and accepted by the Parties. Each Party shall record such facilities on a list, made available to the other Party. A Party's list shall be held confidential if that Party so requests. Either Party may make changes to its list by notifying the other Party in writing and receiving a written acknowledgement. Such acknowledgement shall be given no later than thirty days after the receipt of the notification and shall be limited to a statement that the notification has been received. If there are grounds to believe that the provisions of this sub-Article are not being fully complied with, immediate consultations may be called for Following upon such consultations, each Party shall ensure by means of such consultations that necessary remedial measures are taken immediately. Such measures shall be sufficient to restore the levels of physical protection referred to above at the facility in question. However, if the Party on whose territory the nuclear material in question is stored determines that such measures are not feasible, it will shift the nuclear material to another appropriate, listed facility it identifies.

2. Nuclear material, non-nuclear material, equipment, components, and information transferred pursuant to this Agreement and any special fissionable material produced through the use of nuclear material, non-nuclear material or equipment so transferred shall not be transferred or re-transferred to unauthorized persons or, unless the Parties agree, beyond the recipient Party's territorial jurisdiction.

ARTICLE 8 - PHYSICAL PROTECTION

1. Adequate physical protection shall be maintained with respect to nuclear material and equipment transferred pursuant to this Agreement and nuclear material used in or produced through the use of nuclear material, non-nuclear material or equipment so transferred.

2. To fulfill the requirement in paragraph 1, each Party shall apply measures in accordance with (i) levels of physical protection at least equivalent to the recommendations published in IAEA document INFCIRC/225/Rev.4 entitled "The Physical Protection of Nuclear Material and Nuclear Facilities," and in any subsequent revisions of that document agreed to by the Parties, and (ii) the provisions of the 1980 Convention on the Physical Protection of Nuclear Material and any amendments to the Convention that enter into force for both Parties.

3. The Parties will keep each other informed through diplomatic channels of those agencies or authorities having responsibility for ensuring that levels of physical protection for nuclear material in their territory or under their jurisdiction or control are adequately met and having responsibility for coordinating response and recovery operations in the event of unauthorized use or handling of material subject to this Article. The Parties will also keep each other informed through diplomatic channels of the designated points of contact within their national authorities to cooperate on matters of out-of-country transportation and other matters of mutual concern.

4. The provisions of this Article shall be implemented in such a manner as to avoid undue interference in the Parties' peaceful nuclear activities and so as to be consistent with prudent management practices required for the safe and economic conduct of their peaceful nuclear programs.

ARTICLE 9 - PEACEFUL USE

Nuclear material, equipment and components transferred pursuant to this Agreement and nuclear material and by-product material used in or produced through the use of any nuclear material, equipment, and components so transferred shall not be used by the recipient Party for any nuclear explosive device, for research on or development of any nuclear explosive device or for any military purpose.

ARTICLE 10 - IAEA SAFEGUARDS

1. Safeguards will be maintained with respect to all nuclear materials and equipment transferred pursuant to this Agreement, and with respect to all special fissionable material used in or produced through the use of such nuclear materials and equipment, so long as the material or equipment remains under the jurisdiction or control of the cooperating Party.

2. Taking into account Article 5.6 of this Agreement, India agrees that nuclear material and equipment transferred to India by the United States of America pursuant to this Agreement and any nuclear material used in or produced through the use of nuclear material, non-nuclear material, equipment or components so transferred shall be subject to safeguards in perpetuity in accordance with the India-specific Safeguards Agreement between India and the IAEA [*identifying data*] and an Additional Protocol, when in force.

3. Nuclear material and equipment transferred to the United States of America pursuant to this Agreement and any nuclear material used in or produced through the use of any nuclear material, non-nuclear material, equipment, or components so transferred shall be subject to the Agreement between the United States of America and the IAEA for the application of safeguards in the United States of America, done at Vienna November 18, 1977, which entered into force on December 9, 1980, and an Additional Protocol, when in force.

4. If the IAEA decides that the application of IAEA safeguards is no longer possible, the supplier and recipient should consult and agree on appropriate verification measures.

5. Each Party shall take such measures as are necessary to maintain and facilitate the application of IAEA safeguards in its respective territory provided for under this Article.

6. Each Party shall establish and maintain a system of accounting for and control of nuclear material transferred pursuant to this Agreement and nuclear material used in or produced through the use of any material, equipment, or component s so transferred. The procedures applicable to India shall be those set forth in the India-specific Safeguards Agreement referred to in Paragraph 2 of this Article.

7. Upon the request of either Party, the other Party shall report or permit the IAEA to report to the requesting Party on the status of all inventories of material subject to this Agreement.

8. The provisions of thisArticle shall be implemented in such a manner as to avoid hampering, delay, or undue interference in the Parties' peaceful nuclear activities and so as to be consistent with prudent management practices required for the safe and economic conduct of their peaceful nuclear programs.

ARTICLE 11 - ENVIRONMENTAL PROTECTION

The Parties shall cooperate in following the best practices for minimizing the impact on the environment from any radioactive, chemical or thermal contamination arising from peaceful nuclear activities under this Agreement and in related matters of health and safety.

ARTICLE 12 - IMPLEMENTATION OF THE AGREEMENT

1. This Agreement shall be implemented in a manner designed:

(a) to avoid hampering or delaying the nuclear activities in the territory of either Party;

(b) to avoid interference in such activities;

(c) to be consistent with prudent management practices required for the safe conduct of such activities; and

(d) to t ake full account of the long term requirement s of the nuclear energy programs of the Parties.

2. The provisions of this Agreement shall not be used to:

(a) secure unfair commercial or industrial advantages or to restrict trade to the disadvantage of persons and undert akings of either Party or hamper their

commercial or industrial interests, whether international or domestic;
b) interfere with the nuclear policy or programs for the promotion of the peaceful uses of nuclear energy including research and development; or
c) impede the free movement of nuclear material, non nuclear material and equipment supplied under this Agreement within the territory of the Parties.

3. When execution of an agreement or contract pursuant to this Agreement between Indian and United States organizations requires exchanges of experts, the Parties shall facilitate entry of the experts to their territories and their stay therein consistent with national laws, regulations and practices. When other cooperation pursuant to this Agreement requires visits of experts, the Parties shall facilitate entry of the experts to their territory and their stay therein consistent with national laws, regulations and practices.

ARTICLE 13 - CONSULTATIONS

1. The Parties undertake to consult at the request of either Party regarding the implementation of this Agreement and the development of further cooperation in the field of peaceful uses of nuclear energy on a stable, reliable and predictable basis. The Parties recognize that such consultations are between two States with advanced nuclear technology, which have agreed to assume the same responsibilities and practices and acquire the same benefits and advantages as other leading countries with advanced nuclear technology.

2. Each Party shall endeavor to avoid taking any action that adversely affects cooperation envisaged under Article 2 of this Agreement. If either Party at any time following the entry into force of this Agreement does not comply with the provisions of this Agreement, the Parties shall promptly hold consultations with a view to resolving the matter in a way that protects the legitimate interests of both Parties, it being understood that rights of either Party under Article 16.2 remain unaffected.

3. Consultations under this Article may be carried out by a Joint Committee specifically established for this purpose. A Joint Technical Working Group reporting to the Joint Committee will be set up to ensure the fulfillment of the requirements of the Administrative Arrangements referred to in Article 17.

ARTICLE 14 - TERMINATION AND CESSATION OF COOPERATION

1. Either Party shall have the right to terminate this Agreement prior to its expiration on one year's written notice to the other Party. A Party giving notice of termination shall provide the reasons for seeking such termination. The Agreement shall terminate one year from the date of the written notice, unless the notice has been withdrawn by the providing Party in writing prior to the date of termination.

2. Before this Agreement is terminated pursuant to paragraph 1 of this Article, the Parties shall consider the relevant circumstances and promptly hold consultations, as provided in Article 13, to address the reasons cited by the Party seeking termination. The Party seeking termination has the right to cease further cooperation under this Agreement if it determines that a mutually acceptable resolution of outstanding issues has not been possible or cannot be achieved through consultations. The Parties agree to consider carefully the circumstances that may lead to termination or cessation of cooperation. They further agree to take into account whether the circumstances that may lead to termination or cessation resulted from a Party's serious concern about a changed security environment or as a response to similar actions by other States which could impact national security.

3. If a Party seeking termination cites a violation of this Agreement as the reason for notice for seeking termination, the Parties shall consider whether the action was caused inadvertently or otherwise and whether the violation could be considered as material. No violation may be considered as being material unless corresponding to the definition of material violation or breach in the Vienna Convention on the Law of Treaties. If a Party seeking termination cites a violation of an IAEA safeguards agreement as the reason for notice for seeking termination, a crucial factor will be whether the IAEA Board of Governors has made a finding of non-compliance.

4. Following the cessation of cooperation under this Agreement, either Party shall have the right to require the return by the other Party of any nuclear material, equipment, non-nuclear material or components transferred under this Agreement and any special fissionable material produced through their use. A notice by a Party that is invoking the right of return shall be delivered to the other Party on or before the date of termination of this Agreement. The notice

shall contain a statement of the items subject to this Agreement as to which the Party is requesting return. Except as provided in provisions of Article 16.3, all other legal obligations pertaining to this Agreement shall cease to apply with respect to the nuclear items remaining on the territory of the Party concerned upon termination of this Agreement.

5. The two Parties recognize that exercising the right of return would have profound implications for their relations. If either Party seeks to exercise its right pursuant to paragraph 4 of this Article, it shall, prior to the removal from the territory or from the control of the other Party of any nuclear items mentioned in paragraph 4, undertake consultations with the other Party. Such consultations shall give special consideration to the importance of uninterrupted operation of nuclear reactors of the Party concerned with respect to the availability of nuclear energy for peaceful purposes as a means of achieving energy security. Both Parties shall take into account the potential negative consequences of such termination on the on-going contracts and projects initiated under this Agreement of significance for the respective nuclear programmes of either Party.

6. If either Party exercises its right of return pursuant to paragraph 4 of this Article, it shall, prior to the removal from the territory or from the control of the other Party, compensate promptly that Party for the fair market value thereof and for the costs incurred as a consequence of such removal. If the return of nuclear items is required, the Parties shall agree on methods and arrangements for the return of the items, the relevant quantity of the items to be returned, and the amount of compensation that would have to be paid by the Party exercising the right to the other Party.

7. Prior to return of nuclear items, the Parties shall satisfy themselves that full safety, radiological and physical protection measures have been ensured in accordance with their existing national regulations and that the transfers pose no unreasonable risk to either Party, countries through which the nuclear items may transit and to the global environment and are in accordance with existing international regulations.

8. The Party seeking the return of nuclear items shall ensure that the timing, methods and arrangements for return of nuclear items are in accordance with paragraphs 5, 6 and 7. Accordingly, the consultations between the Parties shall address

mutual commitments as contained in Article 5.6. It is not the purpose of the provisions of this Article regarding cessation of cooperation and right of return to derogate from the rights of the Parties under Article 5.6.

9. The arrangements and procedures concluded pursuant to Article 6(iii) shall be subject to suspension by either Party in exceptional circumstances, as defined by the Parties, after consultations have been held between the Parties aimed at reaching mutually acceptable resolution of outstanding issues, while taking into account the effects of such suspension on other aspects of cooperation under this Agreement.

ARTICLE 15 - SETTLEMENT OF DISPUTES

Any dispute concerning the interpretation or implementation of the provisions of this Agreement shall be promptly negotiated by the Parties with a view to resolving that dispute.

ARTICLE 16 - ENTRY INTO FORCE AND DURATION

1. This Agreement shall enter into force on the date on which the Parties exchange diplomatic notes informing each other that they have completed all applicable requirements for its entry into force.

2. This Agreement shall remain in force for a period of 40 years. It shall continue in force thereafter for additional periods of 10 years each. Each Party may, by giving 6 months written notice to the other Party, terminate this Agreement at the end of the initial 40 year period or at the end of any subsequent 10 year period.

3. Notwithstanding the termination or expiration of this Agreement or withdrawal of a Party from this Agreement, Articles 5.6(c), 6, 7, 8, 9, 10 and 15 shall continue in effect so long as any nuclear material, non-nuclear material, by-product material, equipment or components subject to these articles remains in the territory of the Party concerned or under its jurisdiction or control anywhere, or until such time as the Parties agree that such nuclear material is no longer usable for any nuclear activity relevant from the point of view of safeguards.

4. This Agreement shall be implemented in good faith and in accordance with the principles of international law.

5. The Parties may consult, at the request of either Party on possible amendments to this Agreement. This Agreement may be amended if the Parties so agree. Any amendment shall enter into force on the date on which the Parties exchange diplomatic notes informing each other that their respective internal legal procedures necessary for the entry into force have been completed.

ARTICLE 17 - ADMINISTRATIVE ARRANGEMENT

1. The appropriate authorities of the Parties shall establish an Administrative Arrangement in order to provide for the effective implementation of the provisions of this Agreement.

2. The principles of fungibility and equivalence shall apply to nuclear material and non-nuclear material subject to this Agreement. Detailed provisions for applying these principles shall be set forth in the Administrative Arrangement.

3. The Administrative Arrangement established pursuant to this Article may be amended by agreement of the appropriate authorities of the Parties.

IN WITNESS WHEREOF the undersigned, being duly authorized, have signed this Agreement.

DONE at, this day of , 200 , in duplicate.

FOR THE GOVERNMENT OF THE UNITED STATES OF AMERICA:

FOR THE GOVERNMENT OF INDIA:

AGREED MINUTE

During the negotiation of the Agreement for Cooperation Between the Government of the United States of America and the Government of India Concerning Peaceful Uses of Nuclear Energy ("the Agreement") signed today, the following understandings, which shall be an integral part of the Agreement, were reached.

Proportionality

For the purposes of implementing the rights specified in Articles 6 and 7 of the Agreement with respect to special fissionable material and by-product material produced through the use of nuclear material and non-nuclear material, respectively transferred pursuant to the Agreement and not used in or produced through the use of equipment transferred pursuant to the Agreement, such rights shall in practice be applied to that proportion of special fissionable material and by-product material produced that represents the ratio of transferred nuclear material and non-nuclear material, respectively, used in the production of the special fissionable material and by-product material to the tot al amount of nuclear material and non-nuclear material so used, and similarly for subsequent generations.

By-product material

The Parties agree that reporting and exchanges of information on by-product material subject to the Agreement will be limited to the following:

(1) Both Parties would comply with the provisions as contained in the IAEA document GOV/1999/19/Rev.2, with regard to by-product material subject to the Agreement.

(2) With regard to tritium subject to the Agreement, the Parties will exchange annually information pertaining to its disposition for peaceful purposes consistent with Article 9 of this Agreement.

For	For
The Government of India:	The Government of the United States of America:

Remarks by the Editor

On August 1, 2008, the IAEA approved the safeguards agreement with India after which the United States approached the Nuclear Suppliers Group (NSG) to grant a waiver to India to commence civilian nuclear trade. The 45-nation NSG granted the waiver to India on September 6, 2008 allowing it to access civilian nuclear technology and fuel from other countries.The implementation of this waiver makes India the only known country with nuclear weapons which is not a party to the NPT and CTBT, but is still allowed to carry out nuclear commerce with the rest of the world.

On October 8, 2008, President Bush signed legislation to enact the landmark US-India Civilian Nuclear Agreement.

On October 10, 2008, the 123 Agreement between India and US is finally operationalised between the two countries after the deal is signed by External Affairs Minister Pranab Mukherjee and his counterpart Secretary of State Condoleezza Rice in Washington D C.

VII

INTERNAL SECURITY

ARMED FORCES (SPECIAL POWERS) ACT, 1958 (ACT 28 OF 1959)

An Act to enable certain special powers to be conferred upon members of the armed forces in disturbed areas in the States of Assam, Manipur, Meghalaya, Nagaland and Tripura and the Union Territories of Arunachal Pradesh and Mizoram

Be it enacted by Parliament in the ninth year of the Republic of India as follows:

1. Short title and extent:

   (1) This Act may be called the Armed Forces (Special Powers) Act, 1958.

   (2) It extends to the whole of the States of Assam, Manipur, Meghalaya, Nagaland and Tripura and the Union Territories of Arunachal Pradesh and Mizoram.

2. Denitions: In this Act, unless the context otherwise requires,

   (a) "armed forces" means the military forces and the air forces operating as land forces, and includes any other armed forces of the Union so operating;

   (b) "disturbed areas" means an area which is for the time being declared by notification under S. 3 to be a disturbed area;

   (c) All other words and expressions used herein, but not defined and defined in Air Force Act 1950 or the Army Act 1950, shall have the meanings respectively attached to them in those Acts.

3. Power to declare areas to be disturbed areas.—If, in relation to any State or Union Territory to which this Act extends, the Governor of that State or the Administrator of that Union Territory of the Central Government in either case, is of the opinion that the whole or any part of such State or Union Territory, as the case may be, is in such a disturbed or dangerous condition that the use of

armed forces in aid of civil power is necessary, the Governor of that State or the Administrator of that Union Territory or the Central Government, as the case may be, may, by notification in the Official Gazette, declare the whole or such part of such State or Union Territory to be disturbed area.

4. Special Powers of the armed forces.—Any commissioned officer, warrant officer, non commissioned officer or any other person of equivalent rank in the armed forces may, in a disturbed area:

(a) if he is of the opinion that it is necessary so to do for the maintenance of the public order, after giving such due warning as he may consider necessary, fire upon or otherwise use force, even to the causing of death, against any person who is acting in contravention of any law or order for the time being in force in the disturbed area prohibiting the assembly of five or more persons or the carrying of weapons or things capable of being used as weapons or of fire arms, ammunition or explosive substances;

(b) if he is of the opinion that it is necessary so to do, destroy any arms dump, prepared or fortied position or shelter from which armed attacks are made or are likely to be made or are attempted to be made or anystructure used as a training camp for armed volunteers or utilised as a hideout by armed gangs or absconders wanted for any offence;

(c) arrest without warrant, any person who has committed a cognisable offence or against whom a reasonable suspicion exists that he has committed or is about to commit a cognisable offence and may use such force as may be necessary to effect the arrest;

(d) enter and search without warrant any premises to make any such arrest as aforesaid or to recover any person believed to be wrongfully restrained and conned or any property reasonably suspected to be stolen property or any arms, ammunition or explosive substances believed to be unlawfully kept in such premises, and may for that purpose use such force as may be necessary.

5. Arrested persons to be made over to police.—Any person arrested and taken into custody under this Act shall be made over to the officer in charge of the nearest police station with the least possible delay, together with a report of the

circumstances occasioning the arrest.

6. Protection to person acting under Act.—No prosecution, suit or other legal proceeding shall be instituted, except with the previous sanction of the Central Government, against any person in respect of any thing done or purported to be done in exercise of the powers conferred by this act.

7. Repeal and Saving:

   (1) The Armed forces (Assam and Manipur) Special Powers Ordinance, 1958, is hereby repealed.

   (2) Not withstanding such repeal any thing done or any action taken under the said ordinance shall be deemed to have been done or taken under this act, as if this had commenced on the 22nd day of May,1958.

THE ARMED FORCES (JAMMU AND KASHMIR) SPECIAL POWERS ACT, 1990

(21 of 1990)

An Act to enable certain special powers to be conferred upon members of the armed forces in disturbed areas in the State of Jammu and Kashmir

Be it enacted by Parliament in the forty first year of the Republic of India as follows:

1. (1) This Act may be called the Armed Forces (Jammu and Kashmir) Special Powers Act, 1990.

   (2) It extends to the whole of the States of Jammu and Kashmir.

   (3) It shall be deemed to have come into force on the fifth day of July, 1990.

2. In this Act, unless the context otherwise requires:

   (a) "armed forces" means the military forces and the air forces operating as land forces, and includes any other armed forces of the Union so operating;

   (b) "disturbed areas" means an area which is for the time being declared by notification under section 3 to be a disturbed area;

   (c) all other words and expressions used herein, but not defined and defined in Air Force Act 1950 or the Army Act 1950, shall have the meanings respectively assigned to them in those Acts.

3. If, in relation to the State of Jammu and Kashmir the Governor of that State or the Central Government, is of the opinion that the whole or any part of the State is in such a disturbed or dangerous condition that the use of armed forces in aid of civil power is necessary to prevent—

   (a) activities involving terrorist acts directed towards overawing the Government as by law established or striking terror in the people or any section of the people or alienating any section of the people or adversely affecting the harmony amongst different sections of the people;

(b) activities directed towards disclaiming, questioning or disrupting the sovereignty and territorial integrity of India or bringing about cession of a part of the territory of India or secession of a part of the territory of India from the Union or causing insult to the Indian National Flag, the Indian National Anthem and the Constitution of India,

The Governor of the State or the Central Government, may, by notification in the Official Gazette, declare the whole or any part of the State to be a disturbed area.

Explanation—In this section, "terrorist act has the same meaning as Explanation to Article 248 of the Constitution of India as applicable to the State of Jammu and Kashmir.

4. Any commissioned officer, warrant officer, non commissioned officer or any other of equivalent rank in the armed forces may, in a disturbed area:

(a) if he is of the opinion that it is necessary so to do for the maintenance of the public order, after giving such due warning as he may consider necessary, fire upon or otherwise use force, even to the causing of death, against any person who is acting in contravention of any law or order for the time being in force in the disturbed area prohibiting the assembly of five or more persons or the carrying of weapons or things capable of being used as weapons or of fire-arms, ammunition or explosive substances;

(b) if he is of the opinion that it is necessary so to do, destroy any arms dump, prepared or fortified position or shelter from which armed attacks are made or are likely to be made or are attempted to be made or any structure used as a training camp for armed volunteers or utilised as a hideout by armed gangs or absconders wanted for any offence;

(c) arrest without warrant, any person who has committed a cognisable offence or against whom a reasonable suspicion exists that he has committed or is about to commit a cognisable offence and may use such force as may be necessary to effect the arrest;

(d) enter and search without warrant any premises to make any such arrest as aforesaid or to recover any person believed to be wrongfully restrained and conned or any property reasonably suspected to be stolen property or any arms, ammunition or explosive substances believed to be unlawfully kept in such premises, and may for that purpose use such force as may be necessary and seize any such property, arms, ammunition or explosive substances;

(e) stop, search and seize any vehicle or vessel reasonably suspected to be carrying any person who is a proclaimed offender, or any person who has committed a non-cognisable offence, or against whom a reasonable suspicion exists that he has committed or is about to commit a non-cognisable offence, or any person who is carrying any arms, ammunition or explosive substance believed to be unlawfully held by him, and may, for that purpose, use such force as may be necessary, to effect such stoppage, search or seizure, as the case may be.

5. Every person making a search under this act shall have the power to break open the lock of any door, almirah, safe, box, cupboard, drawer, package or other thing, if the key thereof is withheld.

6. Any persons arrested and taken into custody under this Act and every property, arms, ammunition or explosive substance or any vehicle or vessel seized under this act, shall be made over to the officer in charge of the nearest police station with the least possible delay, together with a report of the circumstances occasioning the arrest or as the case may be, occasioning the seizure of property, arms, ammunition or explosive substance or any vehicle or vessel, as the case may be.

7. No prosecution, suit or other legal proceeding shall be instituted, except with the previous sanction of the Central Government, against any person in respect of any thing done or purported to be done in exercise of the powers conferred by this Act.

8. The Armed forces (Jammu and Kashmir) Special Powers Ordinance, 1990, is hereby repealed.

Not withstanding such repeal any thing done or any action taken under the said ordinance shall be deemed to have been done or taken under the corresponding provisions of this Act.

Sd

GOVERNMENT OF JAMMU AND KASHMIR CIVIL SECTT, HOME DEPARTMENT

SRO NO. SW 4 DATED: 6-7-1990

In exercise of the powers conferred under section 3 of the Armed Forces (Jammu and Kashmir) Special Powers Ordinance 1990, the Governor of Jammu and Kashmir hereby notifies the areas given in the schedule to this notication as disturbed areas.

Sd/-
Additional Chief Secretary (Home)
Jammu and Kashmir Govt.

SCHEDULE

1. Areas falling within 20 kms of the Line of Control in the Districts of Rajouri and Poonch.
2. Districts of Anantnag, Baramulla, Budgam, Kupwara, Pulwama and Srinagar.

Sd/-
Addl.Chief Secretary (Home)
J&K Govt.

IMPORTANT NOTE

This SRO has been issued under the Armed Forces (Jammu and Kashmir) Special Powers Ordinance 1990, the ordinance has been repeated by "Armed Forces" (Jammu and Kashmir) Special Powers Act 1990 under section 8(2) of the Act. This SRO issued under the ordinance is valid and shall remain in force because section 8 of the act deals with repeal and savings.

BRIEF DESCRIPTION OF THE FOREIGNERS ACT, 1946; ILLEGAL MIGRANTS (DETERMINATION BY TRIBUNALS) ACT, 1983 (IMDT) AND ASSAM ACCORD, 1985

THE FOREIGNERS ACT, 1946

The Foreigners Act, 1946 regulates the entry into, stay in and exit from India of all foreigners except in case of the State of Assam in which case the IMDT will have overriding effect.

The Foreigners Act, 1946 empowers the Central Government to make orders with regard to all foreigners or with respect to any particular foreigner or any prescribed class or description of foreigners for prohibiting, regulating or restricting their entry into India or their departure from India or their presence or continued presence in India. Broadly the following types of orders could be enforced after due observance of legal process:

- Entry/departure at prescribed times and points.
- Restriction on residence.
- Restriction on movements.
- Prohibiting him from meeting or associating with a particular class of people or visiting some specified places.
- Prohibiting him from indulging in a particular type of activity.
- Preventing him from possessing certain type of articles.
- Regulation of general conduct.
- Requiring him to provide identication.
- Medical examination.

The orders also cover the internees; crews of aircraft, ships etc; instructions to hotels where the foreigners reside and so on. Under this act the burden of proof with regard to bonades lies with the individual. The act is comprehensive and has stood the test of time even though it has undergone a number of amendments.

IMDT ACT

This Act provides for the establishment of tribunals for the determination, in a fair manner, of the question whether a person is an illegal migrant to enable the Central Government to expel him from India and for related matters. Central Government may appoint as many tribunals as it deems necessary. Each tribunal will comprise of two members. Each member of the tribunal should have been a district judge or an additional district judge. The tribunal shall have the same powers as are vested in a civil court under the Code of Civil Procedure, 1908. In addition the Central Government may, by notification, establish for each state an Appellate Court to decide on appeals led against the orders of the tribunals. The members of the Appellate Court (minimum two) should be or should have been a judge of the High Court.

The illegal migrants as defined in the Act are the ones who have entered into India illegally after 25th March 1971. If a question arises whether a person is or is not an illegal migrant, and an application is made to the Central Government, after due consideration the Central Government may refer the matter to a tribunal, irrespective of other national provisions in vogue. The application will be made by a person from the same police station jurisdiction where the alleged illegal migrant resides, along with an affidavit witnessed by two persons from the same police station jurisdiction, accompanied by a fee to be prescribed which will not be more than Rs 100/-. The application shall be made on a prescribed form and shall be certied as true in all respects by a person from the same revenue sub-division.

The Act extends to the whole of India but would be applied to states on notification by the Central Government. For State of Assam it has come into force with effect from 15 October 1983.

This Act, operating in Assam to check the illegal Bangladeshi migration, has been struck down by the Supreme Court on 12 July 2005 as it s procedure was cumbersome and not practical. The Foreigners Act of 1946 is being amended to curb the illegal migration in to India.

ASSAM ACCORD, 1985

In order to reduce the menace of illegal migrants/foreigners, the representatives of all Assam Student Union and All Assam Gana Sangram Parishad on one hand and the representatives of the Central Government and the Government of Assam on the other hand signed an Accord in presence of Shri Rajiv Gandhi, the Prime Minister of India on 15 August 1985. According to this Accord, the foreigners were categorised as follows:

- Those who came before 1 January 1966—Deemed to be Indian citizens.

- Those who came between 1 January 1966 and 25 March 1971—To be deprived of voting rights for ten years.

- Those who came after 25 March 1971—To be deported.

In future, stringent measures were to be adopted to prevent illegal migration, the border surveillance was to be improved to check infiltration and Indian citizenship would only be granted by the Central Government. The Government will also give due consideration to the effective implementation of the IMDT.

VIII

NATIONAL SECURITY COUNCIL (NSC) RESOLUTION

CABINET SECRETARIAT RESOLUTION
New Delhi, the 16th April, 1999

No. 281/29/6/98/TS.—The Central Government had set up in April, 1998, a Task Force under the Chairmanship of Shri K.C. Pant to work out the constitution, role and functions of a National Security Council. The recommendations of the Task Force have been considered and the Central Government has resolved to hereby constitute the National Security Council (NSC), consisting of:

(i) Prime Minister	Chairman
(ii) Minister of Home Affairs	Member
(iii) Minister of Defence	Member
(iv) Minister of External Affairs	Member
(v) Minister of Finance	Member
(vi) Deputy Chairman, Planning Commission	Member

2. The National Security Council (hereinafter referred to as the Council) shall, as and when necessary, invite other Union Ministers to attend its meetings. It may also invite experts and specialists to its meetings for consultation.

3. The Central Government recognizes that national security management requires integrated thinking and co-ordinated application of the political, military, diplomatic, scientific and technological resources of the State to protect and promote national security goals and objectives. National security in the context of the nation needs to be viewed not only in military terms but also in terms of internal security, economic security, technological strength and foreign policy. The role of the Council is to advisethe Central Government on the said matters.

4. With a view to fullling its role, the Council shall deal with the following broad subject areas, namely:-

   (a) external security environment and threat scenario;

(b) security threats involving atomic energy, space and high technology;

(c) trends in the world economy and economic security threats in the areas of energy, foreign trade, food, nance and ecology;

(d) internal security, including counter-insurgency, counter-terrorism and counter-intelligence;

(e) patterns of alienation emerging in the country, especially those with a social, communal or regional dimension;

(f) security threats posed by trans border crimes such as smuggling and traffic in arms, drugs and narcotics; and

(g) co-ordination in intelligence collection and tasking of intelligence agencies so as to ensure that intelligence is focussed on areas of concern for the nation.

5. The Council shall have a National Security Adviser who shall function as the channel for servicing the National Security Council. Shri Brajesh Mishra, Principal Secretary to the Prime Minister shall, in addition to his duties as the Principal Secretary to the Prime Minister, act as the National Security Adviser.

6. The Council shall be assisted by the Strategic Policy Group (SPG) which will be the principal mechanism for inter-ministerial coordination and integration of relevant inputs in the formulation of national security policies. One of the priority tasks of the SPG will be to undertake the long-term strategic defence review. The SPG will be chaired by the Cabinet Secretary and shall consist of:-

(i) Chief of the Army Staff, Chief of the Naval Staff and Chief of the Air Staff;

(ii) Governor of the Reserve Bank of India;

(iii) Foreign Secretary;

(iv) Home Secretary;

(v) Finance Secretary;

(vi) Defence Secretary;

(vii) Secretary, Department of Defence Production and Supplies;

(viii) Scientic Adviser to Raksha Mantri;

(ix) Secretary (R), Cabinet Secretariat;

(x) Secretary, Department of Renenue;

(xi) Secretary, Department of Atomic Energy;

(xii) Secretary, Department of Space;

(xiii) Director, Intelligence Bureau; and

(xiv) Secretary, National Security Council Secretariat.

Representatives of other Ministries/Departments may be invited to SPG meetings, as and when necessary. The Cabinet Secretary or the National Security Adviser may direct for the convening of the meetings of the SPG from time to time.

7. The National Security Advisory Board (NSAB) approved in December 1998 is to advise the Council on issues relating to national security which may be referred to it by the Council may continue to function. The Board consists of a Convenor and other persons of eminence outside the Government with expertise in the fields of foreign affairs, external security, defence and armed forces, strategic analysis, economics, science and technology, internal security, and related areas. The maximum number of members of the NSAB including the Convenor shall be thirty.

8. (i) The Council shall have a separate Secretariat. The existing Joint Intelligence Committee (JIC) will be re-structured and renamed as the National Security Council Secretariat (NSCS). The erstwhile functions of the JIC relating to intelligence analysis and assessment shall continue to be performed by the NSCS.

(ii) All Ministries/Departments shall consult the Secretariat on matters having a bearing on national security.

(iii) The NSCS will prepare or cause to be prepared papers for consideration of the SPG or the NSC.

(iv) An officer of the level of Secretary to the Government of India, designated as Secretary, NSCS, will head the Secretariat.

(v) The NSCS will be located in the Cabinet Secretariat and will also service the SPG and the NSAB.

9. This supersedes the resolution of the Government of India 50/4/18/88-TS dated 24th August, 1990 and Cabinet Secretariat Office Memorandum No. 50/4/5/95-TS dated 6th June, 1995 on the subject.

PRABHAT KUMAR
Cabinet Secretary

BIBLIOGRAPHY

A Appadorai, Selected Documents on India's Foreign Policy, 1947–72, Vol 1

AG Noorani, The Henry L Stimson Centre, Easing the Indo–Pakistani Dialogue on Kashmir: Confidence Building Measures for Siachen Glacier, Sir Creek and Wular Barrage Dispute

Avtar Singh Bhasin, Nepal's Relations with India and China

Bell, Tibet: Past and Present

Bindra, Indo Bangladesh Relations

Birbal Nath, Kashmir The Nuclear Flash Point

BL Sharma, The Kashmir Story

Dawa Norbu, Tibet the Road Ahead

Deendayal Research Institute, Indo-Soviet Treaty, Reactions and Reflections

Durga Das Basu, Shorter Constitution of India

Fasahat H Syed, Nuclear Disarmament and Conventional Arms Control Including Light Weapons

General KV Krishna Rao, Prepare or Perish

HE Richardson, Tibet and its History

HS Gururaj Rao, Legal Aspects of the Kashmir Problem

Jasjit Singh, Nuclear India

Jennone Walker, Security and Arms Control in Post Confrontation Europe

Jozef Goldblat and Thomas Bernauer, Third Review of the Biological Weapons Convention: Issues and Proposals

K Raman Pillai, Indian Foreign Policy in 1990s

K Sridharan, Sea Our Saviour

KK Wadhwa, Constitutional Autonomy, A Case Study of J&K

KL Bhatia, Jammu and Kashmir: Article 370 of the Constitution of India

Lt Gen JFR Jacob, Surrender at Dacca, Birth of a Nation

Major General Afsir Karim, Kashmir The Troubled Frontiers

MD Dharamdasani, Sri Lanka An Island in Crisis

Paul Rogers and Malcolm Dando, Directory of Nuclear, Biological and Chemical Arms and Disarmament

PL Bhola, Pakistan–China Relations

Rahul Roy-Chaudhury, India's Maritime Security

Rajesh Kadian, India's Sri Lanka Fiasco

Rajesh Kadian, Tibet, India and China

Ram Rahul, Modern Bhutan

Rear Admiral CH Stockton, Outline of International Law

Robert H Donaldson, Soviet Policy towards India: Ideology and Strategy

Saswatu Chanda & Alok Kumar Gupta, The Ganges Water Sharing Treaty: Genesis and Signicance

SC Bhatt, The Triangle India–Nepal–China, A Study of Treaty Relations

SD Muni, Foreign Policy of Nepal

Suresh K Sharma, Usha Sharma, Kashmir and the World

TB Millar, Current International Treaties

UN Institute for Disarmament Research, Disarmament Forum Two- 1999

UN Institute of Disarmament Research, The Third Review of the Biological

Weapons Convention: Issues and Proposals

US Arms Control and Disarmament Agency, Arms Control and Disarmament Agreements

Verinder Grover and Ranjana Arora, Events and Documents of Indo–Pak Relations

VH Coelho, Sikkim and Bhutan

Vijay Sakhuja, Cold War in Arabian Sea

(an Article in Strategic Digest—June 2001)

VP Dutt, India's Foreign Policy in a Changing World

YA Korovin, Prof SB Krylov, Prof FI Kozhevnikov, SV Molodtsov, KY Chizhov, YM Shurshalov; International law

www.ingramcontent.com/pod-product-compliance
Lightning Source LLC
Chambersburg PA
CBHW080934240926
51849CB00003BA/452
* 9 7 8 9 3 8 0 1 7 7 1 7 5 *